ALSO BY ROBERT KANIGEL

Eyes on the Street

On an Irish Island

Faux Real

High Season

Vintage Reading

The One Best Way

The Man Who Knew Infinity

Apprentice to Genius

Hearing Homer's Song

HEARING HOMER'S SONG

The Brief Life and Big Idea of

Milman Parry

Robert Kanigel

ALFRED A. KNOPF   NEW YORK   2021

THIS IS A BORZOI BOOK
PUBLISHED BY ALFRED A. KNOPF

Library of Congress Cataloging-in-Publication Data
Names: Kanigel, Robert, author.
Title: Hearing Homer's song : the brief life and big idea of
Milman Parry / Robert Kanigel.
Description: First edition. | New York : Alfred A. Knopf, 2021. |
"This is a Borzoi Book" | Includes bibliographical references and index.
Identifiers: LCCN 2020038085 (print) | LCCN 2020038086 (ebook) |
ISBN 9780525520948 (hardcover) | ISBN 9780525520955 (ebook)
Subjects: LCSH: Parry, Milman. | Classicists—United States—
20th century—Biography.
Classification: LCC PA85.P33 K36 2021 (print) | LCC PA85.P33 (ebook) |
DDC 880.092 [B]—dc23
LC record available at https://lccn.loc.gov/2020038085
LC ebook record available at https://lccn.loc.gov/2020038086

Jacket image: traveler1116 / DigitalVision / Getty Images
Jacket design by Tyler Comrie

Manufactured in the United States of America
First Edition

"Tho' much is taken, much abides."

ALFRED, LORD TENNYSON, "Ulysses"

Contents

PART ONE

Edifice

YOUNG ALBERT AND MR. PARRY

When she asked where they were going and why, Milman Parry's daughter, Marian, would recall,

> my father explained that Jugoslavia was an uncivilized country
> at the edge of the world, on the border of the Slavic wilder-
> ness which stretched from the Adriatic to Alaska. Since hardly
> anyone could read or write Jugoslavians still had retained their
> oral poetry and their ancient native national civilization. There
> were still heroes, and heroic acts and the ancient heroes were
> celebrated in ballads by guslars, or bards, who knew by heart so
> much poetry that if it were written down it would fill libraries.
> But the whole thing depended, my father explained, on the fact
> that they couldn't write it down; as soon as literacy becomes
> common in a country, everyone gets lazy; they don't bother to
> learn things by heart anymore and poetry is no longer a part of
> their daily life.

In 1934 and 1935, Parry spent fifteen months in Yugoslavia, driving his black Ford sedan from town to town with his young assistant,
Albert Lord. They stopped at village coffeehouses, spread word they
were looking for local singers, recorded the songs they sang while strumming their rude, raspy one-stringed gusles. For a few days, or a week or
two, Parry would stay, then head off for the next town, for Gacko or
Kolašin, Bihać or Novi Pazar. In that hardscrabble, mostly mountainous

backcountry, of roads rutted and electricity scarce, of dialects, religions, ancient wars, and tribal resentments all butting up against one another, they struggled with equipment and supplies and bedbug-infested village inns. They powered their recording instrument with a battery charged by the engine of the Ford, shipped over from the States. Along with their native translator, Nikola, they'd periodically return to Dubrovnik, in a Croatian corner of the Kingdom of Yugoslavia, where Parry's wife, daughter, and son awaited them. Then, the Parry house, halfway up the hill above the city, with its fine views of the harbor and the sea, became headquarters of almost military stamp, as transcribers set to work, typewriters clattering, taking down the words of the old songs.

In the end, Parry would gather half a ton of twelve-inch aluminum discs—phonograph records, the size of old vinyl LPs but in white metal—filled with a young nation's, and an old world's, cultural tradition. But Parry was interested in them not primarily for what they said of Bosnia, Herzegovina, Serbia, Montenegro, and elsewhere in the Balkans, but for what they might reveal, by analogy, of the older world of ancient Greece that had produced Homer's *Iliad* and *Odyssey*. Finally, in a town nineteen hundred feet up into the mountains of northern Montenegro, an old man named Avdo Međedović, singer of tales of weddings and war that took days and days to tell, led Parry to conclude that in him they had found their own living Homer.

In September 1935, the Parrys and young Albert Lord returned to America.

On November 16, Parry, back at Harvard, where he was assistant professor of Greek and Lord was a recent graduate, wrote his sister that his wife was just then in Los Angeles. He gave her mailing address, which was that of his financially distraught mother-in-law.

On November 17, Parry was to give a talk on Yugoslav folk songs at Harvard.

On the eighteenth, he met with a student and reported on his progress.

A day or two later, he left for the West Coast.

On December 3, in a Los Angeles hotel room with his wife, a bullet fired from a handgun, said to have become entangled in his luggage as Parry rummaged through it, struck him in the chest and nicked his heart. He died later that day. He was thirty-three.

When hotel employees responded to Mrs. Parry's call, they assumed she had killed her husband; she was the only other person in their suite. The police, however, concluded otherwise, that it was an accident. No autopsy was performed. No charges were brought. Some would suspect that Parry had committed suicide. Later, among Parry's own children, that their mother had killed him was regarded as a real possibility: Maybe in one of her fits of fierce, irrational rage. Or maybe as cool-headed revenge for real or imagined infidelities, or other hurts he'd inflicted on her over the years. Mrs. Parry and her daughter, twisted by a lifetime's mutual antagonism, were both named Marian. Marian the younger was all but certain her mother had killed her father and held to this view all her life.

On December 5, 1935, Parry's body was cremated in Los Angeles. Two weeks later, back at Harvard, a memorial service was held in Appleton Chapel. In the eulogy it was said that Parry had returned from Yugoslavia "with copious material which no future investigators in his field can afford to neglect. His work will endure long after him."

In early 1936, Mrs. Parry donated most of her husband's books, recordings, and papers to Harvard and, with remarkable efficiency, decamped from Cambridge with her children, moved across the continent to Berkeley, California, returned to school at the university, and in little more than a year had earned the BA degree that pregnancy, marriage to Milman, and life with him in France, Cambridge, and Yugoslavia had interrupted.

Meanwhile, Parry's young assistant, Albert Lord, was left with the Yugoslav materials. After working with the man he would call his "master and friend" for fifteen months, he was now almost alone responsible for making something of them. Parry himself had had no chance to do so. Back in Yugoslavia, the winter before coming home, he'd dictated a few pages of notes and ideas; Lord typed them up. And he had a title for the book he hoped to write, *The Singer of Tales*. Now it was all in the hands of Lord, who, at age twenty-three, was scarcely equipped to tackle the job.

Approaching graduation from Harvard in June 1934, Lord "had not the slightest idea of what to do with himself," reports David Bynum, a student and admiring younger colleague of Lord's from a later period. Yugoslavia had come at an opportune time—immediately after graduation, in the middle of the Depression, a time of few other job prospects.

Lord served Parry as typist, gofer, and "recording engineer," freeing Parry for more substantive and intellectually challenging work. He had "no opportunity whatever, as well as no personal inclination, to inquire or know anything meaningful concerning what Parry was about or why in Yugoslavia." The shiny white aluminum discs were, in their thousands, logistical monster and intellectual mystery.

What transformed this untenable situation was this: However much or little his time in Yugoslavia might make him responsible in the eyes of the world for making something of Parry's work, Lord seemed to feel it did. And he felt it all the more with the passage of time, as a deep, pressing, personal need, one impossible to shirk. He had worked beside Parry for fifteen months; he would help advance and enrich Parry's ideas for more than fifty years. "In spite of moments when it seemed otherwise," Lord would write, "my life has been devoted to Parry's collection and to the work which he had only begun to do."

*

Milman Parry was arguably the most important American classical scholar of the twentieth century, by one reckoning "the Darwin of Homeric Studies." At age twenty-six, this young man from California stepped into the world of Continental philologists and overturned some of their most deeply cherished notions of ancient literature. Homer, Parry showed, was no "writer" at all. The *Iliad* and the *Odyssey* were not "written," but had been composed orally, drawing on traditional ways that went back centuries.

Generations of high school and college students can recall descriptive flourishes of Odysseus, as "much-enduring," or "the man of many schemes"; or of the goddess Athena as "bright-eyed"; or of "swift-footed Achilles." Parry showed that these "ornamental epithets" were not odd little explosions of creativity. Nor, in their repetition, were they failures of the imagination. Nor were they random. They were the oral poet's way to fill out lines of verse and thus keep the great river of words flowing. They were the product of long tradition, and many voices. Parry wrote of the fifth-century BCE Greek sculptor Phidias that his work was not his alone but shot through with "the spirit of a whole race"; much the same, he said, applied to the Homeric epics.

Milman Parry

Homer, of course, was no trifling asterisk of classical studies but stood at the very roots of Western civilization, his epic poems filled with stories of the warrior Achilles and the goddess Athena and the other gods and heroes enshrined on every ancient Greek potsherd, represented in paintings, sculpture, and literature for three thousand years, inspiring Shelley and Keats, Shakespeare and James Joyce. After Parry, just how Homer had come into the world and become embedded in the memory of humankind came to be seen in a new way.

As Walter Ong summed up the case in his groundbreaking 1982 book, *Orality and Literacy,*

> The *Iliad* and the *Odyssey* have been commonly regarded from antiquity to the present as the most exemplary, the truest and the most inspired secular poems in the western heritage. To account for their received excellence, each age has been inclined to interpret them as doing better what it conceived its [own] poets to be doing or aiming at.

That is, they tended to be seen like the poems of one's own age, whatever it was, only better.

But no, said Parry, Homer was different, and not just from the literature of our own time, or from Victorian literature, or from that of the Middle Ages, but even from almost all other ancient Greek literature. A rough, ill-formed thought might place the *Odyssey* and, say, Aeschylus's three-part tragedy, the *Oresteia,* under the same broad heading—ancient "classics," revered literary products of Greece, stalwarts of the Western literary tradition. But Parry showed they were different animals altogether, because Aeschylus *wrote,* as you and I write, while the *Odyssey* was something else entirely, percolating up from oral performance over the centuries, shaped by its own, maddeningly "unliterary" rules: The literary critic sees repetition, stereotype, and cliché as unwelcome or worse. But for on-the-fly oral composition they were virtually essential, *characteristic* of it, understood and expected by audience and performer alike. For Parry they were the clue to how the epic poems had been made.

In time, Parry's ideas came to constitute their own orthodoxy, with scholars questioning them as they would anything else, placing them under relentless scrutiny. And yet in all the years since—it is now nearly a century since Parry first asserted them—they have become one of the cornerstones on which Homeric studies stand. And extended into new realms, they have altered understanding of other early cultures as well—not just in the West but in Asia, Africa, and around the world; and not just in past centuries but our own. Parry's ideas have forced us to rethink the role of books and print generally. The Yugoslav singers, like those of ancient Greece, could not read or write. Milman Parry helped us to imagine, understand, and respect another species of human creativity.

"The effects of oral states of consciousness," Walter Ong has written, "are bizarre to the literate mind."

*

I come to Milman Parry from outside the world of classical studies. While for a dozen years in the early 2000s I held a faculty position at a university, MIT, most of my working life has been spent outside academia altogether, as an independent writer. In the early years, I wrote articles, essays, and reviews for magazines and newspapers. Then, beginning in the 1980s, books—about mentor relationships among elite scientists, about tourism in Nice, about an Indian mathematical genius. A servant to my enthusiasms, I never much restricted myself by subject. In 2007, the object of my fascination became a tiny island community off the far west coast of Ireland, known as the Great Blasket, inhabited by a few hundred Irish-speaking fishermen, visited by scholars, writers, and linguists from all over Europe.

One of these scholars was an Englishman, George Thomson, who first arrived on the island in 1923 and took a lively interest in it for the rest of his life. Professionally, he was a classicist, a student of Greek lyric poetry, of Aeschylus, of Homer. For most of his life he was professor of Greek at the University of Birmingham. Through his books, correspondence, and personal story I found him a warming and inspiring figure. Such were his sensibilities, and such were mine, that I could not confine my interest to his place in the Irish story; I became intrigued by whatever intrigued him. Soon I was reading his translation of the *Oresteia,* from which I came away thrilled by the astonishing transformation wrought by Athena in the third play, where vengeance metamorphoses into something like justice. From Aeschylus, then, it was on to the *Odyssey* and the *Iliad* through the lustrous and lucid Robert Fagles translations; these were my first forays into Homer since junior high school. Ultimately, I was caught up in Thomson's ideas about the Homeric Question, the fertile, endlessly fascinating, centuries-old debate about who Homer was, when and where he'd lived, and what it meant, if anything, to attribute to him the authorship of the ancient epics. And the Homeric Question, in turn, led me to Milman Parry.

As one over-neat formulation of his achievement put it, Parry "never solved the Homeric Question; he demonstrated that it was irrelevant." Jettisoning contradictions in Homer that to his mind weren't contradictions at all, he opened the world of classical scholarship to new notions of literary creation. And he did so in a peculiarly single-minded way that made for its own, charmingly geekish story: In the decade after first asserting his ideas, Parry enriched his original insights with such deep analysis of the hexametric line in which the epics were written, such abundance of detail, such obsessive regard for closing off alternative explanations, that, in a scholarly world riven by fractious debate, few could doubt their truth, leaving others to pick at the periphery of his big idea. Classicists today refer to "before Parry" and "after Parry." They speak not of Parry's "theory," or "argument," but of his "discovery." This isn't *quite* true, but it is true enough, many of his demonstrations and proofs seemingly airtight.

Over the years much attention has been paid to Parry's ideas; less to the progression of his thought set against the times and places in which he lived, or the sensibilities and personal history of Parry himself. This book is a story of intellectual discovery rooted in a field, classical studies, often relegated in the popular imagination to the outlands of the irrelevant and the obscure. But success in any field, however recondite, is always a story of humans at work, in all their hope and glory, and in the face of all their foibles and excesses. Homer and ancient Greece stand near the center of this book; but nearer still is Mr. Parry himself. Our story plays out in the times and places in which he lived—across just a dozen years in the 1920s and 1930s, in California, in Paris, at Harvard, and on the Balkan peninsula, where Parry went to test his ideas on a living tradition.

Hearing Homer's Song is the story of Mrs. Parry, too—Marian Thanhouser Parry, who was with him at the University of California at Berkeley at the time of his earliest insights, and with him, too, at the moment of his death. Their marriage was conventional and distant, at best, but inexorably looms large in this book.

To anyone moved to reflect on the nature of human genius or, less grandly, of intellectual work at its highest and best, it is hard not to wonder about the turns of Parry's personal story. From where do great ideas emerge? What are the conditions of domestic life, of home and family, marriage and children, that nourish or discourage them? Parry could seem to have come out of nowhere. The son of an only intermittently successful druggist, he was the first in his family to attend college. At Cal, he studied Greek. His most important papers, in their precision, detail, and recourse to statistical evidence, bear the stigmata of science. But he was a romantic, too, alive with wanderlust. In Yugoslavia, it would be said of him, he loved "to visit the local pashas and exchange amenities, to ply his *gouslars* with wine and listen to their lies." He was enchanted by T. E. Lawrence and his Arabian exploits. He entertained his children with whimsical stories of Mickey Mouse and Winnie-the-Pooh. His daughter told of being brought up to believe "that Great Literature, Good Taste, and Harvard were the most important things in life"—only to immediately correct herself: "No, the *first* thing was to always try to be a hero."

Parry's stature did not arise all at once but gradually grew after his death. Before 1935, he'd begun to get attention from classicists and linguists, enough to earn him a faculty appointment at Harvard. But in fact it was Albert Lord, saddled with all those aluminum discs in 1935, who would further establish Parry's reputation and fix him in the mind of the scholarly world. Save for their brief time in Yugoslavia, the two never really worked together; they could scarcely be said to have truly "collaborated." Yet Lord would take on the mantle of Parry's legacy, first in his own doctoral thesis and then in a highly successful 1960 book. And along the way, quite independently, he'd take Parry's ideas in directions his master might scarcely have imagined, vastly enlarging their range of application. By the time Lord died in 1991 the two of them would be linked almost as one, "Parry and Lord" as enshrined in its respective corner of the intellectual world as Watson and Crick, discoverers of the structure of DNA, were in theirs.

Parry was dead but, thanks in large part to Lord—one could hardly contend otherwise—he lived on.

2

SINGER OF TALES

In February 1937, after receiving his MA in comparative literature from Harvard, Lord wrote a University of Wisconsin scholar with whom he'd spoken before, Miles Hanley, about making copies of the aluminum records he and Parry had brought back from Yugoslavia (at one point reputedly stored in the boiler room of the university's Widener Library); unwilling to take any chances with the originals, Lord wanted copies to take back to Yugoslavia for transcription.

The following month, he wrote the Harvard faculty committee overseeing the Parry Collection, asking that someone be hired to help him with the cataloguing of it. As it was, the collection was "painful and unmanageable" to work with. On his own, he was progressing "so slowly that it seems rather hopeless." He needed a typist, too. And the apparatus for transcribing discs he planned to take to Yugoslavia later that year was on the blink. Altogether, managing the collection was proving "an impossible task for a single person without aid in the more routine matters."

This was early 1937. In March, Lord was named to Harvard's Society of Fellows, a recently established honorary society for young scholars of promise who, without pressure to take classes or pursue a degree, enjoyed freedom, expenses paid, to roam the intellectual territory of their choice. Lord began his three-year appointment by boarding the *Vulcania* for Europe, bound for Dubrovnik and thence elsewhere in the Balkans to collect more songs like those Parry had gathered two years before. The trip took him to new locations in Albania but also to some of the same spots to which Parry had introduced him. Dubrovnik, he wrote his parents, was "the same charming place it always was, and the family [with which he had stayed earlier] just as before. Not one of them seems a day older or a mite different. . . . Of course . . . one misses the big house down below and the Parrys."

The whole trip would resurrect in him the spirit and memory of Parry.

In August, he returned to Stolac, where he and Parry had been in 1934 and 1935, "to hear the gusle again, ride horseback, and get out of the rut of Dubrovnik routine." There, the day

> was spent in looking up old friends, singers, and sitting about in the cafes, eating cantaloupe and drinking coffee. That night we went to hear one of our guslars sing. It was a glorious experience again, lying at ease on heavy woolen blankets—like those I brought back to America [from his first trip]—hearing our Moslem friend, an old man of seventy, sitting beside his fireplace, on the floor, of course, cross-legged, singing the old songs we know so well.

In early September, now finally in northern Albania, Lord took time to record the events of the past few days. In one village, they'd been entertained "by the chief elder. They killed a sheep in our honor. First, according to mountain custom, we sat on the floor and had a kind of brandy accompanied by raw onions, fresh cheese and roast liver. This took, with conversation, nearly an hour. They never leave a glass empty, or even partly filled. . . ."

By November, with a hundred new dictated texts in hand from Albania, Lord was back in New York. Around this time, he wrote for his Harvard class's Triennial Report that he was working on his PhD, and "probably shall be thus engaged for another two years." He was living on campus, in Kirkland House, just upstairs from Parry's old suite.

Next academic year, he taught a course in Serbian language and literature. It was his first teaching job, he wrote George Herzog, a Hungarian-born Columbia University ethnomusicologist, in November 1938, and "it has proven something of a burden." Then, too, "the business of editing and publishing selected texts from the collection now looms before me."

Lord was in his late twenties, apparently making little progress on his doctoral thesis, trying to manage the Parry Collection's records, songs, and paperwork, and he was tired. Maybe beyond tired. "Despair takes hold of me every now and then, despair that I shall never feel sure enough of myself to publish."

In April 1940, he wrote Herzog, apologizing for not having written. It had been a

> wretched and disappointing winter . . . Early in December I finally succumbed to worry and overwork, and my nerves cracked. After a brief stay in the hospital and short rest at home, I was sent away for a two months vacation. The doctors would not allow me to attend the MLA meetings in late December, nor give my Lowell lectures in February.

Years later, writing to Parry's widow, he'd call it what it was, "a nervous breakdown." No euphemisms, no shame, just the bare fact of it.

Two months later he wrote Herzog again, this time from his family's farm in New London, New Hampshire, a hundred miles from Boston. He was there, he explained, "for a combination of work and rest during the summer months. These were doctor's orders, because I was ill again early this month—nervous exhaustion again." His doctor told him to give up his Harvard research "for the coming year at least." His Society of Fellows appointment would be up the first of September. He needed a change of scene. Maybe he could teach for a while—perhaps classics, or Russian, or Serbo-Croatian: Did Herzog know of a position that would get him out of Harvard, out of Cambridge, and away from pressures and responsibilities for, say, a year?

But it wasn't teaching that got him away. And it wouldn't be for just a year. It was eight years before Lord was back at Harvard.

*

On January 22, 1941—almost a year before the Japanese attack on Pearl Harbor that propelled America into the war—Lord showed up at the Boston naval shipyard in Charlestown for a physical examination by a navy doctor. He was five foot six and a half, 135 pounds, no venereal disease, appendix removed, normal hearing, close to normal eyesight, no evidence of mental or nervous abnormality. He was fine. The doctor judged him capable of performing duties requiring—here he had to choose an adjective—"arduous" physical exertion. Five days later, Lord started on his new job.

From now until long after the end of the war, Lord turned away from the body of work left undone by Milman Parry's death. Occasionally he would deal with matters related to the Parry Collection, such as helping composer Béla Bartók with a volume on Yugoslav folk music. He would translate part of a novel by the Serbian novelist Rastko Petrović, *The Sixth Day,* into English. And, probably in short spurts as his health and navy yard duties permitted, he'd confront his doctoral thesis. But normally, his daily work life left scant time or energy for much else. Rising at 6:30, he'd commute, probably by streetcar and subway, from his parents' house on Franklin Street in Allston, the close-in Boston suburb where he'd grown up, to the sprawling shipyard. There, in that vast

Young Albert Lord, Bijelo Polje,
summer of 1935.

complex of piers, cranes, and dry docks, destroyers and submarines were being built—and, with the onset of hostilities, battle-damaged warships repaired. His first job was that of "under clerk-typist" with the Supply Department, at $1,260 per year. Even then that wasn't much, less than a third of what Parry had made at Harvard. Someone would later suggest that Lord's hiatus reminded him of *Sullivan's Travels,* a popular Depression-era film about a well-off young man's quest to shed privilege and sample the "real" life of ordinary working people. But Lord's shipyard years probably served ends more therapeutic and practical than socially relevant.

With his strong efficiency ratings, Lord earned more as the war dragged on. He was regularly promoted, moving up several grades to "senior property and supply clerk." But he did suffer one telling setback: In 1944, a navy officer assigned to review Lord's ratings by his more immediate supervisors—on, for example, his ability to organize his work—down-rated them across the board; the "outstandings" his civilian supervisor gave him three days earlier became mere "adequates." The officer wrote: "No supervision exercised. Ability only for routine work. Lacks initiative." Subsequently, Lord's ratings, both initial and on review, bounced back up. Yet perhaps the officer was onto something: At least during this period, Lord was not conspicuously ambitious. He was earnest, responsible, careful—even over-careful. Later, certain scholarly rivals made fun of his tendency to balance every idea against its opposite: "But then, on the other hand . . ." This was no serious lack; under the right circumstances it was desirable. But at the navy yard, Lord seemed determined to avoid stress, stay just where he was. A personal history he'd filled out when he started there cited his degrees from Harvard, his language skills in French, German, and Serbo-Croatian. But in the end nothing took him away from his typewriter for long. He knew just what he needed: "For eight years," he'd write later, "I had a vacation from academic life."

*

Finally, as Lord wrote, he felt "ready to return," resigning from his government job in July 1948, almost three years after the end of the war; he took with him, as memento of his shipyard days, a veritable doorstop of solid steel, part of an anchor chain. He completed his PhD the following year. In supporting Lord's application for a Guggenheim Fellowship back in February, Parry's Harvard colleague John Finley noted Lord's 1940 breakdown but reckoned him now "fully recovered." With Lord at the helm, Finley wrote, the Milman Parry Collection would be in good hands, thanks to Lord's "exceptional capacity for the work, a capacity mingledly deriving from his devoted loyalty to Parry's memory, his energetic and systematic mind, and his immersion in the material."

Lord's doctoral thesis was called "The Singer of Tales"—the title Parry had chosen for the book he planned to make from his Yugoslavia research. It told in rich, nuanced detail what Parry had done, what he and Lord had learned, about the lives of the singers, how they grew into their art, and how theirs amounted to a variant breed of literary creativity. His thesis defense was one not in name only but, it would be said, "in the real sense of a new and controversial thesis" that needed defending; several jury members left the room with minds quite altered. Ten years later his thesis came out as a book, much changed, but under the same title. Both bore the stamp of Parry on every page, as homage, reverie, and reminder of all Parry had thought and done more than a quarter century before.

Early in the book, Lord reviewed the confusions, inconsistencies, and scholarly battles bearing on the composition of the *Iliad* and the *Odyssey*—the Homeric Question again—that had raged for centuries. Finally, as if in a fit of scholarly wonder, he declared:

> It is a strange phenomenon in intellectual history as well as in scholarship that the great minds [whose ideas he'd just reviewed], minds which could formulate the most ingenious speculation, failed to realize that there might be some other way of composing a poem than that known to their own experience. They knew and spoke often of folk ballad and epic, they were aware of variants in these genres, yet they could see only two ways in which those variants could come into being: by lapse of memory or by willful change.

They could not, in short, conceive of an oral poetry—that is, one not merely spoken or sung in performance, but *composed* orally, on the fly,

in the heat of the moment, driven by the stern exigencies of an expec-
tant audience. It was a poetry, Parry had all but proved, that could produce an *Iliad* or *Odyssey:* "I believe that the greatest moment in recent
Homeric scholarship was expressed by Milman Parry when he . . . spoke
of his growing realization that what he had been calling traditional was
in fact oral."

No one, least of all Parry, suggested that the songs of illiterate Yugoslav peasants had roots in ancient Greece. Indeed, it wasn't their particular stories and legends that seized Parry's imagination, but *how* they'd
been created—orally, with no fixed text, each rendering of them a little
different and a little new. The work of his Yugoslav singers, then, stood
in compelling *analogy* to that of Homer.

But Greece and Yugoslavia were not home to the world's only traditional societies. Parry realized that oral composition of the Homeric
epics hinted at the oral composition of other traditional works. In one of
the last things he wrote—the fragmentary pages he'd call "Ćor Huso," or
Blind Huso, referring to a South Slavic singer of legendary repute—he
would venture into realms neither Homeric nor Yugoslav. He'd cite
Marcel Jousse, the French Jesuit thinker raised in rural France, away
from books, in a world almost purely oral. He'd refer to an African tribe
whose songs never changed much, "since the penalty of the change of
any syllable was death." He'd tell of the Lomaxes, a family of Smithson-
ian folklorists, who advised him of "variations in the same song by the
same singer" among Negroes in the American South.

Now, in *The Singer of Tales,* and then over the whole course of his
Harvard career, Lord reached far beyond Parry. Within his doctoral thesis, then in his book of the same name, a new creative landscape opened
up, one unlike any inhabited by a John Updike or a Margaret Atwood,
the kinds of writers we mostly *mean* by writers. Here was a quite distinct
force for the making of literary texts, one born in song and speech and
only much later, if at all, reduced to print. It was this alternative creativity that Lord celebrated in *The Singer of Tales:*

> What is called oral tradition is as intricate and meaningful an art
> form as its derivative "literary tradition." In the extended sense
> of the word, oral tradition is as "literary" as literary tradition.
> It is not simply a less polished, more haphazard, or cruder sec-

ond cousin twice removed, to literature. By the time the written techniques come onto the stage, the art forms have been long set and are already highly developed and ancient.

That appeared on page 141 of his book in a chapter entitled "Homer." The next chapter was devoted to the *Odyssey,* the chapter after that to the *Iliad.* All this lay comfortably within the fields of thought Parry had first planted. But now, in Lord's final chapter, came auguries of the intellectual revolution to come. It was entitled "Some Notes on Medieval Epic," and ventured beyond Homer and Yugoslavia. In the years since Milman Parry's death, Lord began, Harvard's Francis P. Magoun had applied the new "oral theory" to Old English. Others had applied it to Middle English romances; and to *chansons de gestes,* French songs from the late Middle Ages. In this chapter he would write of medieval epics like *Beowulf.* The singers he had met in Stolac, Gacko, and dozens of other Yugoslavian towns had created exemplars of artistry much as Homer, and his tradition, had created the *Iliad.* Here, then, through the oral rather than the written, lay a strategy for discovering other such examples of narrative imagination in Africa, the Holy Land, Asia, everywhere. And these, long before the development of alphabets or other writing systems, were as important as any literary culture that came later, and as worthy of study.

Some readers surely balked at the idea. Scholars and writers are apt to dismiss words not immortalized on the page, issuing merely from the lips. People lie, repeat themselves, contradict what they've just said, phumph and jabber endlessly. Singers and storytellers, bombastic preachers, drunken barroom rhetoricians, fast-talking salesmen, Don Juans purveying sugarcoated come-ons—all were past masters of the shady arts of speech. We may listen, but we don't entirely trust; many of us want to see it in black and white, laid out on the page in front of us. Without that reassuring superstructure of print, speech and song can seem deficient.

Some such underlying habit of mind was what Lord helped overturn, his book inspiring a host of thinkers to offer convincingly new interpretations of the terrain between speech and print. In his 1963 book, *Preface to Plato,* Eric Havelock pictured oral poetry in early Greece as the means by which society held and transmitted its collective wisdom; small wonder, then, that Plato famously attacked written poetry, as it risked undermining the social structure of Athens. Then, in 1982, in *Orality and Literacy,* Walter Ong elevated the oral world to a new level of scholarly seriousness. Both thinkers expressed their indebtedness to Parry and Lord.

In 1986, John Miles Foley, a former student of Lord's, founded *Oral Tradition,* a journal expressly devoted to every aspect, in every age, of the oral cast of mind celebrated by Parry and Lord. In 2007, a whole issue of the journal was devoted to Bob Dylan. Richard F. Thomas, who later went on to explore Dylan's debt to the classics in *Why Bob Dylan Matters,* noted Dylan's antipathy to being locked into the studio version of his songs, preferring rather to alter them, often radically, in performance; so there was never any true final version of "It Ain't Me, Babe" or "Tangled Up in Blue." This was something like how Parry and Lord imagined the Homeric epics taking shape, forever altered in performance, inevitably becoming something else, different, and new.

In the same issue, the essayist, photographer, and Allen Ginsberg scholar Gordon Ball offered his argument for why Bob Dylan merited the Nobel Prize in literature. In *literature*? But Dylan was musician as well as poet, his genius taking flight not through language alone but voice, music, performance. Didn't matter, wrote Ball. Music and poetry were forever and indissolubly linked; "poetry depends on oral performance," could never be wholly severed from it. Take Ginsberg's classic "Howl," the long poem that launched the Beat Generation of the 1950s. In such a poem "what's on the page may only be an approximation, sometimes a dim one, of what's in the air, in the poet's—the singer's—voice." Indeed, on first reading, "Howl" had left him cold; it took hearing it, on the wings of a human voice, Ginsberg's own, to win him over. All this bolstered his argument for Dylan's Nobel. "Let me be clear," he took care to add, "I don't mean to say that the Greek 'singer of tales' " of Lord's classic book, "and 'the vagabond who's rapping at your door,' " from a classic Dylan song, were quite the same. But wasn't he?

In 2016, Dylan did win the Nobel Prize for literature. "It was a decision that seemed daring only beforehand," Horace Engdahl, then permanent secretary of the Swedish Academy, observed at the Nobel ceremony, "and already seems obvious." Homer, Parry, and Lord would all be mentioned when it came time to publicly explain the academy's decision. "If people in the literary world groan," said Engdahl, "one must remind them that the gods don't write, they dance and they sing."

The world looked different when you saw it from a perch other than that of the lone writer sitting down with a manuscript to cudgel into shape, or that of a reader who, for pleasure and understanding, reflexively turned to books. In a traditionally literary world, you read, study, underline, consult, take notes. Once smitten by an author, you track down other examples of his or her work. Or, struck by a particular point, you turn to the author's bibliography, to lead you back to corroborations and challenges to it. Amid such moments of literary life, you might imagine Jane Austen taking up her pen to resume her story of Darcy and Elizabeth Bennet; or Gibbon, among his books and papers, gathering his notes on the rise and fall of Rome. So instinctively do we sense this long train of books, texts, annotations, pens and pencils, typewriters, printing presses, and the other paraphernalia of print, that it can be hard to think of literary creation in any other way.

Parry's successors over the three-quarters of a century and more since his death challenged that unthinking primacy. Lord, bearing Parry's legacy—and suffering under the weight of it—projected his mentor's ideas into the great world of scholarship. From him, and his students, and students of his students, tentacles of influence radiated out from Parry's original work, first through the "Yugoslav analogy," then to one epoch and civilization after another: The quest to understand Homer became, through Lord's intellectual leadership, a new discipline— variously "oral tradition" or "oral studies"—that has been harnessed on behalf of the Old Testament, jazz improvisation, hip-hop, and other ancient, medieval, and modern traditions. "From that pioneering effort" by Parry and Lord in the Yugoslavia of 1935, John Foley summed it up in *Homer's Traditional Art,* emerged a "field of vast proportions, affecting scores of cultures all over the world and throughout history."

"Working from the clues he left," wrote Lord of Milman Parry in *The Singer of Tales,* "I have tried to build an edifice of which he might approve."

PART TWO

California

[1902–1924]

3

DOWN IN THE FLATS

The San Francisco earthquake of 1906 did not leave East Bay communities like Oakland untouched. The roof of the Empire Theatre collapsed, killing five members of its burlesque troupe. Brick walls crumbled, plate glass windows shattered, streets filled with rubble. Compared to San Francisco, however, the damage was contained and Oakland was able to shelter tens of thousands who fled there by ferryboat from the stricken city across the bay. Many never went back. Between the 1900 and 1910 censuses, Oakland's population swelled from 67,000 to 150,000. It was a new city, building, growing, annexing adjacent farmland.

On a cloudy day in 1912, from the corner of 4th Street and Broadway in downtown Oakland, someone snapped a picture looking south across the city: We see horse-drawn wagons, streetcar tracks, one- and two-story buildings, a pair of poor hotels, the Roma and the Italia, twenty-five cents and up for a room. In the distance, toward an inlet of San Francisco Bay, a forest of sailing ship masts rises over the horizon. In these earliest years of the twentieth century, Oakland was no longer the Wild West, but you didn't need much imagination to fire up visions of it. In 1910, Buffalo Bill's Wild West and Congress of Rough Riders visited town; Bill Cody, in goatee and long flowing white hair under his cowboy hat, and American Indians in full regalia, lined up in front of the Oakland Tribune building for a publicity shot. The Transcontinental Railroad, the laying of whose golden spike famously cinched the Atlantic and Pacific coasts in 1869, had its western terminus in Oakland; the first trains pulled up at 7th and Broadway, a mile from where the Parry family lived, at 478 22nd Street, when Milman was born in 1902.

His boyhood played out in no one family home; the Parrys rarely stayed more than two or three years anywhere, moving up a little, or trying to, with each new place. Mostly, they remained within a small, fitfully urban trapezoid of a district that fanned out north from downtown Oakland, between Broadway and Telegraph Avenue, an old stagecoach route that shot up the East Bay to Berkeley. The area, which seems to have gone by no particular designation, roughly corresponds to, or abuts, neighborhoods known today as Northgate, Waverly, Koreatown, Pill Hill (for its several hospitals), and Automobile Row (for the car dealerships that sprang up after 1912 along Broadway). It was a neighborhood of modest frame houses, small shops, and storefront factories, all an easy walk from the drugstore where Milman's father worked during much of Milman's childhood.

The Parry place—wherever exactly it was at any one time—stood far from the brown hills of east Oakland on which would one day perch fine homes, on steep slopes, with striking views of San Francisco Bay. They lived in the broad Oakland flatlands, or flats, where the vernacular architecture, as in much of the East Bay, was the wood-frame house. It was street after street of them, sometimes tucked cozily together, sometimes apart, rarely more than two stories high, occasionally showing off a bit of Victorian gingerbread or southwestern stucco. No big brownstones here, no mansions. By 1910, when Milman was eight, the family moved to 486 24th Street, around the corner from the drugstore, a street of laundries, flats, and squat single-family houses. Three doors down was a "dress shields and suspenders" factory, housed in a frame building little larger than their house. A stable stood across the street. A small sausage factory occupied a site over on Telegraph. Once you got much past 26th Street the neighborhood thinned out; looking north up the gradual slope of Broadway, you'd see as many windmills and water tanks as houses.

Milman's father, Isaac Milman Parry, was born in 1865. Isaac's own parents came from the Midwest, Ohio and Illinois, but were said to go back to the Parrys who'd helped found New Hope, Pennsylvania, where a Parry Mansion dating to 1784 still stands. The Milman name that showed up in every recent generation was owed, Milman Parry's wife would report, to one of the Parry men who "ran away with a Miss Milman." Isaac's wife, born Mary Alice Emerson, was two years older than he. Both were California natives; their own parents, the pioneer genera-

Milman Parry, age fifteen.

tion, had come west across the continent in the mid-1800s. Of the winter rains and floods of his youth, Isaac would tell how "no one expected aid, they rebuilt by helping each other, the pioneers were friendly to each other, they lived simple lives, their houses were plain and easily repaired or rebuilt, there was no gas, no electricity, they had oil lamps, candles, fireplaces, wooden stoves. No rush."

When Isaac and Alice married in 1894, she brought to the new household an eight-year-old son, George, who took his stepfather's surname. Isaac and Alice had four children of their own. Girls Addison and Allison, fraternal twins, were born in 1896. A third daughter, Lucile, followed in 1898. Their fourth child, Milman Paul Parry, the Homeric scholar, was born on June 23, 1902.

Milman was a bright-eyed boy with dark hair and regular features, a little shy of average height. He liked getting out, moving his body. He was a Boy Scout; in a photo taken of him in uniform at age eleven or twelve, he could have been a poster child for the Scouts he looks so fine, happy, and wholesome. Through the local YMCA, he camped, hiked, and swam. In June 1916 he joined 120 other boys for one of the Oakland

Y's annual weeklong outings to the Santa Cruz Mountains, with non-stop sports, swimming, and boating, and visits to the picturesque Pigeon Point Lighthouse. Back in the neighborhood, he was stitched in enough that when a friend, son of an Oakland police inspector, held his annual birthday bash at Piedmont Park, or else at his house down 24th Street from the Parrys, Milman was regularly invited, sometimes going with one of his older sisters.

He was a smart boy, a good student. At Grant School, he was among those fifth and sixth graders accepted for the new Monday morning French program. His final year there, he was one of 248 boys—boys only—culled from schools around the city to collect Rotary Club achievement awards. He played chess; a photo taken around this time shows him near the end of a game, only a few pieces left standing. He and his opponent wear short-sleeved white shirts, ties, high-top shoes, and heavy woolen trousers, all alike enough to be a school uniform. The other boy, about his age, smirks. Maybe he has Milman in check; he seems delighted with himself. Milman does not. He remains lost in the game, engrossed.

4

THE OLD DEAR

In 1950, age eighty-five, Milman's father replied to a grandson's complaint that he had failed to answer his letter. This was true, he allowed, writing back in clear cursive script. But "I have no right to do this," by which he seems to mean setting down his thoughts at all. "I have an inferior complex about my ability to write an interesting letter. . . . I was taken out of school at eleven years of age and put to work to help raise the family income, because of such few years of schooling, I am lacking the ability of expressing myself as well as I desire."

But writing was probably Isaac's only conspicuous academic deficit. "Our father was the 'student'" of the family, daughter Addison, Milman's sister, would write:

> There never was a time, until his death at 92, when he was not studying something. It might be navigation, it might be yoga. In his early twenties, during a few months on naval duty in Japan, he learned to speak that language well. As children, Japanese fairy tales were our delight and sea shanties our lullabies.

During World War II, by then close to eighty, an age when learning a language is notoriously difficult, he went back to Japanese, determined to refurbish his skills for the sake of the war effort. He was forever reading and learning. "He was a very scholastic man," says one grandson, Milman Youngjohn, son of Milman Parry's sister Lucile. "He had no formal education, but he was well educated."

The little houses where the Parrys lived bubbled over with book learning. When Milman was five they lived near one of the classic Carnegie libraries, and Saturday afternoons often found him or his siblings there. Around the house they'd play a game in which one of them recited a poem until he or she could progress no further, at which point one of the others carried on. On their parlor wall, Addison remembered, "a sepia Galahad in his purity reproached us, and a panel of American poets, Emerson, Whittier, Bryant, Longfellow, and Lowell, reminded us daily that life was real, life was earnest."

As for Milman's introduction to the classics, it seems to have come via a University of California professor, John Mills Gayley, who in 1893 had come out with a popular introduction to the classic myths laced with illustrations, engravings, and maps. It was forever getting revised and updated, and when Milman was about seven his father presented him with the latest edition.

One might dismiss all this Culture as like the obligatory piano in the parlor of any respectable Victorian home, a cliché of middle class striving; the sensibilities of the Parry household bent toward the middlebrow. But it was something. And it mattered to Milman and his sisters, enriching each of them in various degrees.

Unfortunately, the respect for intellect that flavored their lives in the Oakland flats didn't align with their modest circumstances. Isaac had this "great scholarly bent," grandson Milman Youngjohn allows, but "little parental sense of responsibility for the four kids." He means this narrowly, in that Isaac felt no burning need to equip them with higher education or otherwise launch them into adult professions. His children "didn't expect a lot from him" because in dollars and cents he simply didn't have much to give them. Youngjohn's sister, Christine Henry, goes so far as to picture Milman's family as "poor and hard-pressed."

At the time Isaac's third daughter was born in 1898, he was working as a nurse at a place called the Alms House in Milpitas, a town at the southeast corner of San Francisco Bay, north of San Jose. Years later he'd work as a prosthetics fitter. Indeed, most of his working life was spent at the fringes of the world of medicine. In October, the California State Board of Pharmacy, meeting in San Francisco, announced nine new license holders, one of them being I. M. Parry. Isaac had graduated from neither college nor high school. Yet the state now anointed him, at

Isaac Parry. His son Milman
took to calling him "the Old
Dear," and the name stuck.

age thirty-three, eight months after the birth of his youngest daughter, a
"registered pharmacist."

Back in 1891, in response to unqualified druggists and their sometimes harmful preparations and prescriptions, the state set out new cre-
dentialing standards. You could become a registered pharmacist if you
were in business at the time the law took effect; you were "grandfa-
thered" into it. Or you could attend a college-level pharmacy school.
Or, as in Isaac's case, you could take and pass a series of exams. The
year before Isaac took the exams, the pharmacy board raised the bar so
that only four in ten applicants passed. One test covered basic grammar
school skills, like reading, writing, and arithmetic. Another was entirely
practical; you had to be able to convert from grams and milliliters to
English weights and measures and back again; measure sugar and albu-
men in the urine; and so on. This was a time before Big Pharma, when
your corner druggist prepared in the back of the store much of what he
sold out front.

License in hand, Isaac moved the family to Sonora County, to a
mountainous back country 125 miles east of Oakland, near the boundary
of what had recently become Yosemite National Park. It was a gold rush
country of log houses, land swindles, and rough justice. Here, daughter

Addison would tell the story, he tried to set up shop in a mining camp; the evidence suggests a place known as Summersville, today a ghost town. But "life there was too hard for our frail mother," recorded Addison, who was around six at the time of the move, precipitating their return to the East Bay—first to Alameda and then to neighboring Oakland.

This was before the coming of the big drug chains, but one East Bay outfit, Bowman Drug, became known for training young pharmacists, and for a time Isaac worked in one of their stores. At various stages of his career, Isaac was clerk, owner, and manager, though not necessarily in that order, and never with complete success. Milman Parry's wife, Marian, would all but dismiss her father-in-law for having "a drugstore of his own which he evidently wasn't successful with, so finally he just was a pharmacist in somebody else's drugstore."

On February 2, 1909, a masked man named James B. Clifton, released from San Quentin penitentiary the Thursday before, walked in off Telegraph Avenue into the von Kieferdorf drugstore at the corner of 24th Street in Oakland, up the length of the store past the display cases to the counter at the back, pointed a gun at the clerk, and demanded money. "He was compelled to take flight," the *Oakland Tribune* reported the next day, "through the courageous actions of I. M. Parry, the clerk, who hurled the first object he came in contact with" at him, a heavy book. "This put the desperado to flight. He ran from the place and shot twice at Parry, but missed. Parry ran after him." Clifton ran out into the street, grappled with a detective who happened to live next door, was arrested, brought up on charges of attempted murder, and sentenced to life in prison.

Most of Isaac's working life was more prosaic. His was an age when many treated themselves with patent medicines like Fletcher's Castoria or Pinkham's Vegetable Compound or, as one account has it, other "gargles, inhalations, enemas, poultices, tonics, elixirs, pills, lotions, syrups, and ointments." In 1911, when Milman was nine, I. M. Parry placed prominent ads in the *Oakland Tribune* for his own hair concoction.

YOUR HAIR CAN BE LONG, LUXURIANT AND GLORIOUS

Let us help you to attain a luxuriant healthy beautiful head of hair. Take our advice, try a bottle of

PARRY'S HAIR TONIC AND DANDRUFF REMEDY.

This tonic costs only 50¢, but every bottle is worth a fortune to your head. Cleans the scalp, feeds the pores, renews life in partly dead hair roots. . . . Phone me now before you forget it, and I'll deliver a bottle to your door.

A few years later, Isaac, by now almost fifty and a little better established, belonged to the local association of druggists. When in 1913 the group met to discuss its recent policy of limiting Sunday hours, Isaac was among those to speak out. "There is absolutely no use to keep the stores open all day Sunday," said he. "Pharmacists are human beings just like other persons and therefore are entitled to at least a few hours of rest on Sundays." No need to extract a few more dollars from the long week.

For Isaac Parry, no dark bass notes drift down to us of laziness or

Your Hair Can Be Long, Luxuriant and Glorious.

Let us help you to attain a luxuriant, healthy, beautiful head of hair. Take our advice, try a bottle of

Parry's Hair Tonic and Dandruff Remedy.

This tonic costs only 50c, but every bottle is worth a fortune to your head. Cleans the scalp, feeds the pores, renews life in partly dead hair roots and enables a new growth to appear. Eradicates dandruff and keeps it away. Don't hesitate. Don't take chances. Use a bottle at my risk, and if you are not entirely satisfied, I will refund every cent you paid for it. There isn't anything better and I know of nothing so good. Phone me now before you forget it, and I'll deliver a bottle to your door.

Price, 50 cents a bottle.

I. M. PARRY. Mfg. Chemist,
737 Telegraph Avenue, corner 24th
Phones
Oakland 3574; Home A-3021

In 1911, a neighborhood druggist typically prepared in the back of his store much of what he sold out front. Here, Isaac Parry's own hair tonic.

dissipation, but neither do high notes of burning personal ambition. At the store, manning the counter and compounding prescriptions, he was competent enough. But his was a familiar middle-class story that never reached its third act, Horatio Alger–style, where industry and pluck transcend modest roots. He didn't become rich. He wasn't highly accomplished in ways Milman's future colleagues might have valued.

On the other hand, he carved out a life for himself and his family, retaining the love and respect of his children. At home, certainly, he seems to have been far more approachable than the stereotypically stony nineteenth-century father figure; in a letter to his sister Addison in 1935, Milman would write of his father: "His candor is such that he cannot say the smallest thing without showing his whole state of being." When he was young, Milman took to calling him "the Old Dear," and the name stuck.

In his eighties Isaac sent his grandson Milman Youngjohn a cheerful Christmas card otherwise all sleighs and carolers:

> *Hello Grandson*
> *How is German Dilligence?*
> *Are you getting your name Up?*
> *Are you a good Husband?*
> *Do you live within your income?*
> *Are you always a*
> *Gentleman?*
> *This last question needs*
> *a yes to satisfy*
> *The old Dear*
> *Lots of love to you & Beep.*

This was not some old codger's sanctimonious missive, stresses Mr. Youngjohn, but grandfatherly playfulness, complete with a gentle dig at Youngjohn's own father, known for his Teutonic efficiency. *Here* was his grandfather as he remembered him, never entirely serious. One time Isaac was asked, out of the blue, whether he was Jewish, this despite the family's established Welsh Quaker roots. His reply was vintage Isaac: "Well, the Phoenicians are known to have mined tin in Wales around the time of Christ." Thus, a reply that was not quite a reply, swaddled in a tidbit of sly semitruth.

It's harder to say how Milman's mother, Alice, figured in his life, in part because she died when he was just sixteen. They were close, perhaps more so even than Milman and his father, Marian would guess later. A studio portrait shows Alice in her midforties, wearing a lacy, high-collared dress, Milman about seven, his arm draped casually around her shoulder. He wears a little jacket and looks for all the world like Beaver from the 1950s TV show. They make for an appealing mother-son two-some, if we can count on a posed Victorian portrait to reveal anything at all. But this same photo, when she saw it later, exerted a hold on Marian, too. She wasn't used to seeing her husband looking so easy and relaxed, yet there he was, "snuggled up to her. He was very affectionate and loving as a small child. . . . I don't know when or how the . . . iron entered into his soul."

Marian came to view his mother—through Milman himself, most likely, since she never met her—as a strong, disciplined figure. "She had to be, living the kind of life she did," presumably a reference to Isaac's looser ways. "Our mother was artistic in a rather Jane Austen sense," reported Addison. "She painted well and played the piano." A scrawled

Mother—Alice Emerson Parry—and son.

caption on the mother-son photo reads: "She supported the family giving piano lessons."

Marian would picture the Parrys—their roots back east, with a silly family coat of arms no less, and a tendency to distance themselves from their neighbors—as infected by snobbism: "They felt they were superior," if without obvious reason to think so. Once, years later, their son Adam was having dinner with his aunt Lucile, who'd married the owner of a forty-three-acre orange grove in El Cajon, outside San Diego. "Oh," she gushed at one point, "I wish I had peasant blood." Adam, who could be snarky, fairly choked on his wine: "Well, Lucile, what do you think you have?"

After Milman's death, one of his former students at Harvard, Harry Levin, painted a warmly tinted "Portrait of a Homeric Scholar" that spoke of Milman's presumably "overburdened adolescence"; it left him, wrote Levin, with "the emotional grasp of one who has supported himself since the age of thirteen." This is not exactly true; his parents supported him. Yet it nods to a truth—that Milman's equivocally middle-class upbringing conferred on him an ancillary education better-off boys sometimes missed: Regularly, especially in the summers, during and after the Great War, Milman worked—at a sawmill in Mount Shasta near the Oregon border; as an electrician's helper; on the railroad; as a "passer-boy" of hot rivets. He did not regret his need to hold down a job, and he would put to good use his practical skills later, in Yugoslavia.

If wealth and gentle breeding didn't pervade the Parry household, a certain "lightness-of-being" did. The Parrys were nominally of Quaker stock, but religion did not intrude much in their lives; "they went to any church they were near," it would be said of them. We don't know just how George, Alice Emerson's son, came to be absorbed into her marriage with Isaac, but it seems he was, easily and completely; when Lucile was married in 1920, she learned for the first time that George, ten years her senior, wasn't her biological brother. And while Isaac would never understand much of what his son achieved, when the first volume of *Serbo-Croatian Heroic Songs* came out in 1954, he asked for an autographed copy from Albert Lord. "Sometimes I think I loved him too much during his life time," he wrote of Milman.

Milman grew up with books, tales of distant places, verbal play, and affection. Whatever he had growing up (save perhaps the cold baths he endured as a child), he flourished in it. "He liked the domesticity that he was used to at home," his wife would say, with his mother and sisters. As a child, sister Addison—who tended to cast a rosy hue on anything related to the family—pictured her brother as "reared in a secure and loving home. Like our parents we faced up quite early to the often harsh aspects of life. More than sisters and brothers," she wrote, "we were comrades-in-arms. No one of us would have turned from life nor let another down." They didn't have everything growing up, or even a lot, but Milman and his siblings had enough.

A few years after Alice died in 1918, Isaac remarried, to a woman named Blanche, who arrived too late to figure much in Milman's life. Figuring more, at least through Marian's eyes, was Addison; with their mother's death, Marian theorized, *someone* needed to step into the maternal role. And Addison, who would never marry, twenty-two at the time, six years older than Milman, was it. To Marian, she was "in a way in love with her brother." Indeed, she'd suggest, with a hint of bitterness or maybe triumph, that her marriage to Milman left Addison "upset by the interruption of their intimacy."

For much of her adult life, Addison worked as a secretary in an academic department at Cal, the University of California at Berkeley, which she briefly attended, hoping to become a teacher. Back at Oakland Technical High School, from which she graduated just as Milman enrolled, she wrote several stories for *Scribe,* the school literary magazine. In one, the hate of two enemy soldiers on the Western Front is transmuted into something like love. In another, the narrator tells of discovering, in a remote Great Lakes camp, an American Indian boy masterfully playing a violin left him by his French father; brought to the big city, his musical light is extinguished. These are not insubstantial stories.

With Addison, probably more than with his other siblings, Milman connected. His letters to her later verge on frothy. "We are having a bit of fairly good weather," he writes Addison from Paris, "that is, what you'd call the worst weather possible in California." Later, from Marseilles, he lavishly describes its Old Port only to interrupt himself:

Fine description, is it not? Another letter like this and I shall be writing travelogues.

What are you doing? Why the devil don't you write me and

say something about yourself. Are you writing? Are you step-
ping out? How old are you? I'd surely like to know how things
are getting along. After all I am your brother, though a very bad
brother, I admit.

Here and elsewhere in his letters from France it's as if he's out to
reproduce the light, even zany, side of their Oakland youth.

The impulse extended even to his father. In Milman's letters, it could
seem that Isaac, thirty-seven years his senior, was just one of the clan,
included among recipients of his lighthearted epistolary treatments.
From Greece, in 1925, Milman comments on his father's letter, which
had been "written on a thin paper of a sort more typically used for other
purposes (those purposes which, according to you, are necessary but
never talked about)." After telling of his travels in Greece, including
references to this "unclean race and its doubtful food," he concludes by
simply asserting, "The Parthenon is good looking."

"So to end this letter, the only one I've written like it, for travel letters are of doubtful value. But for your sake, Old Dear, anything. . . .
Your noblest and most filial, Milman."

5

ARMILIUS THE SAGE

Elementary school for Milman was Grant School, at 29th Street, easy walking distance from the house. Then, beginning in 1916 he was off to Oakland Tech, the new crown jewel of the city's public school system, a mile and a half up Broadway. Tech's earlier incarnation was as a school for the mechanical trades. The yearbook still included gray, leaden ads for machine tool suppliers. Behind the main building, with its façade of white classical columns, stood four low, shed-like shops for woodworking, metalwork, and other mechanical arts.

Tech was a big, roiling place, a modern high school, said to be third largest in the country, its arrival on upper Broadway in 1915 enough of an event to garner a long article in the pages of *The Architect*. For its 2,000 day students, class ranged from 7:30 to 3:30; then came the next wave, the school's 3,000 afternoon and evening students. Milman was there for three and a half years, his time darkened by historical events brought closer to home than students, parents, or teachers might have wished.

The Great War broke out in August 1914, America's entry coming in April 1916, during Milman's first semester. Spy fever closed down the radio club, founded a few years earlier, apparently for fear of wayward or illicit signals. Trenches were dug on the ball fields behind the school to introduce the boys to the Western Front. Required military education included drills and sham bayonet attacks. Mechanical drawing students made blueprints for the Oakland shipyards. A cartoon in Milman's class yearbook showed the devil pitchforking the hated Hun, in his spiked helmet, sprawled in the mud, defeated.

The Armistice of November 1918 brought only partial relief, for it corresponded to the height of the Spanish flu pandemic, which would kill more than fifty million people worldwide. All across Oakland, the flu shattered the normal routines of life. The city's Municipal Auditorium became a huge infirmary. For weeks at a time during Milman's last year, Tech shut down altogether. In October, all Oakland theaters, movie houses, and churches were ordered closed. "After we've washed the dishes we're going to the Red Cross rooms and help make the gauze masks," a Cal student wrote her parents around this time. "Everyone is going to have to wear them tomorrow. . . . The campus will surely be a funny-looking place. I don't think they do any good myself." She was right; later studies showed they little impeded the spread of the uncannily contagious disease. Altogether, the epidemic took fourteen hundred lives in Oakland alone. At its height, on October 25, 1918, Parry's mother died, age fifty-three; her death certificate lists stomach cancer as the cause. She was buried three days later. Funeral services were held at the local undertaker's, Truman's, on Telegraph Avenue, a few blocks from the Parry house.

"The world is a different one from that in which we lived before school closed," the weekly *Scribe* editorialized a few weeks after the Armistice, the epidemic at high tide but the war, at least, thankfully over. "It is a world with a new standard of morals and of life raised forever, a world dominated by a great God-given permanent Peace, brought by the victory of all that is just and right and humane."

The following May, toward the end of Milman's final semester, the *Scribe* reported that graduating seniors were "a brainy lot," with 85 of 155 grads planning to enter college in the fall. Of those, 14 aimed to become teachers, 8 lawyers, 6 doctors, 11 engineers, most of the remainder bound for "commercial and office work." None voiced plans to become a classical scholar.

Yet it would not have been so wayward or surprising had someone done so. Greek wasn't in the Tech curriculum, but Latin was; three teachers, all unmarried women, shouldered the classroom load. The most energetic among them seems to have been Elsie Henrietta Martens, likely the unnamed Latin teacher who, Addison wrote, had "glimpsed [Milman's] potentialities" at Tech. The semester before his arrival at Tech, Martens had started up a Latin Club.

LATIN CLUB'S LIVELY PLANS

Members to Laugh and Feast as Ancients Did

Thus were the club's intentions announced in the *Scribe*. "Now, Latin will no longer be a dreaded, dry as dust subject. . . . Plans for socials, entertainments and dances, together with the learning of songs and games, will soon be in progress, which will develop in time into the acting of plays and holding feasts similar to those held in the early days of Rome."

Miss Martens followed through. "Twenty-seven members of the Latin department enjoyed a picnic hike to Redwood Canyon last Saturday, coming home tired but happy on the last afternoon train." Latin-themed jokes appeared in the *Scribe:*

TEACHER: Give the principal parts of a first conjugation verb.
FIRST LATINIST: Tell me one!
SECOND LATINIST: D. . . . if I know.
FIRST LATINIST: Damifino, damifinare, damifinavi, damifinatum.

Milman took four years of Latin, along with four of English and one of French. He also took algebra, geometry, trigonometry, chemistry, and two years of history. Plus a year of typewriting; Tech liked to show off its 116 typewriters, ranged across three large rooms, much as schools today celebrate their computers. The Remington and Underwood companies each sponsored typing competitions. Given Milman's later reliance on his typing skills, the class may have done him as much good as some of his academic subjects.

We can't know for certain whether Miss Martens's Latin Club drew in Milman, for in his class yearbook, where most seniors listed activities and accomplishments, he didn't bother, just as he wouldn't in college. Addison, photographed for the yearbook three years earlier in a dark sailor's top and cheerful neckerchief, listed Honor Society, Tennis Club, *Scribe,* and Historical Society as among her interests. Milman was represented only by his photograph; his haircut, a severe razor cut along the sides, swept up into a pompadour on top, suggests he was not immune to fashion.

Insisting that the war had bestowed on all "a broader and finer vision of the part it is our privilege to play in a democracy," and with hope that "the lessons of war are not forgot in the hour of peace," Milman's Class of June 1919 dedicated its yearbook to "The New Order of Things."

On June 6, Milman was among nineteen boys and twenty-nine girls awarded the Gold T, the school's top scholastic honor.

On June 30, he applied for admission to the University of California at Berkeley (which until 1919, when Los Angeles became the second, was the sole Cal campus), and that fall enrolled. The university, which had moved from Oakland in 1873, was just up the Telegraph Avenue streetcar line from the Parry house on 26th Street; he could have walked the four miles if he'd been of a mind. In the middle of campus stood the Sather Tower and the new university library, its great columns gleaming in the California sun. To the west, down the hill, was downtown Berkeley. Above, the campus climbed into the verdant hills and the mountain gorge that was Strawberry Canyon. From here, Milman could look down on the East Bay flats from which he'd come and to which he would return each day after class.

He was serious enough at his studies, getting decent if not stellar grades, including As in Greek both semesters his first year; he also took economics, political science, Latin, English, and public speaking. And each term those first two years he took the equivalent of a half course in military skills as a member of ROTC; a photo dated 1920 shows Milman in uniform; it seems a bit crumpled, actually, not quite ready for inspection. Early on, he changed his major from pre-law to Greek. Later, someone would call Parry "one of those rare and happy scholars who early find an absorbing and fruitful field of study." But he didn't find it *that* early. Just now, in his first and second years at Cal, he could hardly have named his career path with confidence.

It was still a time for experiment and adventure. When he was about eighteen, he hopped a freight train, bound for his newly married sister Lucile's house in Texas, twelve hundred miles away. If anyone discouraged him from doing it, no evidence comes down to us. Addison packed him some lunch, waved goodbye, and the next thing we know, Milman was being dropped off in the middle of the desert, near tiny Clint, Texas, at Lucile's. Her son, Milman Youngjohn, reported how "this scruffy looking kid shows up," he's taken into the house, and his father turns to Lucile: 'This man says he's your brother.'" She scarcely recognized him.

Milman in uniform, a little after the
end of World War I; at Cal, military
training was mandatory.

Milman was in a bad way, couldn't hold down his food. But after a brief
recuperation his sister and brother-in-law dropped him off at the station
and he was on his way back to Oakland.

Sometime in 1921, Milman got the writing bug. That September's
issue of the Cal literary magazine, *Occident,* carried his fantasy, or fable,
or reverie, or whatever it really was, entitled "Tales of Armilius the Sage."
It began:

> From his earliest youth the sage Armilius had studied all wis-
> dom, with this one hope: that he should find the Key to Immor-
> tality. All ancient lore he read, and all the learned discussions of
> the doctors of his own time, and as the years went by Armilius
> the Sage became famed throughout the world for his learning.

What followed were seven brief fables presumably owed to this
Armilius, about whom we learn only that he grapples with the riddles
of human existence. Armilius recounts the History of the King's Beard,

tells of thirty-seven dragons who weep at another dragon's death, of a pig named Alexander, of the battle between Mind and Heart within Armilius himself, and finally of his own death, when he finds the Key to Immortality in the life of his son and his son's son. These tales owe nothing to any historic or mythical figure I can trace. They are rendered in a peculiar faux-archaic language and can seem like nothing so much as a sophomoric romp—a sophomore being about what Milman was at the time—or perhaps, in the spirit of his father, a playful literary put-on. But there is enough in them to see hints of a serious young man who, not entirely at home in his own time, not yet having found his way, is trying on masks, searching for who he is, or who he is to become. A teller of tales? A searcher of ancient truths? An original and authentic intellectual voice?

His mind was loading up with new knowledge. But otherwise, Milman's first four semesters at Cal probably left him little changed from the boy he was at Tech. He was still living at home in Oakland. Though he had made Greek his major, he was momentarily distracted enough by the idea of becoming a physician that, in early 1922, he would sign up for a course in anatomy before precipitately dropping it. Mostly, he went to class, gathered credits, marched toward his BA.

But then, between the spring of 1922 and the summer of 1924, everything changed. He met a woman with whom he became intimate. He got her pregnant and married her. He became the father of a little girl. He found himself part of a campus bohemian element whose leader, a celebrated anthropologist, may have served as life model for him. He earned his bachelor's degree. He took some time off, wrote a paper about Homer, and got his master's degree. After yet more uncertainty and much disappointment, muddied by money and its insistent demands, he boarded a ship with his wife and baby and sailed for France.

6

MRS. PARRY

In a story Marian Thanhouser, the future Mrs. Milman Parry, wrote for *Occident*, the Cal literary magazine, in 1920, Mrs. Warren is a widower, living with her twenty-year-old son, Donald. He is in love with Esmè Searle and hopes to marry her. How ridiculous! she thinks. Why, he is still a child. She glances at his framed baby picture, "sturdy in tiny overalls, and with mussed hair." Marry this Esmè, whom he'd met at an art tea? "A girl who frequented studios, who wore jade earrings and lip-salve—who used theoretic idealizing of love to sanction her abandonment to every emotional adventure she might manage." No, it was impossible.

Just then, the doorbell rings and Esmè stands before her. "Oh, Mrs. Warren," she cries, "you are his mother. You will understand. You must have felt it, too: I can't marry him. It's not that he's too young. I'm too old."

Well, not so very old, Mrs. Warren tries to reassure her.

" 'I'm twenty-four,' says Esmè Searle. 'A woman of twenty-four—a boy of twenty.' " How could she, Mrs. Warren, understand how a woman could feel old at twenty-four? And how could she tell Donald it was over? She begs Mrs. Warren to do it for her.

After she leaves, Mrs. Warren stands by the window, "full of pity for everyone in the world. The dead leaves played in an eddy of sun and glinting dust. The church bells pealed golden through the pale golden air. . . . How should she tell him?"

Marian wrote this story before she met Milman, but the story's themes of age and experience, and some of the details, too, seem to uncannily prefigure their actual courtship.

A photo portrait from a trip to Atlantic City, when she was still only thirteen, shows Marian on the cusp of young womanhood. She is with her mother and a family friend, the three of them artfully arranged for the camera, turned out in furs and flowered hats. Marian was from a well-off Jewish family in Milwaukee. Her father, Frank Thanhouser, had enrolled at Harvard, but dropped out when he married Marian's mother, Mildred. Mildred was the daughter of a Milwaukee department store magnate, Max Landauer, a force in the local Jewish community and a major philanthropist. Marian was their only child.

Marian came to see herself, in her mother's eyes, as weak, sick, and dependent. At one point, Mildred decreed that she not go to school at all and had her tutored at home instead. It was awful, Marian would remember. She had no friends. Her mother, a formidable figure, was forever out and about, active in clubs, while Marian was stuck at home.

When she had her tonsils taken out, she came out of the operation briefly paralyzed. But she recovered, and finally went to Milwaukee's Riverside High School, whose yearbook anointed her "our class poet." Several of her poems appeared in national publications.

> *Sometimes at night I heard the dark,*
> *Wide and wind-shaken, calling me.*
> *I should get up, and flying high*
> *Above the tree-tops to the sea,*
> *Scream till the waves scream back at me.*

She dedicated one poem to Rupert Brooke. In it, she spoke of "life's one and valiant truth / The strenuous abandonment of youth."

Once out of high school, she was held back by a host of real or imagined medical problems. She grew tired easily. She was never diagnosed with tuberculosis, yet heard it said that her lungs were not healthy and pink but a sickly gray. A year late, she enrolled at the University of Wisconsin at Madison, where she came down with the Spanish flu. At one point, she was down to eighty-five pounds: "I had to be taken care of and put to bed." Several of her friends died, but she recovered. Finally, in 1920, she was hauled off to mild, mellow California and the university at Berkeley. It was all for her health, Mother told her.

The young Marian Thanhouser, the future Mrs. Parry, with her mother, Mildred, and a family friend in Atlantic City, New Jersey, 1912.

Mildred, forty-eight, with most of a bachelor's degree from Vassar in hand, enrolled at the same time as her daughter. She loaded up on economics, political science, and philosophy, finally earning a BA a year and a half later, then began taking graduate courses. During much of this period, mother and daughter lived together, for some time at Cloyne Court, a renowned local architect's eruption of cedar shingles up the hill near the northeast corner of the campus, today student housing, back then a residential hotel.

When Marian presented her academic record to Cal in January of

1920 she'd already accumulated twenty-four college credits at Wisconsin, mostly in English and French. But now, at Cal, Mother insisted, she needed to take it easy, on account of her health; she must not burden herself with a full load of courses. Marian's transcript shows that she'd attend classes for a semester, take off the next. One day, about two years after arriving in California, Marian groused to a friend that she'd grown weary of her old, stale life, of "being ill and trying to get strong and somehow never getting strong." She'd had enough of the whole business, it went so far back. But wasn't Marian quite "comfortable"? ventured her friend. Didn't her family have money? Why not just buy her way out of her lassitude? Maybe she needed "some really . . . interesting clothes"—no more of the same old pleated skirts and sweaters! So Marian splurged on a new wardrobe. And she bought a dog, a German shepherd named Argus, whom she began taking to class with her: "I put on a sort of show."

And one day, Milman Parry was there to see it.

Marian had become friends with the Classics department secretary, a young woman named Harriet, who administered the department library. Classics faculty had their offices in Wheeler Hall, the great classical revival building that had gone up near the heart of the campus a few years before. But the department library, its shelves laden with Homer, Plato, and Euripides, occupied a suite of rooms elsewhere—in the southwest corner of the university library, on the third floor. In one of them, students in the department would congregate. It was a lovely refuge, on sunny afternoons bathed in light from the big windows overlooking the campus. Marian had no business being there but Harriet had the keys, so there she was. And there—the spring of 1922 seems the best estimate for when—she met Milman.

He was good-looking, his features regular, his long face with just a hint of Lincolnesque gauntness, sometimes a pipe planted between his teeth. Maybe not the all-time handsomest man on campus, Marian would say, but close. But "it was our tastes and things" that brought them together. One of the first times they got a chance to really talk she was taking Latin and having trouble with Cicero's "De Senectute," a reverie on aging and death. Milman, with four years of Latin at Tech and now more at Cal, helped her make sense of it. They both loved the outdoors. They'd hike up behind the campus, past the broad swath of country that would soon become the Coliseum, wandering through Strawberry Canyon, with its beds of boulders, tangles of creeper and fern, canopies of willow and oak. "We just got along so well."

Marian was lovely with dark, Mediterranean features, thick brown hair, great big eyes. She was no intellectual, but did not lack intellectual gifts. She was doing well enough at Cal. Her poetry was of its time—and good enough, as we've seen, to be published in its time. Back at Wisconsin she'd been an "ardent" student; this was her word. At one point, she'd worked day and night on a paper on Emily Dickinson, hoping to land a coveted spot on the school's literary magazine. "I was very ambitious and I wanted to be 'a big woman on the hill'"; the Dickinson paper would do it. But it didn't. More than six decades later, she'd still ask herself why—a few punctuation errors too many, maybe; or, the professor who liked her work out of favor among the other faculty. "It was a very, very bitter disappointment to me."

Now, at Cal, she wrote several pieces for *Occident,* which, all through the buoyant early 1920s, luxuriated in artful covers, quality paper, generous editorial resources. Its stylized logo was a rendering of the ship Ulysses sailed back from Troy, captioned with a quote from Tennyson: "To strive, to seek, to find, and not to yield." It was *Occident* that carried Marian's story of Mrs. Warren and Esmè. For another piece, she interviewed an alum, Jay Stowitts, a track star during his time at Cal who later gave himself over to ballet and joined the dance company of the Russian ballerina Pavlova, touring the world with her. "Stowitts, through whose brain now whirl masques and pantomimes, kept facts and statistics in so orderly a manner" back at Cal that he'd been named to the economics honor society. He was an unusual subject, and Marian handled him gracefully.

Milman was further along in his studies than Marian, closer to earning his BA. But in other ways, he couldn't help but remind you of Mrs. Warren's boy: he was so very, very young. He tried to act older, gave out his age as more than it was. But when, early in their relationship, Marian met Milman's father, Isaac blew the boy's cover, and said of his son, *Why, he isn't even 20 yet!* In 1981, in a series of interviews over three days that Marian gave Pamela Newhouse, a young classics scholar interested in writing a biography of Parry, Milman's youth makes for a recurrent theme. Her mother seemed to like him well enough, but with the caveat that, after all, "he was very young"—maybe too young to imagine permanently with her daughter; she'd be better off back in Milwaukee marrying one of the local businessmen. At nineteen or twenty, Milman was not a member of one of Cal's residential clubs, like Dahlonega on Channing Way, or Tilicum on Durant Avenue; he still lived at home, and may have been romantically and sexually unseasoned. Now, in the hands of a woman three years his senior and her new friends, he was drawn into waters he was not quite ready to navigate.

Marian had become one of a group of students, faculty, and hangers-on centered around two Berkeley anthropology professors, Robert Lowie and, especially, Alfred Kroeber, that made for its own little bohemia. The Berkeley campus would one day include a Kroeber Hall and a Lowie Museum; "All my friends turned into buildings," she liked to say later. For now, though, the anthropology crowd was a source of stimulating friendships, easy companionability, and "advanced" views on sex. "We were the children of this, you know, circle," said Marian of Milman and herself, the two of them among the youngest in the group.

One of Marian's close friends was Raina Prohme, a redheaded spark-plug of a crusading journalist from Chicago recently drawn to the Bay Area. Her own involvement with the anthropologists had spurred an interest in cultures and religions, and would ultimately draw her to China and its revolutions; Marian would be there to see her off when the *Tenyo Maru* sailed with her to Asia. Raina seems to have been loved and admired by men and women alike. But not by Milman. Introduced to the group by Marian, he'd formed a dislike of Raina, and she of him. Eight years older than he, she had firm views and a vivid personality, neither of which, it seems, young Milman found attractive.

Marian and Milman were living through what historians would anoint as the Roaring Twenties, the era of the flappers, with women ostensibly freed from corsets and crusty nineteenth-century mores. Bedding one's boyfriend "wasn't in the air among my mother's friends' daughters," Marian would say, but in their own little bohemia, things were different. Their crowd included men and women "of a good deal of sophistication and . . . some of them [were] quite wild." In this looser setting, the two of them soon embarked on an affair in which, she'd say, "I was more or less the leader." An only child, her mother the family's dominant force, all her life she'd been caught up in girl things. Now Milman's "masculine reactions," his sheer, square-jawed maleness, seemed exotic to her. It was great fun, she'd say, of those early days.

But then, in the spring, about a year after they'd met, Milman having earned his BA and been inducted into Phi Beta Kappa, "it turned out I was pregnant."

The news did not go over well with him. "That's the beginning of the baby and the end of me," she'd report him saying.

"He was just so young," recalled Marian, as if to excuse the unthinking cruelty of the remark. At least from the vantage point of old age, youthful trials behind her, she made it sound as if it hardly troubled her. After all, "it was more in line with my business to have babies sooner or later."

On May 11, 1923, in San Francisco, they married. Her mother gave them money for a honeymoon, during which they hitchhiked down the Pacific coast to Carmel, about a hundred miles south of Berkeley.

Marian around the time of her marriage to Milman in 1923.

They camped out, which left Marian impressed with her new husband's Scouts-bred skills. She wasn't used to roughing it but took to it well enough that, one night, when it turned dark and cold and Milman suggested they board a passing bus, she objected, "No, no, we're not going to take that bus." So they stuck to the plan, got picked up by a succession of friendly drivers, and finally made it to Carmel. There her mother had a rented house, with its warm bathroom, waiting for them. Later they hitched their way up the mostly still wild Carmel Valley.

So, that spring and early summer of 1923, they were a young married couple with a baby on the way. Their first home was an apartment on La Vereda Road in the Berkeley hills, near campus. Milman took a few graduate courses that spring, but in the summer took a leave from the university. When they learned of a place near Santa Cruz, a former poultry farm, they picked up and moved there. It was beautiful up in the mountains, Marian would say later; but the caption on a snapshot from the period, showing her sitting, curled up on the worn wooden step of their cabin, describes her as "pregnant and depressed." Meanwhile, Milman sometimes grew bored and needed a dose of "civilization," so would head into Berkeley for the day. Finally, after an awkward and unwelcome approach to Marian by a friend's brother, they felt compelled to move again. This time it was to a place at the far end of the Bay Area from Santa Cruz, Mill Valley, across the Golden Gate (not the great bridge, yet unbuilt, but the break in the headlands between bay and ocean) in Marin County. In Mill Valley, they moved into a furnished cottage on Molino Avenue, at the top of a flight of too many steps, and waited for the baby. For the birth itself, they went into San Francisco. Their daughter was born on January 28, 1924. They named her Marian; for reasons unknown, they took to calling her Wux.

It was early in this fraught and restless period that Milman showed up at the door of Ivan Linforth, one of his Greek professors. He was finished with classical studies, he told him. He was going to become a writer. He had by now contributed several essays to *Occident,* which had named him one of its (eleven) associate editors. Though he'd skipped the graduation ceremony for his BA, he was one of four writers credited with his class's Senior Extravaganza, a Cal theatrical tradition; that year's production, "But It Wasn't," set Athlete, Poet, and Businessman all vying for the hand of the fair maiden. A 1923 *Blue and Gold* yearbook photograph shows Milman, hands behind his back, with his three co-writers, looking bored, or at least fashionably indifferent. But he must have enjoyed the work, the camaraderie, and any modest acclaim that fell to him. For it was around then, probably late spring of 1923, that he approached Linforth and apprised him of his plans to become a writer. A writer, in particular, like a certain well-known Irish essayist (whose name, unfortunately, is lost to us). Spending much time in the company of Aeschylus, Linforth was given to understand, would corrupt his natural talent and style. It sounded to Linforth like a fait accompli; this was what young Parry had decided. From what he'd seen of him in class, Parry was a good student, but not one whose merits seemed so extraordinary that he, Linforth, should try to argue him out of it. He wouldn't try. He didn't try.

The next time Parry and Linforth met was in the fall, the fall of the great Berkeley fire; whipped by fierce winds coming out of the east, the conflagration left much of the city north and east of campus a smoldering ruin of stone chimneys, all that was left once the frame houses, more than six hundred of them, burned down around them. Milman and Marian, whether in Mill Valley by now or still in Santa Cruz, weren't affected. But for Linforth the fire would have all but date-stamped his memory of this second meeting with Parry. Now, he'd recall, Milman no longer talked of a writer's life. He seemed to have forgotten the idea entirely. Now all he could talk about was Homer.

7

MILMAN ON THE BEACH

Homer was the veritable First Cause of the Western literary tradition; author of the *Iliad* and the *Odyssey*, the two great epic poems of gods and goddesses, heroes and war. "Epic" because they were long, 25,000 lines of ancient Greek verse making up the two of them. Epic because they told of honor, high ambition, bravery, the yearning for home, all on huge poetic canvases.

> *As soon as Dawn with her rose-red fingers shone again*
> *I dispatched some men to Circe's halls to bring*
> *the dead Elpenor's body. We cut logs in haste*
> *and out on the island's sharpest jutting headland*
> *held his funeral rites in sorrow, streaming tears.*

[FAGLES *Odyssey*, 12, 10]

Each was composed in a regular, little-varying poetic meter known as dactylic hexameter. In each, themes were repeated, speeches were repeated, heroes were identified with repeated "epithets," like "swift-footed Achilles" or "wily Odysseus," the repetitions themselves a kind of music, adding to the poems' mesmerizing impact when they found a receptive ear.

The *Iliad* is about Achilles, who, angered by what he deems an injustice done him, refuses to lend his matchless warrior skills to the siege of Troy. The *Odyssey* is about Odysseus and his adventures during a ten-year journey home from Troy to Ithaca and his wife, Penelope.

Once, the Homeric epics were the one sure element of a reputable education. Even those with thin memories of Homer might dimly recall Greek ships hauled up onto the beach opposite the heights of Troy; or Odysseus slaughtering Penelope's suitors, the slack, selfish men who'd defiled his palace in Ithaca. Both poems have large casts of characters, long speeches, blood, gore, nobly expressed feeling, and memorable scenes—of Odysseus tied to the mast of his ship in order to resist the seductive call of the Sirens; of Achilles dragging the dead body of Hector around the walls of Troy—that have worked their way into the West's collective memory.

> *But he raged on, grimly camped by his fast fleet,*
> *the royal son of Peleus, the swift runner Achilles.*
> *Now he no longer haunted the meeting grounds*
> *where men win glory, now he no longer went to war*
> *but day after day he ground his heart out, waiting there,*
> *yearning, always yearning for battle cries and combat.*

[FAGLES *Iliad*, 1, 581]

Not every ear over the past three millenniums has been receptive to Homer, whether in Greek or in translation, especially in settings awash in schoolhouse scoffery: Even with a devoted teacher, many a high school student, stuck with Odysseus on Calypso's island, or witnessing another bronze spear splatter another poor brain on the plains of Troy, has had his fill of Homer, with no wish for more. Homer doesn't take with everyone. But surely, that summer of 1923, he took with Milman Parry.

For three years, Milman had been caught up in Greek studies at Cal. Even without taking a course dedicated solely to the *Iliad* or the *Odyssey*—as it appears he did not—he'd certainly read some of the "books," or chapters, of the epics; Homer's language was often used to teach ancient Greek. But now, it seems, Milman fairly devoured Homer, something there, in the poet's language, intriguing and delighting him, striking him in ways he was eager to think about.

> *Now,*
> *the lustrous queen soon reached the hidden vault*
> *and stopped at the oaken doorsill, work an expert*

sanded smooth and trued to the line some years ago,
planting the doorjambs snugly, hanging shining doors.
At once she loosed the thong from around its hook,
inserted the key and aiming straight and true,
shot back the bolts—and the rasping doors groaned
as loud as a bull will bellow, champing grass at pasture.

[FAGLES *Odyssey,* 21, 50]

According to Sterling Dow, a Harvard classics professor who in the early 1960s spoke with Cal's Ivan Linforth, "Parry had some ideas about Homer, and asked if they might make an acceptable M.A. thesis." Yes, Linforth replied, he thought they might. That summer Parry had given himself, in abject surrender, to Homer. And those marathon sessions with the *Odyssey* and the *Iliad,* lying on a Los Angeles beach (as Linforth told it and Dow recorded it), had driven him back to classical studies.

In the summer of 1923, it needs saying, Milman Parry was no real scholar, however ordained to become one he might later seem. But the academic field into which he stepped in the fall of 1919 and pursued through his undergraduate years had taken with him, deeply. Back at Tech, he'd studied Latin, not Greek. But in his freshman year at Cal, Milman took two big five-credit courses, curricular gateways into ancient Greek studies. He must have had some premonition to enroll in the first place, as the class was a real time sink, meeting for an hour every day, through the week and across the whole academic year, with tons of reading, the familiar "Roman" alphabet soon surrendering to the thetas, phis, and epsilons of the Greek alphabet. Parry had entered Cal as a pre-law student. But almost immediately, his sister Addison, who lived with him at home on 26th Street, would report, Greek "became his deep and abiding love. I think it was the sheer beauty and grandeur of spoken Greek—and the great delight the Greeks found in simply being alive—that attracted him in the first place."

Early on, in ancient Greek, Milman must have felt like a newcomer to town at a big, raucous party where he knows no one, lost in a blur of new faces, names, and unfamiliar references; but linger in town and the blur may resolve, the once alien becoming friendly and familiar. For the newcomer, ancient Greek is its "case" endings—nominative, genitive, dative, accusative, vocative—that establish a word's function in a sentence. Ancient Greek is Pericles's funeral oration from Thucydides; Agamemnon's fatal return to the House of Atreus in Aeschylus's *Oresteia;* the tedious yet oddly thrilling Catalogue of the Ships from the *Iliad;* Odysseus wandering through Hades, speaking with the dead. All, in time, to many a seasoned classicist's eyes and ears, warmly endearing.

Across his undergraduate years, Milman would take no fewer than fifteen courses in Greek, forty college credits in all, plus seven in Latin. So, by the summer of 1923, BA in hand, he was long past that first party, where he'd known no one; now, more or less, he knew everyone. Over the intervening years, names, eras, ideas, and works of literature had become sharply distinct; he'd be able to refer to them knowingly for the rest of his life, in time even the most recalcitrant ideas becoming friends.

At Cal, during these years, Classics was an established, high-profile department. Its reputation rested on the intellects and sensibilities of four men—Allen, Jones, Calhoun, and Linforth—who, according to one self-admiring departmental history, at least, made for "as excellent a Greek faculty as has ever been found anywhere."

James Turney Allen earned his doctorate at Yale and was an authority on Greek tragedy and comedy but also on the physicality of the Greek theater, down to taking measurements and absorbing construction details of the Theatre of Dionysius in Athens. An actor whose histrionic bent was said to have served him well in the classroom, he directed the inaugural play at Cal's Greek Theatre, Aristophanes's *The Clouds,* in 1903. He was also the author of a widely used textbook of beginning Greek.

Roger Jones, a young assistant professor during his time at Cal, with whom Milman may have become something like friends, was an Ohioan with a doctorate from the University of Chicago. He was a scholar of Plato known for stressing the unity of Platonic thought, and much interested in the structure and syntax of Greek and Latin.

Then there was George Calhoun, chair of the department around this time and whose book, *A Working Bibliography of Greek Law,* Milman helped him with enough to earn a written acknowledgment. Later, the older man would help line up a job for him, cite his work, and debate its fine points in print. Calhoun, whose doctoral dissertation bore the title "Athenian Clubs in Politics and Litigation," was an authority on Greek government, economics, and law. But later, conceivably under Milman Parry's influence, he would turn to Homer.

Ivan Mortimer Linforth, whose office was directly across the hall from Calhoun's on the top floor of Wheeler Hall, was perhaps the star of the department. Like Parry, he was a California native and a Cal grad. Completing his master's and doctoral degrees by 1906 was apparently enough to get Latin out of his system, and for the rest of his long scholarly life he turned to matters Greek, especially Greek religion. For his maiden effort in Greek, he published a book, *Solon the Athenian*. He was a champion of Sophocles, and around the time Parry was his student, worked on papers about how Herodotus, the fifth-century BCE Greek historian, treated the gods in his work. In the classroom, it was said of Linforth, "he taught Greek not as a foreign language, but as what could become for his students, as it was for him, almost a second native language."

During his undergraduate years Parry probably took courses from all of these men. As the breadth of their interests testified, there were many ways to be a Greek scholar. But though they might seem removed

Ivan Linforth, professor of Greek at Cal, perhaps the first to hear young Milman Parry's ideas about Homer.

from the everyday turns of life, their devotion to their singular interests differed little from that of, say, a pro athlete for her sport, or a police detective for the vagaries of the criminal underworld. Ancient Greek was difficult and "dead"? To them it was anything but; they had *that* in common. As they did in having let some narrow, seemingly boyish enthusiasm—classical scholarship was almost a wholly male preserve— flame into a doctoral thesis demanding their best energies across a span of years.

*

"Ancient Greece" was not a point in time, like a birth, battle, or death, but spanned perhaps thirteen hundred years, from Bronze Age Mycenae to the Greek world and culture that remained as Rome ascended to its own heights.

Popularly, and for good reason, "the glory that was Greece" conjures up the fifth century BCE. That was the time of the philosophers Socrates and Plato; the historians Herodotus and Thucydides; the sculptor Phidias; the dramatists Aeschylus, Sophocles, and Euripides; the wars with Persia and between Athens and Sparta. Half a millennium forward extends "ancient Greece" to Alexander the Great and the Hellenistic period following it, into the first and second centuries BCE, when Greek roots nourished Rome. All this counts as "historical," in that books and other written records document much of it. We know that the battle of Thermopylae took place in 480 BCE, that Socrates died in 399, that Alexander swept into India in 326. Details about particular people, places, and events come down to us, with greater or lesser accuracy, much as in our own day.

But Greek civilization stretched back the other way, too, back from the golden age of Greece in the fifth century, back before the coming of the Greek alphabet, adapted from the Phoenician, in about 750 BCE. By historians' consensus, a "dark" age spanned the period from about 1100 to 800 BCE. Before that, back to about 1600 BCE, stood Mycenae, a rich Bronze Age civilization that spread from the Peloponnesian peninsula to the whole Aegean world. There an early written language, known as Linear B, later understood to be an early form of Greek, seems to have been used mainly to record palace inventories—so many amphorae in the king's storehouse, so many chariot wheels—before dying out a few hundred years later. It is sometime during these centuries, perhaps around 1200 BCE, that a siege of Troy, in modern-day Turkey, the historical substrate of the *Iliad,* is thought to have taken place.

> *Now the great array of gods and chariot-driving men*
> *slept all night long, but the peaceful grip of sleep*
> *could not hold Zeus, turning it over in his mind . . .*
> *how to exalt Achilles?—how to slaughter*
> *hordes of Achaeans pinned against their ships?*
> *As his spirit churned, at last one plan seemed best:*
> *he would send a murderous dream to Agamemnon.*
>
> [FAGLES *Iliad,* 2, 1]

And what could be said of Homer, teller of this tale, along with that of the *Odyssey,* those founding texts of the Western tradition, sometimes deemed a kind of secular bible? No one knows. By Richard Martin's reckoning in a recent introduction to Richard Lattimore's translation of the *Iliad,* seven places in Greece—Smyrna, Chios, Colophon, Salamis, Rhodos, Argos, and Athenai—have over the centuries claimed Homer as their own, none of them convincingly. Aristotle, in the fourth century BCE, wrote of Homer. So did the Jewish historian Josephus in the first century CE. Some have wondered whether the two epics were composed by different people. Others, noting aberrations and linguistic infelicities, imagined the epics as cobbled together, sometimes unartfully, from numerous original sources. The identity of Homer, who or what he was; whether one person, two, or more; when he lived; how he or others composed the *Iliad* and the *Odyssey;* and even what it *means* to have composed them, have for millenniums been raised as questions, answered, refuted, new challenges thrown down, new evidence gathered in rebuttal. Indeed, for literary works so ancient, so cherished, and so widely read, it's remarkable that such scholarly conundrums—collectively referred to as the Homeric Question, further addressed later—were still, by 1923, big, broad areas of debate. Even with the coming of Milman Parry, they have not been, and may never be, entirely resolved.

Still, the deference accorded his name helps establish Homer as "real," in some sense, as the epitome of genius, as if a god himself. Despite all nuanced debate, that one supremely gifted poet wrote two great epic poems was for centuries taken for granted by many if not most classical scholars. In antiquity, writes Richard Martin, "not even the most hardened cynic doubted that Homer the master poet once existed." Likewise in the centuries since: Most ordinary readers and students dipping into the epics, or reading them in their entirety, would have given such questions, even were they aware of them, little thought. Odysseus's escape from the Cyclops commands more devoted attention. So does the making of Achilles's shield in the *Iliad*. Or Priam's heart-rending embassy to Achilles, seeking his son's mutilated body. In Parry's time, certainly, most readers would have assumed, imagined, or stoutly insisted that, whatever the implements of writing available to him, Homer, whoever he was and whenever he lived, once sat down to write the two poems attributed to him. Mary Shelley wrote *Frankenstein*. Shakespeare wrote *Macbeth*. Plato wrote *The Republic*. And Homer wrote the *Odyssey* and the *Iliad*.

But Milman Parry would show that "he" didn't write them, couldn't have written them, that in their earliest form, they weren't "written" at all. Another, quite different creative process was at work. This idea, which first snuck up on Parry in California, which he set down in raw form in the master's thesis he proposed to Ivan Linforth in 1923 and later developed and refined in Paris, would shoot out tendrils of insight and understanding far beyond the world of classical studies and inspire new ways to understand early civilizations and their literature.

*

In 1981, when Pamela Newhouse interviewed Parry's wife, she also spoke with others knowledgeable of Parry's life and work. One of these was Sterling Dow, a Harvard professor who, based on his conversation with Professor Linforth back in 1964, told her, in her words, "how this inspiration came to Milman about Homer . . . that somehow there was literally a moment when he got it." And more, that the moment came while Parry, lost in Homer, lay out on a Los Angeles beach. In fact Parry may never have been to Los Angeles, much less read Homer on one of its beaches.

Dow had been in Berkeley in the spring of 1964 to give that year's

Sather Lecture and, when he could, gather biographical materials to serve some yet undefined project devoted to Parry, by this time a legendary figure. Linforth, forty years after Parry's time at Cal, was one of Dow's chief informants, one of the few people on campus apt to remember Parry. Of course, at eighty-five, he may not have had a perfect memory. But Dow's own papers suggest that he, Dow, did not always record facts with unerring accuracy either. Conceivably, California's many Spanish place-names ran together in his easterner's memory. More likely, it was because Los Angeles was on his mind, determined as he was to unravel the circumstances of Parry's death, in Los Angeles, a quarter century before.

Somehow, then, he got it wrong; almost certainly, there was no Los Angeles beach. But that Dow or Linforth erred doesn't discredit the larger truth implicit in the story of Parry on the beach reading Homer— that whatever happened that summer happened, if not in a single place, or at a single moment, or on a single day, then yet, on the scale of Parry's brief, truncated life, almost all at once.

Indeed, that the insight owed to a particular moment in time rests not alone on Linforth's memory, or Dow's; Parry himself said as much. When, in 1928, in Paris, Parry introduced his doctoral thesis, he declared that "the idea of this book"—his Cal master's thesis writ large—"first occurred to me on the day" he first saw Homeric literature in a new light. Maybe there was no true, perfect, single *moment*. And yet the nascent idea apparently did come to him, full-blown, bathed in something like the glow commonly thought to surround literary, artistic, and scientific discovery. These days, the idea of the eureka moment is sometimes belittled, real creativity in the arts and sciences seen as more complex and more collective, nothing reducible to a lightning bolt of sudden awareness. And in its fullest development, Parry's discovery did hew closer to this more nuanced vision.

Still, it seems plain, something remarkable did happen one day in 1923 to Milman Parry.

8

GLAUKOPIS ATHENE

The thesis Parry wrote in the summer and fall of 1923, which earned him his master's degree that December, was called "A Comparative Study of Diction as One of the Elements of Style in Early Greek Epic Poetry." Parry's paper expressed the understanding he had reached—on that "one day"—that the *Iliad* and the *Odyssey* (along with a few other specimens of early Greek literature, together known as the Epic Cycle) had in common something that Greek literature coming later, even a little later, did not: They had become what they were through some shadowy "traditional" process, not by individual talent and craft alone. Crudely—but perhaps suggesting the sheer effrontery of Parry's claim—they just *were,* having evolved in ways he would spend the rest of his life trying to demonstrate and define. He wrote now:

> Just as the story of the Fall of Troy, the tale of the House of Labdakos, and the other Greek epic legends were not themselves the original fictions of certain authors, but creations of a whole people, passed through one generation to another and gladly given to anyone who wished to tell them, so the style in which they were to be told was not a matter of individual creation, but a popular tradition, evolved by centuries of poets and audiences, which the composer of heroic verse might follow without thought of plagiarism, indeed, without knowledge that such a thing existed.

There is raw assertion in Parry's thesis, and suggestions of scholarly grandstanding, but also a scaffolding, if a light one, of evidence. And the evidence he uncovered, right there in the words themselves, attested to certain patterns in the older Homeric works that were less prevalent in those coming later. In particular, he wrote, a "traditional" epic had an "almost formulaic quality," where it regularly used certain words and phrases in certain predictable ways—monotonously, one might object, or compulsively, but also, to good effect, hypnotically.

One of numerous examples was *glaukopis Athene,* which means gray-eyed Athena, or bright-eyed, or flashing-eyed Athena. The goddess of wisdom, daughter of Zeus, Athena appears again and again in the *Odyssey,* on her own, or disguised, to help Odysseus when he needs her most. As for the word *glaukopis,* it has been amply studied, but its meaning is not the issue here. What is, is the two, *glaukopis Athene,* together. The phrase shows up often in both the *Iliad* and the *Odyssey* (twenty-nine and thirty-eight times respectively). And it does so regardless of whether that moment in the story has anything to do with Athena's eyes, whether gray, flashing, or otherwise remarkable. Moreover, it shows up not at random but usually at the end of a line—actually, almost nowhere else, as if to fit a cozy little pocket expressly made for it.

The *Odyssey* and the *Iliad* have been translated into English and other languages in poetry and in prose alike; but in ancient Greek, they were poetry, pure and simple. Poetry normally conforms to particular metrical schemes—in the case of the Homeric epics, one known as dactylic hexameter, which hews to a variety of constraints related to Greek's "long" vowels and "short," appropriate places to break the line, and so on. What Parry asserted now was that *glaukopis Athene* and many other such "ornamental epithets," as he'd call them, showed up where they did, in "prescribed position and order," regardless of the dictates of the story itself. "They flow unceasingly through the changing moods of the poetry, inobtrusively blending with it, and yet, by their indifference to the story, giving a permanent, unchanging sense of strength and beauty."

By their indifference to the story! Parry was saying that these phrases told us nothing—at least then and there, where they appeared—about the goddess, hero, ship, or city they ostensibly described, but simply fit the line; they *sounded* right. The word *neos,* ship (or *naus,* related to "nautical" or "navy" in English), crops up often in the *Iliad;* the Greek warriors reached Troy by boat. About one-third of the time, in more than two hundred instances, *neos* gets an adjective. And of those two hundred, only once, noted Parry, does the adjective contribute to the scene or story.

That one exception, *hekatozugos,* refers to a ship with a hundred thwarts, or benches, for rowers: We must cease our bantering, Aeneas challenges Achilles: "Plenty of insults we could fling against each other / enough to sink a ship with a hundred benches!" Here *hekatozugos* exemplifies a ship's bigness, helps *make* it big. But all those other adjectives modifying *neos* in the *Iliad*? Like *melaina,* black; and *glaphura,* hollow; and *thoe,* fast; and *koronis,* curved; and sixteen others? In no case, when the poet tells us of black, hollow, fast, or curved ships, does their blackness, hollowness, swiftness, or shape figure in the story; rather, they note qualities that are fixed and immutable.

Indeed, appearing when they do, such repeated epithets can even seem at odds with the story. Wrote Parry, plainly aware of the contradictions: "Ships are swift, even when drawn up on land; and raiment is gleaming, although it is ready for the wash."

In both the *Iliad* and the *Odyssey,* Athena is sometimes called Pallas Athena; by one account, "Pallas" was a woman Athena killed accidentally and honored by adopting her name. When this epithet is used, wrote Parry, it is not

> for the sake of introducing her in emphasized augustness [or for any other such purpose]. She was called Pallas because there was space which had to be filled in so that *Athenaie* could fall into its natural place and the hexameter flow smoothly on. And anyone who doubts the truth of this is welcome to refute us by rewriting that sentence, either with the omission of Pallas or with the substitution of other words.

Much of the language in the *Iliad* and the *Odyssey,* he was saying, was "dictated by convenience." *Whose* convenience? Well, it would seem, the poet's—though that would turn out to be only partly correct.

*

In 2001, a scholar tracing the development of Parry's thought, Juan Garcia, was struck by how often Parry referred to "race" in his master's thesis—six times in one brief section alone. It was a time before Nazi racial theories had put the word itself into disrepute, a time when the walls of classical studies were being infiltrated by insights from outside the traditional domain of Greek and Latin language and literature. As from archaeology: In the late nineteenth century the remains of Troy, of Mycenae, and of the Minoan civilization on Crete had all been unearthed. But also from the relatively new discipline of anthropology, the study of humankind—of tribes, races, social groups, and "primitive" peoples in something like their original environments.

At Cal, in the early twentieth century, anthropology was represented by the towering figure of Alfred Kroeber, who had made his name through the study of American Indian society in the Pacific Northwest. Kroeber drew students intrigued by visions of exotic cultures in faraway places—and, as we've seen, bred a coterie of devoted admirers. Marian took four semesters of anthropology at Cal, Milman three—not the usual diet for a classics major. Given the research trips he would later make to backcountry Yugoslavia, the field of anthropology was a natural place to seek influences on Parry. But Garcia showed you needn't look so far to the future to find this anthropological stamp on him: Just look to his master's thesis, begun months after completing his final anthropology course.

Homer alone was not the subject of Parry's thesis, but rather the world he came from; that itself corresponded to an anthropological worldview—the individual, yes, but the group, more. Ten times, by Garcia's count, Parry contrasted the individual artist—so venerated in modern culture, so looming, so large—with the social group of which he was part. At one point, Parry wonders whether he is being "overzealous" in finding beauty in words selected "not by careful choice for the sake of their meaning, but by pure metrical convenience?" It might seem so, "if we are judging by modern individualistic standards." But no, not if we think in terms of what he called the "racial artistic tradition."

To make this point Parry turned to ancient Greek sculpture, whose artistry, he said, emphasized not innovation, but "convention, tradition." Greek sculptors, almost as one, drew from fixed themes, their subjects represented in traditional and familiar ways. So, for example, Phidias, the towering master of ancient Greek sculpture, had in a celebrated work known as the *Lemnian Athene*—a rendering of which appeared in a book Parry's father had given him as a child—depicted a peaceful Athena, one

> with uncovered head and closely-bound hair circled by a festal fillet, who holds a spear in one hand and a helmet in the other, and wears the aegis in unwarlike fashion aslope her breasts. Moreover, the expression of the statue, a repose of body and face which by its very quietness indicates a divine strength and intellect, was an expression which, at the time, any carver of divinity must represent to the best of his ability.

Phidias might seem far from Homer, but now Parry tightened the knot on his argument: "By following this tradition of design and expression Phidias has filled his work with the spirit of a whole race," in a way most apt to "represent the beauty, the strength, the calmness of her nature." Not Phidias alone had created this Athena but, rather, "the Greeks in collaboration with Phidias. . . . He has blended his own genius with that of his race, so inextricably that the two are hard to distinguish."

So it was, said Parry, with Homer. His formulaic diction "was not a device for mere convenience, but the highest possible development of the hexameter medium to tell a race's heroic tales."

Parry had, I think, a temperamental affinity for the ideas he would develop in his thesis, even before he wrote it; he had grown impatient with literary self-indulgence. Among his likely contributions to *Occident* were two brief essays, resonating almost as one, in which he disdains the shimmering superficialities of 1920s America. In one of them, "The Morning After," appearing in December 1922, well before his summer on the beach with Homer, Parry insists "there is no such thing as modern literature," only good and bad. Humans are biologically much the same across the ages; the truths of ancient writers are truths today: "The theme of Sophocles, that there is a natural punishment for the breaking of a civic or a social law, is perfectly applicable to present-day society." The author scorns the "rampage of adolescent originality" of his own day, its thin and bogus creativity based on nothing more profound than the excesses of the night before.

It is hard not to see this essay as billowing up from some of the same waters as those of his master's thesis. Faced with "the unrestricted range of style in contemporary letters," and the modern writer's emphasis on differentness and "originality," he wrote, Homer and his contemporaries would have been bewildered. For them, it was more natural by far to give themselves over to their own tradition, to the "established limits of form to which the play of genius must confine itself." Here were limits and constraints, then, not to resent, resist, or defy, but to embrace.

We are left to visualize, and respect, an author who doesn't cast incessantly for the next word, subject, or idea; who doesn't grasp at ever new ways to tell his story; who doesn't forever reach for addendum or correction. Rather, Parry wants us to imagine a seemingly "non-creative" means of composition embedded in the stories of one's people, one's tribe:

> An audience of the period of epic poetry would have been dumbfounded had they heard a rhapsodist recite a piece whose story was altogether his own invention. They would probably have been more amazed [yet] if he had used a new method of telling, say having some minor character tell the story so that everything is seen through his eyes, a method often adopted by modern writers. And if he had made the theme of his story a study of the mental processes of the main character. . . . But it was not done. As a matter of fact, they could no more imagine such things than they could modern machinery. Homer [and the other early writers, if that's what they were] had to take their stories from legend and from no place else. They had to tell them in the grand manner, in which almost all the characters are eminently noble and speak as beautifully as the poet can contrive.

This is an alien and uncomfortable idea, and would probably have been just as much so in 1923, when Parry wrote his thesis: Great art might depend on more than unconstrained creativity.

*

During the whole time Milman worked on his thesis, he and Marian were newlyweds and Marian was pregnant. Through it all, she had scant idea of what he was doing. "I never asked him what this master's thesis was about," she'd comment ruefully in 1981 to Pamela Newhouse. "But," she'd add, as if to excuse her seeming incuriosity, "he never said to me—you'd think he would have—'I have a special idea about Homer.' You'd think that he would have talked to me about it. That's something I don't understand, really I don't."

Would he have talked with her about it had she asked?

Well, she replied to Newhouse's question, he did occasionally read something to her in Greek, but it was just for the sound of it. She did not know the language.

"I can't imagine," said Newhouse, "what his reason might have been for not telling you, unless he just thought you wouldn't be interested."

"Well, I never asked, I guess."

*

When it came time to submit the thesis, the way Addison Parry told it later, her brother had just minutes to get it in before it was due. "Milman tore from his apartment, sprang onto the tail of a moving van and, triumphantly waving the manuscript, rode down Euclid Avenue to the campus," handing it in just in time. Discrepancies dog this story, as Addison herself acknowledged: "All families have tales about each other [that] they repeat among themselves with delight." Still, she felt it was more true than not, Milman himself hailing his as "perhaps the most 'noble' submission of a Master's thesis ever made!"

Its forty pages had few footnotes, the author little inclined to picture himself as perched on the shoulders of others. Mostly it was a straightforward essay, coupled to six appendices in which Parry supplied numerical corroborations—as, for example, his Appendix IV, on the adjectives used with *neos,* ship. For the main text, about twenty-five pages, the few Greek words were written in by hand. The fifteen pages of appendices, more densely Greek, were typed on a Greek-character typewriter. Three professors, Linforth and James T. Allen from Classics, and Robert Winslow Gordon, a Harvard-educated English professor who was to become a well-known folklorist, weighed in with their approval.

Once accepted and deposited in the library, the thesis was forgotten, perhaps never seen by a living soul for forty years.

Then, in 1964, Sterling Dow, who had earlier assumed it was missing or lost, unearthed it from the Berkeley stacks. From the library entry
directing him to it, he could see it was related to Homeric poetry. He
had no inkling that Parry's famous Paris thesis of 1928 had its origins in
it; some modest schoolboy exercise was all he expected. "But the first
few pages show that this expectation was incorrect. On the contrary, the
great discovery is there—firm, detailed, bold." (It wasn't the last time
Parry's work would be reckoned not as theory, suggestion, or hypothesis
but as "discovery.")

A few years later, the Oxford classicist Hugh Lloyd-Jones got his
hands on it: "An astonishing piece of work," he wrote Milman's son,
Adam: "Imagine it being written by a man of twenty!"

In time, it would be seen for what it was, a road map to Parry's future
work. But even this early, it was easy to discern the thorny problem it
posed: Read his thesis wrong, jump to conclusions too precipitately, and
you could write off Homer altogether, as a stickler for tradition, handing down old stories, his vision sadly constrained. No, Parry wrote, alert
even now to this perception, Homer must be read differently, entirely so,
even from all other ancient Greek texts.

> Probably there are few things more necessary to the apprecia-
> tion of Greek epic poetry than an understanding of the quality
> and value of this traditional element in the style, this necessity
> of the composer to follow certain very definite lines. Explana-
> tions of it have often been taken for granted, or vaguely guessed
> at, especially in discussions of the "Homeric question"; it has
> never been properly explained. And yet it is the very point where
> modern critics must change their attitudes if they would under-
> stand the epics as their original audiences understood them.

Modern critics must change their attitudes? This tone of unbridled
confidence, even arrogance, did not characterize the thesis as a whole.
And future colleagues would not see much braggadocio in him. But he
was right: "Change their attitudes" is just what a whole generation of
scholars would have to do.

PART THREE

Paris

[1924–1928]

9

THE PARIS DEAL

At the time he received his BA, Milman Parry still had no definite idea of what he was to do with himself. He'd done well at Cal, coming away with a Phi Beta Kappa key. But he was not particularly set on the life of a classical scholar. As recently as the fall of 1922, he'd seriously enough considered a career in medicine to sign up for an anatomy course, only to petition out of it later. At least briefly, he'd weighed shipping out to sea, as his father, for some years of no fixed profession, had done before him. He and Marian even talked of moving to New York—though, as Marian would recall, "I don't know what he thought he was going to do" there. On leave from Cal and living in the Santa Cruz mountains with his pregnant wife, he'd worked for the railroad. For at least a year, then, all was uncertain. "Well, why not be a college professor? Anybody can do that." These are the words Mrs. Parry remembered saying to Milman, quite deadpan, while talking with Pamela Newhouse many years later.

Finally, in early 1924, with Parry's master's thesis deposited in the university library, any lingering doubt seems to have been stilled: He would become a scholar, his life that of books and ideas. If the courses he took at Cal during his undergraduate years are any indication, the scholar in him—the real searcher, the close thinker, as opposed to the dutiful, cramming student—had surfaced early. The Classics department set aside one course, Greek 199, as "Special Study for Advanced Undergraduates," for which the student was to go off, read on his own, and "report at regular intervals to the instructor." Parry had taken two 2-credit editions of it in the 1921–22 academic year. Now, with the successful completion of his master's thesis—or more probably in the happy *doing* of it, with all its freedom to follow his own internal compass—things seemed clearer. The arrival of baby Marian, in January, about a month after the awarding of his MA, helped galvanize him, too: No more talk of running off to sea. A scholar's life was now the goal in the Parry household, a life like that of Linforth, or Calhoun, or perhaps Alfred Kroeber, the anthropologist.

But the meanest of practical obstacles stood in the way. The family, now three, was living in Mill Valley, getting by on his paltry assistant-ship; for the spring term of 1924, Milman was listed in the University Register as "assistant in Greek," teaching a little and taking a few graduate courses himself. If he was to find anything like a proper academic career path, he needed a doctorate and, first, the financial support to pursue it. Accounts of distinguished scholars at places like Princeton or Harvard can make it seem that money's unhallowed hand never corrupted the purity of their intellectual lives. But Milman's circumstances permitted no such nose-in-the-air stance. His father had managed his working life with something short of high ambition and large success. Most of Milman's future colleagues at Harvard didn't have fathers who'd been shot at in botched robberies; the Old Dear was a character, a likable personality, but no source of patronage. So now, drawn to a life of scholarship and the intellectual terrain of ancient Greece, Milman was on his own.

As for Marian, the only job she'd ever held was reading aloud to a blind student. She'd not even done much ordinary housework, never so much as ironed a shirt. Maybe, she thought, she could land a writing job, "because that was the thing I had been trying my hand at," and had vague hopes of pursuing. For now, Milman had his modest assistantship. But his eyes, like those of the other budding classicists in the department, were on the future: Of those competing for limited departmental funding, said Marian loyally later, "Milman was by far the best of them." But nothing materialized.

And, just possibly, she worried later, it was her own fault, for what she conceived as her loose ways among the anthropologists' crowd. "Mr. Linforth highly disapproved of me . . . because it was pretty obvious that [she and Milman] were living together" before their marriage in 1923. Linforth, according to one of his later students, Joseph Fonten-rose, was "distinguished in appearance, rather handsome, a man of quiet

dignity . . . with a quiet but ready wit." Marian acknowledged his fine
looks. But to her, "it was as though he were carved out of a block of
something . . . very cold." He and his wife saw themselves as somehow
"the guardian of the morals of the classics department." And this, Marian would worry, led to Milman's failure to get fellowship support for
his doctorate.

So they looked to Europe, an option Marian managed to make seem
an answer to her own inadequacies: "I found domesticity quite difficult," she would say, "and we didn't have enough money ever to have
a maid in the United States," whereas Europe meant ready, low-cost
household help. During these years, of course, Europe was everything
young Americans of their aesthetic and intellectual sensibilities could
want. "We came to feel," Malcolm Cowley wrote in *Exile's Return* of his
generation of young American college students (roughly Milman's own)
and its impatience with American ways, "that wisdom was an attribute
of Greece and art of the Renaissance, that glamour belonged only to
Paris or Vienna and that glory was confined to the dim past." For reasons
unclear, Milman didn't look to Germany, its hoary philological tradition and prestigious centers of classical learning making it a seemingly
natural choice. But wherever Milman did look—that is, by introducing himself, writing letters, submitting applications—he got nowhere.
Again and again, as Marian remembered, "Milman was getting these
letters of refusal."

He placed especially great stock in an important fellowship at a Bel-
gian university. Failing to get it left him, according to Marian, "heart-
broken. . . . We were right in the country and it was so beautiful and
there were all these fields and fields of poppies and lupine around. . . .
He went out away from the house in the tall grass and I followed him
out there and well, he was crushed." It wasn't as if he couldn't land some
sort of job. The economy was booming; jobs were plentiful. But now,
compared even to just the year before, things had changed: "He didn't
want just any job. He wanted this training." He wanted a scholar's life.

And so Marian gave it to him.

The way it comes down to us, both through family lore and Marian's
own words in 1981, Mr. and Mrs. Parry struck a deal: She had a modest
inheritance through her father, who'd died when she was sixteen. Now
twenty-three, she went to her uncle—who, as its administrator, hadn't
much troubled himself to increase its worth in the years since—to claim

it as her own. The amount, though not huge, was substantial enough to finance their bargain: She would support them while he earned his doctorate. Once he got it, landed a faculty position, and could support the family, she would go back to school and earn her bachelor's degree—for which she had most of the needed credits but, for now, would abandon. They wouldn't need outside support for Milman's work. "We'll go on our own."

Go to Paris, that is.

Paris was in the American air. "After the war," wrote Malcolm Cowley, "one heard the intellectual life of America unfavorably compared with that of Europe. The critics often called for a great American novel or opera; they were doggedly enthusiastic, like cheer leaders urging Princeton to carry the ball over the line; but at heart they felt that Princeton was beaten, the game was in the bag for Oxford and the Sorbonne"—the Sorbonne being just where Milman Parry wound up after leaving Cal.

*

Someday
When you are all alone and far away,
These cool, gray-laden hills will come to mind
And in your memory your heart will find
The half-forgotten picture of that last glad May
And you will grow a little lonely for this hill-bound bay,
Someday.

This is the first verse of a poem, by Ellsworth Stewart, that appeared in the January 1922 issue of Cal's *Occident*. It was entitled "To the Alumni." It can be found among the papers of a woman, Agnes Partin—a year or so ahead of Milman at Cal, bright, ambitious, also Phi Beta Kappa—who wrote warmly spirited letters home to her parents, later collected and published, about her college days.

The poem continues:

Someday
Over the hills and far away,
You will remember moonlight nights and campus trees,

The strumming of a mandolin in minor melodies,
The slanting rain at Sather Gate, acacia bloom on Bancroft Way;
You will remember wistfully the low-hung sun across the bay,
Someday.

In the days, months, and years after he left Cal, Milman Parry may not have much succumbed to sentiments like these. Not when, after his first two years there, any such sweet memories would have had to contend with the more mixed and problematic ones of his affair with Marian, her pregnancy, their hasty marriage, the birth of their daughter, and his life-changing literary and intellectual encounter with Homer—all relics of memory more apt to grab and pull at him than the acacia bloom on Bancroft Way.

*

Leaving Berkeley, that summer of 1924, they went first to Milwaukee, where they stayed at Marian's grandparents' house, saw Marian's old friends and relatives, said their goodbyes. All the time she'd been in California, her mother, Mildred Thanhouser, had remained close by, taking classes with her at Cal. Her marriage, though, as Marian would recount, spelled "the end of California for her." Mrs. Thanhouser had returned to Wisconsin, visiting California only briefly for her granddaughter's birth.

From Wisconsin, the Parrys were off for the East Coast and the Atlantic crossing to France. But not just yet to Paris. They'd chanced upon a magazine article that somehow made the French town of Dieppe, a fishing port on the Normandy coast halfway between Calais and Le Havre, once a favorite of British and French bohemians, seem outlandishly attractive. The ship deposited them in Cherbourg, down the coast from Dieppe. But, caught up in the vagaries of French rail schedules, they wound up far from Dieppe, on a train platform with luggage, baby, and very little French, quite lost. So (wherever they were), they took a room in an expensive hotel they couldn't afford, with a bathroom "big enough for a room [by itself]" and sheets "big enough for sails on a boat."

Madame and Monsieur must be very tired, they were greeted, ever so warmly. Would they care to be served dinner in their room? Why, of course, yes, that was a fine idea.

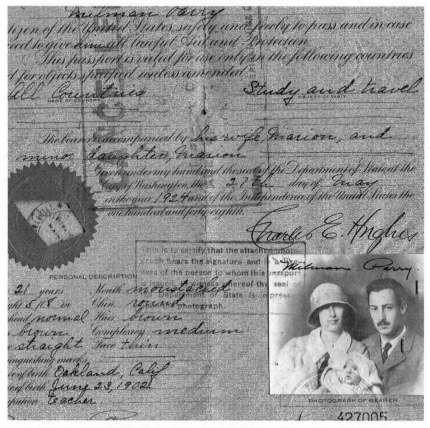

Milman, just twenty-one at the time this passport photo was taken in May 1924, with wife, Marian, and their four-month-old daughter, bound for Paris.

Later, they scoured the town looking for diapers. But neither of them knew the word for them. They'd come with a good supply, but on the voyage over, recounted Marian, "I just threw them over the side of the boat."

Then they got the hotel bill, which made them realize they needed to get out of there "very, very fast."

In Dieppe, her mother's words rang in Marian's ears. *You need a place with good plumbing.* Milman, scouting the town by bicycle, "found a lovely little cottage with pansies in the garden," but not much by way of plumbing. So that wouldn't do. Next they found a good-sized house with a nice apartment, and took that. Of course, "it didn't have any more plumbing than the other."

They hired a woman to help with the baby and teach them a little French. Another woman who lived nearby came around to cook. But the shiny copper-bottomed pans she used soon tarnished, and, well, she could hardly be expected to spend time polishing them, could she? "Pretty soon," Marian would remember, "we were employing the whole neighborhood." Some of the locals wondered, *Monsieur and Madame Parry are perhaps with General Motors?* They were in way over their heads. "We spent in about six weeks, or two months, the money that we intended to spend for a whole year."

After their financially disastrous summer, they moved to Clamart, a suburb of Paris. "We might have lived in Paris," Mrs. Parry would recall, "but I thought it would be better for Marian to live . . . [where] the air would be better for her." Just south of the city, Clamart was by local repute just that—mercifully free of the smoke and congestion that blackened Paris's beautiful buildings and the lungs of its inhabitants.

As with many an American, they were humbled by French, the language. Milman, who arrived in Europe with what his son, Adam, would describe as "a most imperfect knowledge" of the language, enrolled in classes with Alliance Française. Marian learned what she could from people helping her with housework. In Clamart, she took a few lessons, only to find them depressing. "They consisted of little dictations of such statements as, *A bird has not an arm, it has a wing.*" Years later, after Milman's death, in her new life in California, she'd make a living as a French teacher. For now, though, as she wrote Milman's sisters, if French was going to be just more "awful torture . . . I don't believe I'll ever learn it." Around the house, the two of them didn't even try to speak it.

Clamart could seem almost the country, yet was just seven minutes from Gare Montparnasse, one of the city's main train stations; virtually instant access to Paris was one of the town's selling points. From the little Clamart station you could see the Eiffel Tower looming as large as it did in most of Paris itself. It was a town of little pretension, where people lived on quiet streets of two- and three-story houses faced with *meulière,* a rough-surfaced volcanic-like stone, pocked with large and small holes, that looked like it could have come from the moon. After the Russian Revolution, just a few years before, Clamart had attracted a few émigré intellectuals. And an Armenian immigrant, a physician, had helped make the town a refuge for survivors of the Turkish genocide of the early 1920s. But mostly, Clamart was a town of ordinary Frenchmen and -women, many of whom worked in local mines, nearby farms, or for several large *blanchisseurs,* or launderers, whose great loads of washed linens were trucked daily into the city. Rents were low, which, after the Parrys' free-spending summer, counted for much.

Two main streets ran close together through town, almost in parallel, from the *mairie,* or town hall, at one end, to the *gare,* the little train station, at the other. The *gare,* already the third in the town's history, was a whimsically charming little structure with a peaked, vaguely oriental-flavored entrance that would survive until the early 1960s. From here, Milman—but not so often Marian, at home, with the baby—would be whisked off to Gare Montparnasse. From there he could hop on the Métro, the Paris subway, and soon be wherever he wished in the great city.

10

A WORLD TO HIM

"Here it is about three o'clock and nearly dark outside," Marian wrote Milman's sisters Addison and Allison near Christmas of 1924.

> We have cleaned up the living room, putting all the diapers in an inconspicuous corner and have drawn the long faded pink curtains which descend from the ceiling and cover the French windows. Milman (would you have dreamed this of your brother?) is washing the baby's bottles while I write and the baby is in her pen, talking to herself and playing with all manner of household objects.

Marian added that she'd "had the last week-end 'off'—that is I went to Paris Friday night and stayed till this morning (Sunday) in a little hotel," having spent the day before with an American girlfriend in the Bois de Boulogne, the great park on the west side of Paris. "We saw all the fashionable horses, dogs, babies and people out for walks." The babies: "rosy in hand-embroidered silk coats and caps, sitting up in shiny carriages with nursemaids in blue capes and blue long veils pushing them." She and her friend enjoyed a picnic lunch, bought fruit from an old woman lost in layers of apron and sweater. "It was great fun, for the sun was shining for once in an age." In the evening she met Milman for dinner and a show, a comedy they actually understood.

These events, coming early in their Paris years, were not, it should be said, typical—neither Milman's bottle-washing, nor Marian's weekend in Paris. The tip-off, of course, comes in Marian's aside that she'd had the weekend "off"; her *real* job was back in Clamart with the baby. Years later, Marian would report: "He gave me one day off a week."

*

Milman's grandson Andrew Feld, an English professor and poet at the University of Seattle, asserts that the choice of the suburban locales in which the Parrys lived, first Clamart and later Sceaux, may have had less to do with sheltering their child from Paris's foul air and more with leaving Milman freer to meet women in Paris. Feld could not verify this assertion except to say that his mother—Milman's daughter, Marian (Wux)—said as much. "This is something our mother told us many times." An infant and toddler during the Paris years, and just eleven at the time of her father's death, she was too young to have seen much at first hand; however, the story takes on weight, says Feld, because for his mother to say it suggests "that perhaps her father was not entirely the god-like figure she generally thought he was." In an interview in 2016, near the end of her life, Marian Parry Feld, an accomplished artist and illustrator of children's books who by then, in her nineties, showed evidence of intellectual decline and memory loss, made it plain she felt no great warmth for her mother: Whatever her father's infidelities, she made it sound, they were the all but inevitable result of marriage to a raging, hateful woman—a picture at many removes, it should be said, from the woman Pamela Newhouse remembered earnestly answering her questions in 1981.

All families have their stories. Some are true, some not. Some may be true and yet, a century later, unverifiable. But even stories that fall short of demonstrable fact can hint at larger truths. For the Parrys in Paris, one such truth is that whether or not Milman enjoyed mistresses and affairs, he sampled widely of the pleasures Paris offered, while Marian did not; his experience was richer, fuller, more exciting, while hers was cramped.

Her husband's freedom to explore Paris was a theme of Mrs. Parry's own recollections from 1981. If you were narrowly enough focused or unadventurous enough, you might live in Paris and scarcely let it touch you. But Milman, Mrs. Parry made clear, was neither: "You can't imagine what [being in Paris] meant to someone who was just very, very young," she would say of her husband, who was only twenty-two when they took the ship over. "It was just a world to him that opened up." Today, Hemingway and Gertrude Stein, James Joyce and Picasso, Janet Flanner and F. Scott Fitzgerald and the rest of the familiar contingent of artists, writers, bon vivants, and bohemians make for our vision of Paris in the 1920s. Those were the Crazy Years, one great cultural meme, mythologized, memorably squeezed through Woody Allen's cinematographic lens a few years ago in *Midnight in Paris*. But only later did it congeal into stereotype and cliché; Paris was real enough.

One hundred twenty thousand people lived in the 5th arrondissement, one of Paris's twenty, home of the Sorbonne, at the time Parry was there; they sold groceries, served wine, posed for pictures, drove wagons, strolled through the Jardin des Plantes. The cafés and bookstores that fulfilled the legend were part of its everyday life. The impossibly narrow streets were there, the broad boulevards, the Seine never far distant. The Panthéon, bearing the remains of Voltaire, Rousseau, and Victor Hugo, stood in its grandeur over rue Soufflot. Paris, wrote Malcolm Cowley, "was a great machine for stimulating the nerves and sharpening the senses. Paintings and music, street noises, shops, flower markets, modes, fabrics, poems, ideas, everything seemed to lead toward a half-sensual, half-intellectual swoon." In 1925, at the Théâtre des Champs-Élysées, the dancer Josephine Baker offered her magnificent nude body to her audience and the world. Hemingway's *The Sun Also Rises* came out in 1926, leaving Paris to guess the real-life identities of its leading characters. In 1927, Charles Lindbergh crossed the Atlantic in his little plane, *The Spirit of St. Louis,* setting down at Paris's Le Bourget Field; in Montmartre clubs, people stood to offer champagne toasts, in thanks to Lindbergh for bestowing on humankind "the continent of the sky."

Parry soaked up Paris, or as much as he could, given that he had a wife and child at home and, presumably, eventually, a doctoral thesis to write. During his time there, he was often at the theater. He became a fan of Parisian celebrities like the actor Sacha Guitry. He met the artist Marie Laurencin, an important figure in the Parisian avant-garde, a successful painter, an early cubist; Parry would return from Europe with a number of her drawings, which Mrs. Parry would later have a grand-daughter sell for her. "Even more than the University and its methods," a former student of Parry's later at Harvard, Harry Levin, would write of him,

> French thought and life had their effect on so suggestible an intelligence as his. There he must have acquired that feeling for tradition which continued to haunt him, that ability to deal with the past through association of ideas, that same sense of the cultural continuity of Mediterranean civilization, from the Trojan War to our own day, which is present in the thought of Paul Valéry, the critic with whom he was most in sympathy.

After the immediate postwar slack, and all through the 1920s, the French economy boomed. Prices could seem high to Parisians but to Americans, at twenty-one francs to the dollar, the city was a delicious bargain. The city was more international than other large European cities; out of a thousand residents, sixty-seven were foreign, versus twenty-two in London or eleven in Berlin. To the Sorbonne—the traditional name for the Université de Paris, the great medieval university at the heart of the Latin Quarter, occupying a vast block off rue Saint-Jacques, and home to twenty thousand students—they came from all over. Many, inevitably, were there to pick up undergraduate *licences* and other routine credentials to qualify them for jobs in the French academic system. But the Sorbonne was a hotbed of *higher* learning. Parry was there for a doctorate, and the city brimmed over with others doing the same thing. A Budapest woman, Liliane Olah, was consumed with the life of a certain Madame de Montesson, an eighteenth-century poet. Aaron Zeev Aescoly-Weintraub, a young man from Lodz, Poland, was at work on a critical essay about the Kabbalah and that corner of orthodox Judaism known as Hassidism. P. A. Lascaris, from Greece, was working on "The Aesthetic Education of the Child." From around the world they came, to work closely with famous Sorbonne scholars, giving themselves over to a subject that obsessed or delighted them. When they could pull away from their work, their minds and bodies, ideas and enthusiasms, the books they read and those they wrote, all fed the literary and intellectual ferment of Paris.

Of something of this, Milman Parry tasted. Less so did Marian, tied up as she was with Wux, perhaps eight or nine months old when they moved to Clamart. Letters home to America told of their "rosy and angelic" baby's progress. Family snapshots from a little later show Marian piloting her through her first steps. Their apartment in Clamart often drowned in diapers, every chair or table impressed into service to dry, even the baby's playpen periodically upended into a drying rack. Marian didn't get into Paris much for the theater, she'd say, not for lack of interest, but because how could she? How could she and still be up at six in the morning for the baby? Here, then, was the most familiar story of all—young wife turned toward the baby, husband toward the great world outside.

But this early on, at least, their first year as parents, the split didn't much bother Marian. Their conventional arrangements were perhaps welcome, their separate roles affording them separate satisfactions, if not intimacy. Yes, Marian stayed at home with the baby, with little social life, alone. Yes, Milman was gadding about Paris, meeting people and going places about which she probably knew little. And yet, she'd claim of this period, they were happy, and, "well, unified and, you know, we just really got along very well."

In the letter to his sisters in which she told of Milman's unaccustomed nod to gender equality, she added: "Milman gets his revenge tomorrow when he goes to Chartres for a few days to study the cathedral there."

STUDENT WITHOUT A SCHOOL

The great cathedral in Chartres, about sixty miles southwest of Paris, might in all its Gothic glory have merited "study" by Milman, but it didn't much bear on Homer, the Greeks, or epic poetry. His surviving letters home to California during this period scarcely mention any work he might have been doing. He was not enrolled anywhere yet. He was tourist, explorer, and language learner more than student. Any progress he and Marian had made with the ordinary business of life—finding places to live, seeing the sights, caring for their baby, navigating through their third year as a married couple—didn't directly advance Milman's academic goals. Just now, if he was a student at all, he was a student without teachers, a student without a school.

Parry shared Paris with something like fifty thousand other Americans, at least five thousand of them "more or less serious" students. So estimated Hugh A. Smith of the American University Union, a group founded during the Great War to help American students grapple with the living reality of Paris. Usually, money was not the problem, Smith noted; university fees in France were low, even for foreigners. But a university education in France "demands much more determination, intellectual effort, and especially more mental and moral order or self-control."

Back at Cal, Milman had been able to check off the courses he needed to graduate, take them, pass them, and earn a degree. In America, Smith wrote, "the student has only to follow the chalk marks. He even knows in advance exactly how many hurdles he may knock down, and still get his letters at the end of the year." Not so in France. There were no well-marked lanes for the runners. Provided he passes the "rigid, comprehensive exams at the end, no one asks where or how he has spent his time." If he wanted a doctorate, he registered and declared his intentions, but needn't attend a single lecture.

> All he has to do is to write a good, original thesis, have it accepted by a very critical committee of French professors, get it printed, and be prepared to defend it, in the whole body of knowledge it represents, before a comprehensive examining committee. But he must do this largely through his own efforts.

In America he might be pulled along, ministered to by deans, advisers, and professors "who herd him down the academic lanes." In France he had to search out the right classes, professors, and readings, and snuff out the "temptation to procrastinate that naturally besets him who has only a distant goal to reach."

Such were the traps and difficulties Milman faced in France. Paris was a promised land of the intellect, filled with storied institutions—the Sorbonne, the Collège de France, the École Pratique des Hautes Études, and numerous others. What Parry needed was help to penetrate the French system, find the right mentors. Was his primary object that of putting his own stamp on an ancient discipline? Or was it to provide for himself and his family by earning the degree that would get him a good job? Didn't matter: Whether his motivations were entirely high-minded or bore a tincture of the practical, he needed help.

Early on, even perhaps back in California, Parry had come upon the work of Victor Bérard. Just past sixty when Parry met him in Paris, Bérard was a serious classicist, the *Odyssey* his lifelong interest. But he was no solitary scholar, cut off from the life and light of his time—not someone, it would be said, "locked in his study, for whom antiquity is the object of arid studies." Back in 1912, he'd cruised by sailboat along the shores of the Mediterranean looking for places mentioned in the *Odyssey*, like Calypso's grotto; James Joyce, who'd been living in Paris, working on *Ulysses*, published in 1922, was said to have used Bérard's *Les Phéniciens et l'Odyssée* as prompt, or inspiration, for Leopold Bloom's odyssey in Dublin.

Bérard was very much the public figure. A politician and diplomat, he served after 1920 in the French Senate, representing his native Jura. He was "a big handsome man, with a brain bursting with intellectual enthusiasms and rash hypotheses," according to American novelist Edith Wharton. He had no end of opinions, and liked to express them. Swept up in the anti-German fever of the Great War, he'd contended that one of Germany's most renowned commentaries on the *Odyssey,* Friedrich August Wolf's *Prolegomena à Homère,* had been stolen from French scholars.

Bérard's ideas about the *Odyssey* were popular in Paris in the mid-1920s. His *L'Introduction à l'Odyssée,* the first volume of which was published in 1924, the year Milman and Marian arrived in France, included a bibliography to Homeric study that Parry would rely on to help frame his own work. But just now, Bérard meant more to him than the sum of his books and ideas. Sometime early in 1925, Parry asked Bérard to take him in hand as thesis adviser.

Even had Parry no personal introduction to him, Bérard would not have been hard to track down. Each year the Université de Paris issued a *Livret de l'Étudiant,* or student handbook, that told how to enroll, supplied a university calendar, introduced its many sister institutions in Paris, and, especially useful for Parry, listed most of the professorate of Paris, with their home and office addresses and hours. You could riffle through a current *Livret* and find Marie Curie herself, Nobel Prize winner for discovering radium; she was there at her office at the Radium Institute on rue Pierre-Curie, 10 to 12 on Tuesday and Friday mornings. The same *Livret* listed Bérard, of the École Pratique des Hautes Études, a few blocks from the Sorbonne, available Monday and Tuesday mornings at 10. Also possible, suggests Bérard's grandson, Étienne Bérard, is that they met at Bérard's house on rue Denfert-Rochereau, where, on Sunday afternoons, he'd often host a *table ouverte,* an open table, to receive friends, colleagues, political figures, and students. These were not always decorous affairs but often scenes of spirited, freewheeling debate, with colleagues and friends opposed to Bérard's sometimes idiosyncratic ideas as welcome as those who favored them.

One way or another, Parry found a way to approach Bérard with his request. And when he did, Bérard turned him down.

On leave for the academic year 1924–25, Bérard may have been too immersed in his own work, resolved not to be bothered; he was just then caught up in bringing out the second volume of *L'Introduction à l'Odyssée,* as well as *Les Navigations d'Ulysse.* Or he may simply not have been interested, or interested enough, in young Parry's ideas. He may even have taken an antipathy to them; his approach to the *Odyssey,* says his grandson, was to come at it from several perspectives at once—historic, geographic, phonetic, topographic, philological—while Parry's was single-mindedly through the words themselves; for Bérard that could seem hopelessly narrow. Monsieur Parry, he was said to object, wore "blinders."

Indeed, Bérard's may have been no gentle rejection. Milman was not merely disappointed, his wife would recall, but undone, quite crushed. Three years later, by then having completed his thesis and ready to publicly defend it, he agonized that Bérard might find a way to show up and again quash his hopes.

*

"Sorry you can't see this place," Milman wrote sister Addison from a hotel in Marseilles in June 1925, probably soon after hearing from Bérard. "It would delight your little exotic heart. I myself had no idea at all of what a Mediterranean port could be: there is more heat and blue sea and squalor and races than you can imagine jumbled into one place." He was captivated.

> This hotel (I have an excellent room for 40 cents a night) stands on the Old Port, the same that was first used when the Greeks founded the city 2700 years ago. The port is packed with fishing boats, tugs, launches, everything. . . . The most unusual part of the town though is the Old City, just to the west of the Old Port: everyone sits in the street trying to keep cool: children playing by the hundreds around the knees of nursing mothers . . . negresses Arabs greeks Turks, little girls singing "sur le pont d'Avignon," communist crowds singing l'Internationale, beggars showing their sores for alms (a quarter of a cent satisfies them), a great misshapen Negro with a willow wand pretending to be a wizard (he is sprawled in a trance in a little cement

square beside a fountain where women are washing clothes).
All this at one time within a radius of about thirty feet. Lots of
color, but God, such a horrible life for everyone, especially the
children.

Milman was bound for Greece. Marian's mother and grandmother
had recently arrived from the States and the three women, along with
the baby, headed off together to Switzerland for the summer. Milman
was off alone, on the adventure of a lifetime. And Marian *wanted* it
for him, she claimed later. "I had, I think, almost a motherly desire to
have him have all these experiences," including the chance to travel,
especially to Greece, where he'd never been and never would be again.
Maybe that's all it was for him, those three months in 1925, a young
man's golden opportunity—but after Bérard's rebuff, maybe it was also
a chance to heal.

While in Athens, Parry met up with an old classmate from back
at Cal, Oscar Broneer, a Swede some years older than he, destined for
a distinguished career as an archaeologist; Marian remembered him as
"just as heavy and doughy as a doughnut, a good enough soul." At Cal,
Broneer hadn't much liked Parry, though Parry—well practiced on those
clattering typewriters at Tech—had typed Broneer's master's thesis for
him. He'd remember Parry as often unprepared, too willing to bluff his
way through a seminar. But now, in Athens—and again, later, when
they met in Paris—Broneer found his former classmate changed for the
better. Some of Parry's juvenile arrogance had worn away. Perhaps chas-
tened by Bérard's rebuff, or by the rigors of marriage and fatherhood, or
both, he seemed more likable, and more mature. When Broneer counseled Parry to give up his plans for jouncing across Greece on the back of
a mule and instead go by bicycle, Parry sensibly changed course.

The city and its surrounding region, Attica, were small, Milman
wrote Addison from Athens on June 29. "But this little place is so filled
with names and stories, every little lump of rock, every little creek, littler
ones than that which flowed in the old days behind our house on 426
26 Street, has some story, some piece of life, some intelligent incident
connected with it."

In August, back in Athens, Milman wrote his father about his trip
thus far:

A month at Athens . . . thence by bicycle to Megara, where the old costumes are held in honor; Korinth where are the excavations, or better and more expert to call them digs; to Mykenae and the plain of Argos, the center of the power that sacked Troy across the Aegean; Argos the city, Nauplia (a bunch of other little places in between whose names are found in Homer, not in maps); Tripolis in Arcadia (the bed tried to crawl away from under me here); Sparta, where the bed was full of lice which drove me to sleeping on the walls of the ruins of Mistra, a medieval Byzantine city on a great bluff that kicks out below Taygetus. . . . From Sparta I headed towards Olympia, or rather Pylos, but the road ended up in the mountains of Kostantia, and after a rather hard try at pushing the bike over mule trail I gave in and paid a dollar for the rent of a mule and its owner.

The trip could seem to cover a lot of ground but, across almost three months, the daily distances were manageable by bike.

On the Greek island of Leukas, checking in to a guesthouse, he meets "a sleepy girl, unbeautiful, draped only in a single black dress," who asks how many beds he wants. The girl is curious about his little knapsack and wants to see it. As she lifts the flap and finds his sweater, stuffed on top, he doesn't object. "She takes it out and puts it on, her full body stretching it out as never it was stretched before."

He finds himself on a train. "From the sweating compartment, eight places and eleven people . . . I do not look [out], I only sweat and, head against the wooden seatback, doze out as much of this cramped journey as I can. It is better this way," he adds: The tourist in him has finally been shed, "and I can be more like the men of Georgitsi," who'd been surprised at how he'd marveled at Mount Taygetus, mentioned in the *Odyssey*. For them, it was "just taken as being there."

The trip's most recent leg, Parry reported to his father, had taken him, aboard a fifteen-foot fishing boat, to Ithaka, Odysseus's home and ultimate destination in the *Odyssey*. But then he'd come down sick. "Somewhere around here, among this unclean race and its doubtful food I picked up some sort of intestinal fever, and after eight days of the most beautiful loose bowels (matters which people never talk about) I gave up and came back here to Athens and a doctor." Now he was better and ready to set off the next day for Delos. "Three days of sea and sleeping in the sun will doubtless put me up again for a few days more of bicycling to Delphi before the 27th when I sail for Marseilles."

Back in Paris, the fever recurred. By one account, only Marian's last-minute switch to a French doctor from an American one saved his life. Much of that winter Milman was weak, for a time unable to work and, inevitably, discouraged. He was a young man; there was still plenty of the boy in him. He had time, could still shift gears and do something else. But he'd been in France for a year and a half now and, rankled by Bérard's rejection, laid low by illness, he had nothing much to show for it.

"Oh," Marian would lament, "it was hard getting started in Paris."

12

ALMOST EVERY SUNDAY

In the fall after his return to Paris, Milman wrote Addison from 24 rue Davioud, an apartment building set on a narrow street on the far west side of Paris. It's not clear what he or the rest of the family was doing there or how long they stayed; the Parrys in Paris, like the Parrys of Oakland, never stayed anywhere for long. In this letter, Milman said little of himself, but proffered much advice to his sister, twenty-nine, who was muddling over whether to leave her stenographer's job and become a teacher. He himself, Milman wrote, had scant use for business, which left "such beginners as you in the hands of the more or less stupid." Better to find something "that fits your soul a bit better." As a teacher, she could figure on a nice pension and a life better than "writing shorthand for the same company half your lifetime. Put no trust in the business world, because it doesn't give a damn for anyone that doesn't make it do so." Having gotten out of Oakland, gone to college, held an assortment of temporary jobs, and traveled in Europe, Milman apparently felt competent, at twenty-three, to dispense such worldly wisdom to his older sister.

In December, around New Year's, Milman wrote the twins, thanking them for the dried fruit and the novel they'd sent him for Christmas.

On June 5, 1926, about nine months after getting back from Greece, he wrote them again from a *pension* on rue de Fontenay in a suburb south of Paris known as Sceaux. He acknowledged the advice he'd garnered from one of them—he didn't remember which, and said so—that "if you have nothing to tell us just sit down before a post-card and think of the things worth telling." So now, in this letter, he *enclosed* a postcard; it showed rue de Fontenay, its face inscribed with a cross marking "the house inhabited by Milman Parry during his stay in France." Otherwise, he had little to say—except for this bit of choice news in the first line: "Meant to write you long ago but the distractions of writing thesis were too attractive."

So he *was* writing his thesis.

He had formally enrolled at the Sorbonne six months before, on November 26, but may not have previously told the twins and the rest of the family. Since the previous summer and Bérard's brush-off, Milman seems to have volunteered little, any work he was doing shrouded in epistolary silence. He'd referred once in passing to "days of many Greek books and dictionaries." But that, without embellishment, had given way to "Wux grows and talks: all is well: and here again in days of endless greyness I think much of California," whose diamond jubilee, marking seventy-five years of statehood, his father had written him about. Now, though, finally, something definite: He'd started on the thesis for which he'd come to Paris in the first place.

It was probably after returning from Greece, in the fall of 1935, that Parry met the French classicist Maurice Croiset, first of the scholarly triumvirate that would help him refine and enrich the ideas he had sketched in Berkeley and shape them into a doctoral thesis. Maurice was the younger brother of Alfred Croiset, also a classicist, who'd died a few years before. The brothers had collaborated on a five-volume study of ancient Greek literature that had begun appearing back in 1887; it became a classic of French letters and propelled them both into a succession of elite positions in the French academic firmament.

The first volume of their *Histoire de la Littérature grecque* was Maurice's alone and devoted to Homer. For him, there was indeed a Homer, who had, in the *Iliad,* taken existing tales of the Trojan War and made of them, in the words of one account of his work, a "rudimentary epic." Then his successors, the *Homeridae,* added to it and, together, collectively, wrote the Homeric epics. It was unnecessary that Croiset's conclusions prove entirely correct, if anything bearing on the Homeric Question could ever be proved entirely correct; but they did represent a modest break from orthodoxy. "His creed," by one account of his work, "is that of organic growth"—which was not so different from Parry's notion, from his master's thesis, of the slow, incremental workings of "tradition."

Parry, who'd probably read Croiset's work before arriving in France, made himself known to the much older man, perhaps showing up for his Friday afternoon office hours at the Collège de France; Croiset had been its director since 1911. Intellectually, Croiset might seem a good choice to guide Parry to his doctorate. He may have had in hand Parry's academic transcript from Cal, issued while Parry was in Greece. And over the next few years, he would indeed encourage the young American, reading and commenting on parts of his thesis. Yet, he'd have had to explain to the young American, he could not be his thesis adviser. The Collège de France could award him no degree; it awarded no degrees at all, being not even a college in the American sense, but more like a think tank. Parry needed to go across the street to the Sorbonne, the Université de Paris, and talk to Aimé Puech, a professor of Greek poetry there.

In later years, Puech, about sixty when Perry met him, would bask in his pivotal place in the Milman Parry saga; in several accounts, he'd remind readers how Croiset had directed Parry to him, and how he, Puech, had taken him in hand. As for the Bérard unpleasantness, Parry may not have mentioned it to him. Puech's sensibilities were conservative and religious; his most enduring work of scholarship, which he pursued during his time with Parry, was a history of Evangelical literature as it came down to us in Greek. He was perhaps not the most naturally sympathetic to Parry's ideas; a later critic would suggest he may not even have understood them in their full significance. But Puech, who had lost an adult son in the Great War, warmed to the young American: "I was immediately charmed by his youthful ardor, by the elegance of his mind and of his person, and by the clarity with which he already conceived his [research] program. During the time preparation of the thesis required," Puech would write, "I had the pleasure of receiving him, almost every Sunday, and of discussing with him the progress of his work."

Puech lived in a large, almost new apartment building at the southern edge of the Latin Quarter, a ten-minute walk down rue Saint-Jacques from the Sorbonne. Few of the professors or students Parry knew in Paris lived in what Americans would call a house. If you knew nothing else about a middle-class Parisian, it was a good bet he or she lived in a five- or six-story mansard-roofed apartment house, sometimes built around a

Clockwise from upper left: Influences on Milman Parry in Paris: Victor Bérard, his earliest hope for a mentor in Paris; Aimé Puech, his steady pilot toward a Sorbonne doctorate; Antoine Meillet, who helped him see the oral improvisation within Homeric poems; Marcel Jousse, whose ideas introduced Parry to the richness of illiterate cultures; Matija Murko, who pointed him beyond Homer, to the guslars of Yugoslavia.

court, with black ornamental ironwork of greater or lesser charm embellishing its banks of windows. The theme was most evident along the city's broad boulevards but carried over to narrower streets as well. It was everywhere. Within those iconic buildings could be found much variety in the size and comfort of individual apartments. But outside, their consistency of scale gave Paris its "look," the city's remarkable architectural harmony. And in the sheer density of population they bestowed on the city—far higher than, say, London's—they helped give Parisian streets and sidewalks their vitality.

Puech lived in one such place in the Val-de-Grâce corner of the Latin Quarter where, it would be said, "the religious life and university life rub shoulders with one another but don't mix." The area took its name from the vast Val-de-Grâce church—begun as a monastery in 1620, become a military hospital during the French Revolution, later topped by a great dome visible from all over the *quartier*. Here, on Sundays, Parry met with Puech.

Puech was known to be demanding of his students, to have scant tolerance for slapdash work. A few years later he would write an obituary for a colleague in which he said something of how he worked with young scholars. He gave them, he explained, only the most cursory introduction to their disciplines, formally instructed them in almost nothing, and never dictated thesis topics to them: A doctoral candidate, he would write, "can only be truly interested in a thesis he has had a personal role in choosing."

Parry had *that* from the beginning, long before he'd set down in Paris. "He was already master of his ideas," Puech would write. Indeed, Parry knew what he was doing because, in a real sense, he had already done it: The essential ideas running through his two, closely related Paris theses were right there in his master's thesis, the former a monumental elaboration of the latter. When both his master's thesis and his Paris theses, translated into English, were published in book form years later, the master's thesis took up 15 pages, the Paris theses 239.

13

THE HOMERIC QUESTION

Back in Berkeley, Parry had concluded that the Homeric poems were not the work of one man who conjured up stories on his own or, in search of novelty, was determined to tell them in new and distinctive ways. Rather, they grew out of a tradition that placed scant premium on invention or originality, was bent instead on telling old stories in the most noble, affecting—and familiar—way. This, in outline, was the idea Parry advanced across the few pages, and handful of corroborating appendices, of his master's thesis, with only a nod to the scholarship of the past. His Berkeley work could remind you of a musical prodigy who, even as a child, untrained, finds a way to make immortal music. In the case of Parry, this Mozartian inspiration, this flash of insight at age twenty-one, had cast new light on the Homeric epics, affording a surprising glimpse of the world out of which they had come.

But now, two years and five thousand miles from Berkeley, pursuing a prestigious credential in the French capital, much more was expected of him. The Paris thesis would be a ripened, more nuanced exposition of the idea he had first floated back in America. That idea was not by itself so terribly abstruse. But now he would enrich it with examples and counterexamples, weave them into an armature of argument, respond to ideas going back centuries. In this narrow sense it was the opposite of the master's thesis, with its charming Mozartian theme; for now it was its enrichment and development, as much as the original idea itself, that helped establish it in classical scholarship. "His theory of epic composition, together with the supporting field work," wrote Harry Levin in

1937, "must stand among the few humanistic researches of our day that have gained the sort of recognition accorded to a scientific discovery."

Of course, it was almost impossible to imagine scientific "discovery," with its air of certitude, applied to anything Homeric. Too much time had passed—including hundreds of years, at least, in a prehistorical darkness without alphabet, books, or written documents of any kind. So when it came to Homer, what could ever be said with confidence? Even the most basic facts, the crudest chronology, were often uncertain, indistinct, or disputed, questions always more numerous and insistent than answers.

If there was a Homer who'd written, sung, gathered, dictated, or revised the epic poems, when and where did he live?

If there was a historical siege of Troy, in which the *Iliad* was rooted and Odysseus's return from which formed the basis for the *Odyssey,* when was it?

If there was something like an "original" *Iliad* and *Odyssey,* when and how had they come to be?

If they'd been written (as most readers of the epics had little cause to doubt), when and how were they first set down? And if not, how did they take the form known to us today?

These and other questions tantalize in part because the Homeric epics have been reckoned by so many, for so long, as so good, the recipients of perhaps the most abundant allusion and commentary of any individual works of art, ever. About two hundred years ago they began to be subsumed under the heading of "the Homeric Question." As a contemporary of Parry, the Swedish philologist Martin P. Nilsson, wrote in 1933, "The problem is as difficult as it is fascinating. Opinions differ, and not only that but views and methods differ in a most embarrassing manner, so that what is written by one group of Homeric scholars seems hardly to exist for another." Roughly, opinions split, if not always cleanly, between two groups, the Unitarians and the Analysts, each laying emphasis on different sets of facts, each pointing up contradictions and inconsistencies difficult to resolve.

The Unitarians imagined the epics as too fine, too glorious, too ambitious, or just too long to have been written by other than a single great man, whether Homer or someone else. Overall, the epics exhibited remarkable literary integrity, bore the mark of a single creator. Of course, one question billowed up right away: A single creator of *both* epics? Or were we now, already, up to *two* Homers? But either way, how to explain the glaring gaps in what were supposed to be sublime works of literature, textual sites where logic lapsed? And what of sections, of both epics, that by even the most generous criteria could not be viewed as brilliant, or literary, or even just good? Like, say, the Catalogue of the Ships in Book 2 of the *Iliad,* where each tribal contribution to the Greek war on Troy is dutifully listed with the number of ships furnished, page after page of tedious accounting? Or Telemachus's voyage in the first four books of the *Odyssey,* which can seem crudely stitched into the rest of the story. One early scholar to take aim at Homer, a memorably acerbic figure known as the Abbé d'Aubignac, in 1664 dismissed the *Odyssey* and the *Iliad,* in the words of translator Emily Wilson, as "incoherent, immoral, and tasteless, cobbled together out of an ancient folk tradition."

The second camp, the Analysts, or Separatists, saw no one author behind the Homeric texts, viewing them instead as the products of multiple authors in multiple eras. Late in the eighteenth century, the German scholar Friedrich August Wolf, in a work widely viewed as the opening shot in modern Homeric studies, *Prolegomena to Homer,* suggested that what became the epics had first been transmitted in bits and pieces down through the years. In time, they'd come under the eye of literate editors who, in reducing them to written texts, suited them to the tastes of their time. Thus, the epics were each an accretion of different pieces—no one genius, no place for a distinct Homer—stitched together only later. Or else, as variation on a theme, perhaps there was what Wilson pictures as "an original core narrative, an ur-Odyssey, which had been encrusted with many later and clumsier accretions"; in this scenario, the task of later editors was "to strip away the layers of later sub-Homeric narrative and restore the original purity of the poems." Some even settled on a place and time for the restoration, this stitching-back-together—the sixth century BCE, when the Athenian ruler Peisistratos is said to have gathered scraps of epic for performance at an upcoming festival, forming them into something like the texts we have now; this became known, rather grandly, as the Peisistratid Recension.

Of course, the Homeric Question, as its own oddly charming and elusive story, with its own roster of concepts and theories, its own cast of ornery and opinionated characters, can lure us away from the epics themselves—from Achilles and his friend Patroclus, old Nestor, poor foolish Elpenor, Athena and the other gods, Penelope's scheme to out-wit her suitors, ever-scheming Odysseus's astonishing lies. The whole panoply of story and scene risks getting lost in clouds of scholarly argu-ment by Wolf, Wood, and Witte, d'Aubignac and Düntzer, and others among the league of Homeric scholars. When Adam Parry translated and edited his father's papers, he introduced them with a long, detailed review of the Homeric Question, studded with these names and many more. There was no evidence, Adam commented, that at the time his father wrote his master's thesis, "he had so much as heard of the scholars named above." But in Paris, learning all this intellectual history, right up to the late nineteenth and early twentieth centuries, was part of what Milman, in the hands now of Puech and Croiset, had to do.

Yet he never made it seem that the Homeric Question itself lay at the center of his thesis; rather, pursuing his own line of thought to what he saw as its inevitable conclusion, he can seem to fly blithely over the old debate, heedless of the battles taking place on the fetid scholarly plain below. Only later—after Paris, after Yugoslavia (where Parry would subject his claims to the test of lived experience), indeed, after he was dead—would the classical world reach a taunting conclusion: Parry hadn't so much resolved the Homeric Question as shown that it was irrelevant; he had all but eradicated the old dueling dualities, burning them away in the fire of a new understanding.

*

How can we understand "a primitive literature," asked the influen-tial nineteenth-century French historian and philosopher Ernest Renan, "unless we enter into the personal and moral life of the people who made it; unless we place ourselves at the point of humanity which was theirs, so that we see and feel as they saw and felt; unless we watch them live, or better, unless for a moment we live with them." In this question, Parry began his thesis, lay "the central idea which we propose to develop in this volume."

But how to enter into the life of long-gone people? For archaeolo-gists it was easier: You dig up the past, as Heinrich Schliemann did Troy or Arthur Evans did Knossos, and look hard at the stone ruins, epi-graphs, and artifacts you find there. Parry's path toward understanding was through the language of the epics itself, using it to imagine him-self back to a civilization more than three millenniums past. Mostly, he did not focus on the specific content of the poems—gods invoked, battles waged, prayers and rituals depicted; that was a fruitful enough approach, certainly, but not Parry's. In the ancient Greek texts as they came down to him, he was interested in just *how* the stories were told, the words chosen to tell them, their recurring patterns, the positions of words on the poetic line.

This might seem an unlikely strategy; Victor Bérard, as we've seen, seems to have been cold to it. It offered no ruins or shards of fired clay to inspect, no Greek isles to explore by sailboat. Just words. And even the words themselves were, as we've seen, questionable, with scholars left wondering how they'd come down to us, the very sequence of scenes and stories perhaps reworked and reshuffled. Scholars of later poets, even some ancient ones, had histories, documents, personal accounts to go on, notebooks, diaries, drafts. But for Parry, the sole clues were the texts of the *Iliad* and the *Odyssey,* which he was convinced revealed something of how they themselves had come into being; and which said something of the people who had known them, how they thought and how they lived. "Philological criticism of Homer," wrote Parry in his Paris thesis, "is only of value to the extent that it succeeds in reconstruct-ing that community of thought through which the poet made himself understood to those who heard him sing."

According to Harry Levin, who knew him well, Parry saw himself as "an anthropologist of literature."

14

ORNAMENTAL EPITHETS

Parry's "principal thesis"—one of the two his degree required of him—would be called "The Traditional Epithet in Homer."

Today, especially in America, the word "epithet" carries an ugly tinge, connoting abusive personal or ethnic insult, as in "racial epithet." But in more general and neutral use, and all the more back in 1928, "epithet" was simply a word or phrase that goes with a person, place, or thing, like "Richard the Lion-Hearted," or "America the Beautiful," or, as we've seen, "gray-eyed Athena" and "wily Odysseus." In the Homeric epics they're ubiquitous. In the original Greek and in most translations, they are probably the most instantly recognizable feature of the reading experience.

> *Lord marshal Agamemnon*
> *Wind-quick Iris*
> *Wise King Priam*
> *Shining Hector*
> *Thrace, mother of flocks*

That's how one translator of the *Iliad*, Robert Fagles, rendered a few of them in English. Here are a few more, from the *Odyssey:*

> *Odysseus, master mariner*
> *Grey-eyed goddess Athena*
> *Calypso, cunning goddess*
> *Earth-shaker Poseidon*

These epithets took up the center of Parry's thesis, just as they had his master's thesis. Indeed, what he did now could aptly be seen as a reprise of his work at Cal, the Paris thesis an expansion and extension of ideas he'd advanced earlier in Berkeley, only now aiming for sure and certain proof; it was this obsessiveness that most indelibly stamped the Paris thesis, every page of it insisting that there, in its demonstrations, arguments, and evidence, lay the beginning and end of debate.

To recapitulate the idea: People, places, and things appearing in the *Iliad* and the *Odyssey* are often linked to epithets, like those we've sampled. But for Parry "linked" was probably too weak a word, name and epithet virtually one, all but fused together. Epithets for Athena don't "describe" her at one particular instant, but for all time. The goddess Iris, Zeus's messenger, is not "wind-quick" because her speed may be crucial to the moment; she is wind-quick in essence and for all time. Indeed, sometimes epithets run counter to the moment's meaning, as when "swift ships" sit beached along the shore. These "formulae" appear on this line or that, in a particular position in the line, because they fit the line, make it sound right in the original Greek, satisfy its rhythmic demands.

Rhythm, poetry, music: *Dum-diddy, dum-diddy, dum-diddy* . . . such is the normal rhythm of the *Iliad* and the *Odyssey* as they clip across the epic line and down the epic page. This metrical scheme, known as dactylic hexameter, is the mainstay of Greek epic poetry, almost defines it. It is a rhythm that became closely associated with gods and goddesses, heroic actors in heroic times, their stories nobly told. Like the iambic pentameter of Keats, or of Shakespeare in his sonnets, or other metrical schemes more natural in English, dactylic hexameter brings a particular order, discipline, and regularity to the line; it constrains the syllables that can satisfy it.

Hexameter means six "feet"—the basic unit of stressed and unstressed syllables—across the line of verse. Dactylic refers to a particular pattern of syllabic stress, our *dum-diddy*. The words "desperate" and "metrical"—**des**-per-ate and **met**-ri-cal—are both dactyls, a long or accented first syllable, then two more that trail off lightly. In English, accents get vocal stress, are sounded a little louder; in ancient Greek, as the distinction is normally made, they're not so much stressed as subtly lengthened.

This, at least, is dactylic hexameter in raw schoolbook form. In fact, the stress pattern is not quite so constrained as that but allows, in a dactyl's proper place, a spondee, one of dactyl's cousins in the vocabulary of poetic rhythm; a spondee is two equally stressed syllables, as in "dead-head," or "sunshine." Indeed, the last of each hexameter line's six feet is almost always a spondee. So across the line, the beat might go *dum-diddy, dum-diddy, dum-diddy, dum-diddy, dum-diddy, dum-dum*. When teachers of ancient Greek try to pilot their students across this new terrain, they'll sometimes extract a bit of epic and speak or sing it out loud, in what are thought to approximate the intonations of Homeric Greek; these days, you can go online and hear them, the hexametric rhythms, whatever the words mean, mesmerizing. My infant granddaughter, when all else failed, would finally fall off to sleep to them.

Dactylic hexameter's very long line and characteristic rhythm don't work so well in English; Longfellow tried it, with only middling success, in his poem "Evangeline":

This is the forest primeval. The murmuring pines and the hemlocks,
Bearded with moss, and in garments green, indistinct in the twilight . . .

It does better in ancient Greek. In his introduction to Robert Fagles's translation of the *Odyssey*, classical scholar Bernard Knox helps get at just how:

Yet though it is always metrically regular, it never becomes monotonous; its internal variety guarantees that. This regularity imposed on variety is Homer's great metrical secret, the strongest weapon in his poetic arsenal. The long line, which no matter how it varies in the opening and middle always ends in the same way, builds up its hypnotic effect in book after book, imposing on things and men and gods the same pattern, presenting in a rhythmic microcosm the wandering course to a fixed end, which is the pattern of the rage of Achilles and the travels of Odysseus, of all natural phenomena and all human destinies.

The singer, bard, or poet, then, has something to say by way of scene, story, speech, or description. And he must say it within the constraints of dactylic hexameter. The epithetic formulae, then, help suit one to the other, fitting substance to the poetic line.

That "shining Hector" and "rosy-fingered dawn" and the hundreds of other formulae were a fixture of epic poetry had never been in question: "Scholarship has always admitted," wrote Parry, ". . . that Homer's diction is made up to a greater or lesser extent of formulae." In his thesis, he noted the opposition aroused by one of his own advisers, Antoine Meillet of the Collège de France, to his claim that Homeric style was almost *completely* one of formulae; as French scholar Charles de Lamberterie would explain, Meillet had "shocked the delicate sensibilities of humanists who felt that such a position slighted the genius of the Artist."

As he'd begun to do in his Cal thesis, when he'd introduced the metaphor of Phidias's sculpture of Athena, Parry was pushing against what had become, in modern societies, almost the sole credible idea of how artists and writers were supposed to work: The individual author's unconstrained creativity fairly bursts the bonds of song or story. But, Parry had insisted at Cal, and insisted now, that Homer was different, not only from modern poets but from those of ancient Greece only a few centuries later. "The epic poets fashioned and preserved in the course of generations," declared Parry, "a complex technique . . . designed in the smallest details for the twofold purpose of expressing ideas appropriate to epic in a suitable manner, and of attenuating the difficulties of versification."

Now, poets of any age have ideas they want and need to express. They always face the difficulties of versification. Why the need for what could seem an elaborate system that left so little room for individual genius? To what end? If system it was, what did it serve?

*

Parry began with one recurrent pattern common among the Homeric epics: A god or hero says something, to which another character—perhaps the old warrior Nestor, or the goddess Athena, or Achilles—replies. That reply (rendered here in a romanized version of the Greek) typically reads *Ton d'emeibet epeita* . . . , "Then X replied to him. . . ." But "X" was often not just Nestor, Athena, or Achilles, his or her name hanging limply alone. Rather, it would be, say, *hippota Nestor,* the chariot-fighter Nestor; or *thea glaukopis Athene,* the gray-eyed goddess Athena; or *podarkes dios Achilleus,* swift-footed godly Achilles. Twenty-seven different lines in the *Iliad* and the *Odyssey,* Parry found, conformed exactly to this pattern, many of them repeated numerous times. In each case, the epithet formula, in its metrical value, satisfied the hexametric line—whereas the name alone, or with a random adjective, would certainly not. (Nineteenth-century poets, Stanford classicist Richard Martin reminds us in his introduction to Richard Lattimore's translation of the *Iliad,* often used the one-syllable *o'er,* instead of the two-syllable *over,* when needed to suit *their* metrical constraints.)

But this was only a foretaste of what Parry would take on over the next two hundred pages. For one thing, ancient Greek introduced complications through its case endings, changes in spelling, and pronunciation of a noun, including a name, such as Achilles, depending on its grammatical role in a sentence or line of verse. In English, the work of case is most often left to word order: *Achilles stabbed the Trojan warrior.* Or, *The Trojan warrior stabbed Achilles.* Thus, we have two sentences, with identical words and entirely different meanings, distinguished solely by their order in the sentence.

Not so in Greek. Here, Achilles, in the "nominative" case, as the subject of the sentence, stabbing the Trojan, would have one case ending, and would sound one way—*Achilleus.* While the Achilles of the second sentence, in the "accusative" case, as direct object, stabbed by the Trojan soldier, would have a different case ending, *Achillea,* the syllabic sound pattern quite different.

There were three other cases (dative, genitive, and vocative), applying to both names and common nouns, that are basic to reading and understanding ancient Greek. But again, they don't merely look different on the page. They often sound different, typically with differing arrangements of "long" or "short" syllables.

In each instance, the epithets linked to these nouns, Parry showed, "responded" to the case differences, so as to make them fit the rhythm of the hexametric line; that is, the epithet accompanying a name in the nominative case typically differed from one used in, say, the accusative.

Parry's whole thesis lived down in the intricate warrens of the hexametric line, and in navigating through them he relied on specialized vocabulary: For example, a dieresis is a break between adjacent "feet" of the six-foot line; the bucolic dieresis is a break between the fourth and fifth foot.

A caesura is a division not between any two of the six feet but within one; the hepthemimeral caesura comes after the first syllable of the fourth foot.

While daunting to the inexpert, English-speaking ear, such terms

pointed Parry's scholarly reader to a precise position within the line. In
the published thesis, whole charts ranged vertically across the page—for
example, Table I, "Noun-Epithet Formulae of Gods and Heroes in the
Nominative Case: Principal Types." The top of one column would point
to a particular location in the line, such as "Between the hepthemimeral
caesura and the end of the line." Beneath it would appear the pattern of
long and short sounds the formula needed to fit. And beneath that heading would appear epithets linked to Odysseus, Athena, Apollo, Achilles,
or the other gods and heroes. So at one position, Achilles was almost
always called *podas okus Achilleus,* swift-footed Achilles. But in another
position, requiring fewer syllables to fit the line, he was *dios Achilleus,*
divine Achilles. Never would the two be reversed.

In the end, Parry all but proved that for each hero, god, or goddess,
in each grammatical case, in each position in the hexametric line, there
was normally only a single epithet that went with it. Achilles, in the
genitive case, between the penthemimeral caesura and the end of the
verse? That would be *peleiadeo Achileos*—"of Achilles, son of Peleus"—
and nothing else.

Parry's thesis floated freely between the French in which it was written and ancient Greek. It cited works in German and other languages.
It was, in every sense of the word, "technical." All in search of patterns
to explain just what was going on in Homer's magisterial verses. Parry
didn't need to show that the epics were studded with epithets; that was
clear to anyone who'd ever read them. It was what they were doing there
that Parry would explain. Why were they so pervasive?

Conceive Homer as an author from our own world and time, one
who chooses words for their special effect at this or that moment in the
story, and it would be easy to see the epithets as arbitrary or inept. But
Parry was not interested in our world and time; to use his own word,
he sought to "reconstitute" an earlier one. Audiences in earlier times
didn't read or hear the epithets as we do. For them, the epithets were all
but permanently attached to the nouns they graced—*rosy-fingered dawn,
godlike Apollo.* They appeared with them not when the story decreed but
when they were needed to make the poem sound like a poem and not an
unmelodic heap of words. Forget about the literary artist grasping for *le
mot juste;* imagine, instead, the traditional bardic world's common cur-
rency of sound and meaning laid at a poet's feet, the formulaic epithets
used as needed to move the great poem along.

"The fixed epithet is ornamental because it is traditional," wrote Parry. Being "traditional" meant that it was embedded in the lives of the people who heard it, for whom it was forever linked to the people, gods, objects, or places of which it was part. "An epithet is not ornamental in itself," wrote Parry, but only by being used again and again with a hero, god, or place it becomes so. In so doing, it bestows "an element of nobility and grandeur."

*

"As we come to the end of our investigation into the meaning of the fixed epithet in Homer, a question arises," Parry wrote in a brief, inconclusive coda to one part of his thesis: "How should it be translated?" That is, if the epithets worked as he claimed, in their original setting, for their original audiences, but not in the same way for modern readers, how best to translate them?

To point up the problem, he turned to a passage in Book 9 of the *Odyssey,* where Odysseus, he and his crew having suffered terribly at the hands of the Cyclops, rams a burning olive-wood stake through his eye, blinding him. Then, making his escape by clinging to the underside of a ram, Odysseus taunts him:

> "Kyklops,
>
> *If ever mortal man inquire*
> *how you were put to shame and blinded, tell him*
> *Odysseus, raider of cities, took your eye:*
> *Laertes' son, whose home's on Ithaka!"*

This, from Robert Fitzgerald's 1961 translation.

The passage's third line refers to *Odussea ptoliporthion*—Odysseus, raider of cities—one of his more familiar epithets.

The fourth line identifies Odysseus as Laertes's son, from Ithaka.

To Parry, these two depictions of Odysseus differ greatly. The former, the ornamental epithet, simply rounds out the poetic line. The latter, in its just-the-facts exactness, helps deliver a hard, hurtful message to the crippled one-eyed monster: Odysseus haughtily identifies himself, his father, his home, all but signing his name and writing his return address, reveling in vengeful triumph.

How, asks Parry, can a translation express this difference? "How can we render the ornamental meaning of *ptoliporthion* without losing at the same time the particularized meaning of the words of the following line?" Citing also a kindred example in the *Iliad,* Parry writes, "The mind gives up before so impossible a task."

The translators, of course, cannot give up. In Robert Fagles's 1996 translation, the same passage reads:

> "Cyclops—
> *if any man on the face of the earth should ask you*
> *who blinded you, shamed you so—say Odysseus,*
> *raider of cities, he gouged out your eye,*
> *Laertes's son who makes his home in Ithaca."*

In her 2018 translation, Emily Wilson did it like this:

> *"Cyclops! If any mortal asks you how*
> *your eye was mutilated and made blind,*
> *say that Odysseus, the city-sacker,*
> *Laertes' son, who lives in Ithaca,*
> *destroyed your sight."*

In all three cases, a residue of Parry's distinction remains. The epithet, "sacker of cities," appears almost parenthetically, in contrast to Odysseus's bold, taunting signature at the end.

*

It was a whole architecture of understanding and meaning that Parry aimed to demonstrate in Paris, not with a corroboration here or there, as in his master's thesis, but with a wealth, a glut, of evidence. Indeed, what would so stand out from his Paris thesis, drawing due appreciation from most scholars, was the precision and fullness with which he made his case, seeming to slam shut the door on alternative possibilities. His was a truth that could seem "scientific."

In their headings alone, the subsections of, say, Part III of Parry's thesis, "The Epithet and the Formula," suggest his comprehensiveness:

1. Noun-Epithet Formulae of Gods and Heroes; Principal Types, 26 pages; 2. Noun-Epithet Formulae of Gods and Heroes; Less Frequent Types, 16 pages. And so on—epithet formulae for heroines, peoples, countries, ships, horses, and finally 11, the human race; and 12, shields.

To use a word less of his time than ours, Parry shows no sign of "entitlement." He doesn't act as if his mere say-so is enough; rather, that it is his duty to prove, demonstrate, substantiate. His thesis is labored. By the roughest of analogies to American novelists of his era, it suggests the dogged, plodding resolve of a Theodore Dreiser, not the easy Jazz Age insouciance of an F. Scott Fitzgerald. His Université de Paris jury would see his thesis as marked by "a remarkable fullness, in a manner one could term exhaustive." A distinguished classicist of the period, Paul Storey, used the same word. Much later, University of Chicago professor Haun Saussy would laud Parry for his "matchless patience." All are approving appraisals—yet with perhaps a hint of damning with faint praise, as if in sly payback for this brain-curdling intellectual exercise, from which even a devoted scholar might shrink.

An early admirer of Parry's work, a young French classicist named Pierre Chantraine, would write in a 1929 review of the Paris thesis, "One is tempted to reproach in his book its sobriety, if this sobriety didn't also give it its force."

*

In a letter to his sister Addison on October 16, 1926, Milman wrote, "My head is too full of German documentation to feel kindly to the good and gentle world." He may, just then, have been absorbed in the work of several mid-nineteenth-century German philologists. Among these was Heinrich Düntzer, who'd studied Schiller, Goethe, and other classic German poets but who also had much to say of the Homeric epics.

"It could fairly be said," Adam Parry wrote of his father's work, "that each of the specific tenets which make up Parry's view of Homer had been held by some former scholar"; to Düntzer and his 1862 essay, *On the Interpretation of Fixed Epithets in Homer,* Milman Parry owed perhaps his most substantial debt, one he freely acknowledged. The connection Düntzer forged between the epithet and its metrical value, he wrote, was "undoubtedly the most important step since Aristarchus"—Aristarchus of Samothrace, second century BCE—"towards the understanding of the fixed epithet in Homer." Düntzer had argued, just as Parry did now, that the epithet "said" nothing, was there for metrical convenience alone. Many of Düntzer's contemporaries, Parry noted, were shocked at the thought—that Homer, of all poets, might be choosing words without regard to what they meant. Other scholars warmed enough to Düntzer's ideas to reach "the melancholy conclusion that Homer," as Parry put it, "was not what he was thought to be." But in the end, he added, "Düntzer's theory suffered from indifference. His work was not forgotten, but no one carried it on."

In fact, he declared, Düntzer was right. But unfortunately, the German hadn't supplied much evidence for his suppositions. Nor did he much try to explain them. So after Düntzer, scholars had reverted to the same stale old ideas, that the epithets really did mean something to the story: Some of them, wrote Parry with a hint of scorn, were determined "to bring us back to the days when indications of the weather were found in the epithets of the sea." That is, *anything,* to show that the epithets were words like any other, to be taken literally, their role in verse-making unacknowledged or disdained.

Essential to Parry's thinking in both the master's thesis and now in Paris was that behind the Homeric epics stood a traditional culture, not one brilliant individual creator. But this was not entirely new, either. Gilbert Murray, perhaps the leading British authority on ancient Greece, had said as much in 1907. No one poet could be credited with the *Iliad* and the *Odyssey,* he wrote.

> We shall find among the causes of [their] greatness something nobler and more august than the genius of any individual man. . . . Each successive poet did not assert himself against the tradition, but gave himself up to the tradition, and added to its greatness and beauty all that was in him. The intensity of imagination which makes the *Iliad* alive is not . . . the imagination of any one man. It means not that one man of genius created a wonder and passed away. It means that generations of poets, trained in the same schools and a more or less continuous and similar life, steeped themselves to the lips in the spirit of this great poetry. They lived in the Epic saga and by it and for it.

Murray wrote this when Parry was five years old.

But he, like Düntzer, might be seen as simply advancing an opinion, if a highly articulate one. It was just such inspired speculation that Parry hoped to transcend, with a heaping-up of demonstration and proof worked out in minute detail. As James P. Holoka would make the case, Parry removed from Homeric studies "the haze of generalization." It was as if after his master's thesis, Parry had realized—or been made to realize, once he'd met Croiset, Meillet, and Puech—that it was only a starting point. So, this second time around, he set out to do it right.

Of course, almost no one would have realized it was a second time; who, after all, had read the Berkeley thesis? In every public and practical sense, the Paris work represented not the second time his ideas were submitted to the classical community, but the first.

Published in Paris in 1928—by La Société d'Édition Les Belles Lettres, the main thesis available for thirty-five francs, the supplementary for twelve—Parry's opus was not instantly embraced by classical scholars. One reason was that it was so damned difficult. As Adam Parry felt enjoined to point out, "the thoroughness of the argumentation makes the work less attractive." Among its difficulties, certainly, was that it fairly brimmed over with numbers; Parry, as we've seen, counted epithets, tracked how often this one or that appeared in various kinds of poetic situations. The Homeric epics were the holy of holies of the Western tradition, a literary place artists and critics honored, rich with deep truth, yet here, of all places, Parry dared inject statistics, *mathematics*? Indeed, his accounting proved so extensive that his columns of data—and data was what they were—had often to be turned on their side to fit the page, as if they were so many quarterly divisional sales reports.

Parry, who had taken his share of math at Oakland Tech, including algebra, geometry, and trigonometry, may have felt shamefaced about it—that, or he simply anticipated objections. For he gave over a substantial footnote to a full-throated defense: "Must we give reasons for making numerical comparisons?" he began. Numbers, he insisted, were "our only means of verifying with precision what would otherwise remain a vague impression." Yes, he allowed, numbers applied to Homer had sometimes been used to make something out of nothing, sullying their reputation. He promised to avoid such traps.

How did an ornamental epithet get that way? How could Homer's audience become "indifferent to any particular meaning of the epithet"? The explanation, he said, was "ultimately one of numbers": It couldn't be reduced to an equation, but if you'd heard an epithet used in the same way "a sufficient number of times," it lost its immediacy, became linked, indissolubly, with its god or hero, the two become one. How *many* times? At one point, Parry actually toys with a number—"not twice, not thrice, but twenty and thirty times," or more.

In a section of his thesis devoted to "Limits of the Method of Investigation," Parry explained why, while the role of epithets bearing on gods and heroes was easy to establish, those dealing with place-names resisted analysis. The problem was the limited data set; that is, Homer was forever invoking Odysseus, say, but only rarely Ithaca, his home. In short, just as in a medical or social sciences study, the "sample size" on which statistical inferences might be drawn was simply too small.

"Parry's statistical orientation emulated the procedures of the exact sciences," Holoka would write. "Here was no mere impressionistic aestheticism; here was a 'hard science' methodology," one that in those days had barely begun to penetrate the arts and humanities. Holoka would go on to aptly cite an analogy made by French historian and critic Hippolyte Taine: "Why study the [fossil] shell, except to bring before you the animal?" Likewise, "you study the document only to know the man." In short—fossil, document, Homeric epithet—each revealed something beyond itself, told of the larger world of which it was a part.

But as much as Parry brought "science" to Homer, his work was driven by literary and aesthetic values. The noun-epithet formulae figured so prominently in the *Iliad* and the *Odyssey* because they made the lines sound right, natural, instead of the artificial things they were. But just why it mattered that they rolled off the pen, or the tongue, so prettily and so easily, and the great, unexpected truth that signified, was to Parry not yet plain.

15

TRAPPED

It was from around the fall of 1926 through most of 1927 that the Parrys lived in Sceaux (pronounced *so*), a suburb of about five thousand residents, south of the city, that they'd learned of through some American friends. There they'd settled in a *pension,* a boardinghouse a few minutes' walk from the train station, set back by a little courtyard or terrace from the street. The kitchen and main living area were on the first floor; their wallpapered bedroom, crammed with double bed and baby's crib, on the second; and three smaller rooms on the third. "He did a good deal of work upstairs," Marian would recall, "counting all these epithets and everything."

Compared to their early days in France, their circumstances in Sceaux were much improved. Milman was now formally enrolled at the Sorbonne. Endorsements in hand from Croiset and Puech, he'd received a $1,200 fellowship from the American Field Service, established after the Great War to support American graduate students in France. They shared the house on rue de Fontenay with two young police officers and a station agent—"from whom," Milman wrote Addison, "we are learning much bad French"; as well as with the Allards, the *pension*'s proprietors, a couple in their sixties. Mme. Allard couldn't read, couldn't write, but certainly could cook, and seemed to adore their little girl.

Early in their stay, during a run of "still, clear autumn days that I wish would never stop," Marian wrote Addison, they left Wux with Mme. Allard, went into Paris, and wound up at the Luxembourg Gardens, where Milman read and I fell asleep on one of the chairs you rent for half a cent. It is a very exciting place so full of incredibly handsome and well-dressed babies and young men and girls that you want to look at that no matter where you are, you always think better ones are going by somewhere else. There is a sort of melancholy air about it due to the dusty yellow light that comes through the old trees and hangs over the big ponds with a fountain in its center, children's sailboats sailing on it and huge bright dahlias and gray statues all around.

Sceaux was more upscale than humble Clamart, where they'd spent most of their first year. Its links to the levers of power and influence in the capital went back to Jean-Baptiste Colbert, Louis XIV's formidable finance minister, who'd designed a chateau for himself in what became the town's royal park. Tied by train to the capital, Sceaux became a place for sumptuous balls for Paris's elite; Balzac titled one of his novellas *Le Bal de Sceaux*. By the late 1920s, it had become a modern suburb, a means to escape Paris, with its noisy cars, traffic jams, and lung-blackening coal smoke. One Sceaux native, Simone Flahaut, would write of her father, a professor in the Latin Quarter who had moved to the town from Paris a few years before the Parrys did: "There in his garden, he quickly forgot the smoke from the train that fell on Boulevard Saint-Michel [near the Sorbonne] and which was so dense in the Gare de Luxembourg that you couldn't see ceilings, nor the stairs, nor the vault of the station."

Sceaux, then, was a fine place to live, or could be. The house on rue de Fontenay was located a few blocks, half a kilometer, from the town's commercial center around rue Houdan, its shops offering, as one advertised, "everything you need and at the best price." Mrs. Parry could walk there in five or ten minutes or else take the tram and, especially on Wednesday and Saturday market days, find herself amid such liveliness as the town could offer.

But she was miserable. "I was just there with Marian and it was so lonely because the French are very . . . they're not easily . . . they don't make friends." On the street, she'd see one particular young woman with children around the age of her child. "But she'd never say *how do you do* to me or anything. It was just terrible." Terrible for her, certainly, and

Marian with her little girl in Sceaux, a Parisian suburb. "From my window," she would write in a poem, "Everything is in squares / The houses are like blocks / And each backyard is walled in."

no less so for her girl, by now a toddler. Marian "had to live around me, too, as well as I had to live around her, and of course I just wasn't terribly happy there." Indeed, it may be that some of the ill feeling between her and her daughter, which in later accounts seems to verge on bitterness, owed something to that year and a half in Sceaux.

Years after Milman's death, in 1950, his son, Adam, wrote sister Marian, then twenty-six, about how he and his own young wife were thinking of having their seven-month-old son stay with his grandparents in California for a while. Wouldn't be bad, he thought. "Living with the Pfeiffers would be idyllic for him"—and maybe give him and his wife Barbara a fresh start. "Remember how Mother was trapped with you in Sceaux for the years she and Papa were in France?"

In a series of seven linked poems, under the title "Banlieue Parisienne" (Parisian suburb), Mrs. Parry would write of her life in Sceaux.

> *From my window*
> *Everything is in squares—*
> *The houses are like blocks*
> *And each backyard is walled in.*

She writes of "little-town streets" quieter than any country road, their houses shut and silent, and of the train, with its "big twirl of smoke" that took you into the Luxembourg station in Paris.

> *It has the mission*
> *of bringing these shuttered houses*
> *to Paris.*
> *The mother dressed in black with her baby in white*
> *Can leave the still streets*
> *For* Les Galeries Lafayette
> *The young man can hurry, keeping the mud off his spats,*
> *To spend the night with his mistress.*
> *She lives near* L'Étoile *and has a bathroom*
> *And lavender slippers.*

A few months after arriving in Sceaux, Mrs. Parry wrote Addison, who had returned to college:

> I envy you. Are you really walking around with a note book and are all your days nicely marked out like a new chessboard? To change the figure, it seems to me that days not planned from the outside are something like tents with no poles; they flap down all over you. I keep putting up poles, such as the [illegible] for Wux's bath, tea, and the firm resolve to make the beds before breakfast. But there is always a sag.

Marian seemed unable to arrange her life to give satisfaction and pleasure. How much did that owe to being a mother, stuck at home, alone, with a young child, in a foreign country, the whole mix poisoned by her own passivity? How much to a sorely preoccupied husband who seemed little interested in her? "I think he was . . . so absorbed with his own life and this work that he was doing," Marian would say. Sterling Dow pictures him—probably, again, through Marian—as "constantly at work, almost vacationless. On the Paris theses, he wrote well into the night, rising only at noon the next day."

Beyond epithet-counting, Marian knew next to nothing of his work. In recalling the period, she was riddled with self-reproach for it.

We know this because she said so, in her long interview with Pamela Newhouse in 1981, a decade after the coming of the modern women's movement, as the two of them sat in Mrs. Parry's little house on Dwight Way, a brief walk from where Berkeley's Free Speech Movement had been born. "I'm ashamed now," Marian said, "when I see the list of books he read, that I didn't read Renan," the French philologist Milman quoted so often. "It was obvious that Milman had a much better mind than I had, which is kind of a sad thing, but . . ." She let the thought trail off. But if there was a gap between their respective intellects, the roles to which they clung only broadened them. Yes, maybe her intellectual appetites were simply not so urgent as his. But maybe, too, with her attention given over to their girl, she was left little able to think about much else. Milman was working through the ancient Greek, tracing epithets through the Homeric concordances, trying to express elusive ideas in a second language. Sadly, there was little "leakage" of all this intellectual energy into their lives together. It was *his* big idea, after all, not hers.

The Newhouse interview paints Milman as doing little to draw his wife closer, of Marian taking no initiative herself, the two of them edging apart. When, first in respectful reticence and then in evident frustration, Newhouse hears Mrs. Parry express regret over the Paris years, she becomes restive, her questions more intrusive:

NEWHOUSE: The overriding impression I get is that at many points when you were less than thrilled you were not being particularly, well, you were swallowing it.

MRS. PARRY: Yes.

Was Milman aware of her state of mind?

MRS. PARRY: As I told you, I was aware that I was a sort of disappointment to him in the sense that he thought that I would be more interested in intellectual things . . .

NEWHOUSE: But he must have seen that if he were saddled with two little children [just one while in Sceaux] all day long, his ability to pursue intellectual things might be a little hampered.

MRS. PARRY: That's something I really don't know. But I think that I was stupid to . . . handle the problems as I did.

At one point, the wife of Edwin Loeb, one of the anthropologists' crowd at Cal, offered to introduce her to her brother-in-law, Harold Loeb, model for the Robert Cohn character in Hemingway's *The Sun Also Rises,* and founder of an international arts journal, *Broom.* It might have been a real opportunity. But, oh, Mrs. Parry would say later, she didn't like the Loebs—neither her friend's husband nor, likely as not, his famous brother. So she declined. "I can hardly believe I was so negative. . . . I was very, very stupid," she'd admit, "because you may not be in love with [someone], but [through him] you meet other people. . . . The way I did it was just so inane." At another point Milman advised her that an art dealer had signaled Marie Laurencin's wish, or willingness, to paint a portrait of her and the baby. Marie Laurencin, of the Picasso and Apollinaire crowd! But "I even refused to do that. Well, just think what it would have been now to have had a picture by Marie Laurencin."

In fact, Milman was little more sociable than his wife; her reticence and timidity, she'd say, "suited him fine." And they did get out occasionally, of course, once to an ambassadorial reception. But "we didn't know anybody and of course we drank some champagne and walked out again."

Later, she'd comment, "I think Milman could have taken me to meet Meillet . . . if I'd insisted. But I didn't really insist."

So she never met him.

16

SOUTENANCE

Antoine Meillet's voice was soft; best to listen to him in a small, quiet room. His microscopic handwriting was almost illegible. After he died, his diaries would be found "stuffed with linguistic notes written on . . . library loan slips, strips of paper used to roll up newspapers." Behind his big glasses and scraggly dark beard, his eyes shut tight as he spoke, he could seem mild and unprepossessing. But he was perhaps the foremost linguist of his generation, mentor to a whole generation of linguists and philologists, a towering intellectual figure.

Meillet was a generation younger than Croiset, a few years younger even than Aimé Puech. His scholarly pedigree went back to the philologist Michel Bréal and to Ferdinand de Saussure, founder of the French school of comparative linguistics. As a young man he'd traveled to the Caucasus to learn Armenian. He had helped discover a hitherto unknown Indo-European language, "Tokharien B." It was going only a little too far to say that Meillet knew all languages, and how each related to every other. An admirer would remember him from before the Great War, in his apartment, then still on Boulevard Saint-Michel, up each morning at five o'clock, reading and writing, often while he stood. "He did not want to make [his students] imitators," it would be said of Meillet, "but free scientific individuals."

Just how and when Parry first met him is unclear. Elected to the Collège de France in 1905, Meillet was also, during the period Parry knew him, professor at the École Pratique des Hautes Études. He knew Victor Bérard, with whom he exchanged opinions of the young American, pointedly objecting to Bérard's view that Parry was too fixated on Homeric language. And of course he knew Maurice Croiset, both of them being based at the Collège de France, both ultimately serving on Parry's thesis jury. As for Puech, he scarcely mentioned Meillet in his sometimes almost nostalgic reminiscences of his days with Parry, as if trying to keep him to himself. Of Parry's Paris professors, his son, Adam, would write, Meillet was the one "whose ideas were most in harmony with Parry's own," alone among them whose work he'd formally cite. And, as we'll see, he would loom large in Parry's career after Paris.

In 1928, when Parry was finishing up in Paris, Meillet responded to his request for a recommendation letter. He'd be happy to furnish one, he wrote from his apartment on rue de Verneuil, a block back from the Seine in the 7th arrondissement, in his tiny crabbed hand: "We have discussed many times your research on Homeric language." He admired Parry's approach, he said. He appreciated how well Parry knew the language and style of Homer. He had no doubt that Parry would "confer honor" on any university that asked him to teach Greek language and literature.

Some would conclude, reasonably, that it was Meillet who presided over Parry's thesis. But he may have been less caught up in the day-to-day work of directing Parry's doctoral studies, across two and a half years, than was Aimé Puech, a less brightly glowing light in Paris than Meillet or Croiset. Puech was more the proverbial academic worker bee. He had a substantial bibliography of papers and books, including one on early Christian writings in Greek that came out about when Parry's thesis did. But Faculté des Lettres records suggest he may have surrendered more to the Sorbonne's administrative routine—setting budgets, voting on promotions, renaming rooms, showing up for academic ceremonies. A modern scholar, Charles de Lamberterie, would picture him as partial to Parry's work, appreciative of its importance, yet not *entirely* certain just why it was important. In any case, it was Puech who watched over Parry's progress across 1926 and 1927 and into the following year.

Setting out to see Puech on Sundays, Parry would step out from the house on rue de Fontenay and make for Sceaux's little train station, passing by the house where the widowed Marie Curie had once lived with her two daughters and her father-in-law. At the *gare*, the size of a large house, with mansard roof and twin chimneys, he'd board the train for

Paris. After a twenty-five-minute ride through the city's inner suburbs, he'd likely have gotten off not at the Luxembourg station, near the Sorbonne, but at the smaller Port-Royal *gare;* from there, a few minutes on foot would bring him to Puech's apartment in Val-de-Grâce.

Right from the beginning, it seemed to Puech that Parry knew what he was about; Puech talked with him about his ideas, but "less with the intention of modifying them than to lead him to deepen them and draw out their fine shadings." And he helped him, too, with his written French. Parry had come a long way since the summer of 1924. In a letter to Addison in 1926, he'd boast of a compliment he'd recently received for his French. Still, as Sterling Dow would report, probably through Mrs. Parry, the French thesis "cost him much slow and careful labor; and he had help with the final version." Help, certainly, from Puech. "While he spoke French with ease, as he loved just and precise expression," Puech would say of his student, "he consulted me each time he had a scruple of form and questioned me persistently until he came away satisfied."

(Meanwhile, little Marian was growing up fluent in French, her faulty English rendered in an accent "abominable" to her father's ear.)

Parry's thesis, "The Traditional Epithet in Homer," first published in French in 1928 (and in English translation only in 1971), comes down to us as a final fixed work of scholarship. But (like the Homeric epics themselves, if by a different route), it was the product of a lengthy genesis—not just the several years it directly cost its author in France but back to that 1923 summer on the beach in California. If Parry's Cal thesis was just the thin melody of his big idea, the Paris thesis was its richer, fuller orchestration. The false starts, the retractions, the backings-and-forthings that his thesis went through don't come down to us. What does seem plain, however, is that Parry's authorial decisions defaulted to *more*—to approach his subject from yet another angle, close out yet another alternative, build an edifice of ever more unassailable proof.

In January 1927, Parry wrote Croiset with several chapters from his thesis. Croiset wrote back two weeks later saying he'd not finished them yet but that he could see they represented serious, interesting work. "I estimate that you have studied a part of Homeric technique with more precision than anyone else has until now. And I can only urge you very forcibly to continue with what you have started." He'd be glad to meet with Parry anytime he wished and suggested the following Friday morning.

Then, in April, more good news: "My thesis," Milman wrote Addison, ". . . has been accepted as presentable—when finished—for the degree of *Docteur ès lettres* which I find will be a prettier title than *Docteur de l'Université de Paris*." It's not clear how Parry, during the two years or so he'd worked on it, came to seek the more prestigious French credential, which was more typically earned midway through a scholarly career than at its beginning. Surely, it demanded more of him, requiring two theses, principal and complementary, not one, and a committee of five senior scholars, not three, to evaluate their merits. (Its roots went back to an 1810 decree, during the time of Napoléon, which prescribed that one of the two theses be written in Latin, a requirement relaxed before Parry's time.) Far enough along by now, and confident enough of success, Parry looked into getting the two theses printed (another degree requirement), and learned it would be expensive. He hoped to formally defend his thesis the following spring.

"At that moment," he wrote Addison, looking ahead to the following year, "I shall once again become a man instead of being, as for so long, a student: I am getting tired of being a student."

*

It was around this time—much work remaining but Milman's prospects improved, the air in the household a little lighter—that Marian again became pregnant. "Well, that was a little bit of a surprise," Marian would recall.

By then, they had left Sceaux for Paris, where for a time they lived in a little apartment near Notre Dame Cathedral. Great location, crummy apartment is how Marian remembered it; but in any case it was too small now, with a second child on the way. So probably in late 1927, Milman tracked down a larger place for them, in an apartment building on rue Marie-Davy, in the 14th arrondissement, near the Cité Universitaire, the experiment in international education then going up on the outskirts of Paris. They were living here when their son was born on February 1, 1928.

And their son's name? To this simple question, we are reduced to a maddeningly convoluted answer: One night, as Marian told the story, she was exhausted, wholly wrung out, and appealed to Milman: "Look, if you'll cook supper, I'll let you name the baby." He agreed, pronouncing their son's name to be Milman. That's the name appearing on the child's Report of Birth with the American Consular Service dated a few weeks after the event.

So the parents were Milman and Marian, and their children were Milman and Marian.

In fact, their son would, for most of his life, and in most of his professional records, be known as Adam Milman Parry; sometimes he went by Milman, sometimes Adam.

Mr. and Mrs. Parry, we may recall, called their firstborn child Wux. Now, their second became Duppy.

Of course, once at school, Duppy would never do. So Marian took to calling him Mel—which, she belatedly realized, was more typically short for Melvin, who he was not.

In this book, he is Adam.

Sister Marian, almost exactly four years older, would recall the glass doors on their apartment on rue Marie-Davy, "the bassinette all covered with satin ribbons, and the small, squirming Schnoss"—*her* name for her baby brother.

*

What Parry had worked toward all the time he was in Paris was his *soutenance,* or thesis defense. Essentially, it was a culminating oral exam, garlanded with a bit of formality and public ceremony, a perhaps once-in-a-lifetime moment of intellectual glory. Parry's was announced, complete with the titles of his theses, right alongside theater openings and museum exhibitions, in *La Semaine à Paris*. It was set for 1 p.m., Thursday, May 31, 1928, at the Sorbonne.

If you'd gotten this far along, three or four years into your thesis work, it was rare to perform so badly at your *soutenance* as to be turned away entirely without a degree. But that made it no less fraught. After cracking your head on elusive concepts and ideas, writing three hundred pages, struggling over each word and comma, you didn't want to throw it all away in one bad afternoon of mental block and muddle.

While most candidates did get their degrees, the jury had ample room to point up a thesis's failings, and rank it. In the end, they could judge it *très honorable,* or *honorable,* or deny it any special *mention* at all. The sometimes lengthy reports they prepared afterward—usually handwritten in those days—were free to voice every variety of criticism, every want of enthusiasm, every species of discontent. The report for one candidate receiving an *honorable* during the late 1920s noted the "grave faults" of both its theses. Another, for a thesis to which the jury otherwise seemed sympathetic, wished for "an overall picture more vivid than he has offered us." A third, also earning an *honorable,* called the candidate's thesis sober and well conceived, but lamented she still had "difficulty expressing herself fluently in French"; and that her taste for objectivity at all costs inhibited useful discriminations. Richer elaboration of her ideas "would have done her more honor."

Parry's *soutenance,* like most at the Sorbonne, was held in the magnificent Salle Louis Liard, named for a late-nineteenth-century French philosopher and academic administrator. Entering the university complex from rue de la Sorbonne, you'd cross the Cour d'Honneur with its monument to a meditative Victor Hugo, step through the bank of doors of the library, and from there down a few steps into the great amphitheater. It was about sixty feet long and thirty wide, virtually every inch of wall and ceiling covered with warm-toned wood and large, gilt-framed paintings of the Great Men of French intellectual and literary life. Pascal, Descartes, and Racine lined one wall. Tiptoe down the tiny steps that took you to the examination dock at the bottom, turn back toward where you'd come in, and there, on the wall behind you, was Corneille and, on the courtyard side, Molière. If Parry had the least disposition to be intimidated, this was the place for it.

Parry's thesis jury consisted of Meillet, Croiset, Puech, and two younger scholars, the Hellenist Louis Meridier and the linguist Joseph Vendryes; together, Harry Levin would write, they read "like a bibliography of modern classical scholarship." They and Parry met at the bottom of the amphitheater, the hall's two hundred seating places, in gently curved, pew-like benches, rising behind it. As Parry stood facing the jury, the painted portraits looking down on him, midday light from the three great windows facing the Cour d'Honneur over his right shoulder, the dock itself was actually quite intimate. You could speak in normal

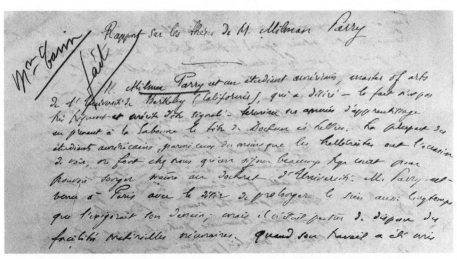

The opening of the jury report on Parry's 1928 doctoral thesis at the Sorbonne; his five readers, it would be said, constituted "a bibliography of modern classical scholarship."

tones to the jury seated in the little semicircle a few feet from you and expect to be heard. In fact, Parry spoke so softly, remembered Marian, who'd gotten someone to watch Wux and Duppy for the afternoon, that she could hardly hear him. Of course, she "probably couldn't have understood it very well even if I could have caught all of the words."

The French flag, the *Tricolore,* graced the proceedings. "That was the first time I ever had the feeling of being in a completely alien country," Marian recalled. "I thought, goodness, what will they do to us?" In fact, to one or two questions, Parry simply didn't know the answers. "Well," Marian thought at the time, "that's the end, he's failed."

He did not fail. Overall, the jury found that Parry presented his work "with ease and precision." But he did not just sail through. His short supplementary thesis, an application of his principal thesis to certain metrical anomalies in the epics, enjoyed little favor among them. Vendryes faulted even its title, "Homeric Formulae and Homeric Meter," deeming it too grand and insufficiently clear. All in all, he and the others judged, it was "less complete and less finished" than the principal thesis.

The principal thesis, on the other hand, was lauded as "one of the most original and most instructive studies published on Homer in some years." Parry's subject was "the most important of all for precise understanding of Homeric style, and viewed a certain way, the most difficult to resolve." As for Parry's statistics, he had approached them with a sensibility "both flexible and broad, avoiding the perils they'd present were they too mechanically applied." In the end, he had all but proven "that Homeric style must be judged from another point of view entirely from that of a modern poet, even that of Virgil."

So they *got it*. They appreciated that "a great number of seeming liberties and metrical oddities" in the epics, the subject of much claim and counterclaim over the centuries, now neatly explained themselves. Parry had swept aside "numerous questions which [no longer] even needed to be asked." He had built a new intellectual edifice, one that didn't imagine some one man's inspired poetic creation but rather a communal, collective, ever metamorphosing one. Set against *that,* one need no longer explain this or that seeming anomaly in the Homeric texts, not when this new outlook, with its altogether different creation story, explained so much by itself.

"With the completion of Parry's dissertation," Stanford University classicist Richard Martin would write, "the real revolution in Homeric studies began." But that revolution, which indeed it proved to be, wasn't embodied in Parry's thesis *quite* as it stood. As the jury's written "reservations" suggested, there were gaps in it, questions without answers, truths implied but not developed or even asserted. For one thing, he'd overstated (though Meillet dissented from this particular criticism) the ubiquity and centrality of the epithet formulae. He'd assumed that the formulae predated the epic poems themselves, whereas just possibly it worked the other way around, the epics spurring formulaic diction. And he had failed to assert outright the conclusion his work seemed to imply—that epic poetry was a recited or improvised poetry.

It was this last that left the deepest impression on Parry.

As summarized in the jury report Puech wrote afterward, the idea could seem a bit murky. But there, in Salle Louis Liard, Parry heard it straight from Meillet. And some months later, in Meillet's published review of his thesis, he heard it again, a vision of Homeric creation by

anonymous bards constrained by the exigencies of oral recitations, chanted to the accompaniment of instruments that marked their rhythm. We have no way of knowing whether the Greek bards used written memory aids or at what date the Homeric poems were set down in writing. The essential facts are that these poems were intended to be recited and that they were based on ancient oral semi-improvisations . . . [the epithet formulae being] necessary for the storytellers who made up their texts as they went along and expected by listeners who found that these formulae eased the effort of following along.

On hand in Salle Louis Liard the afternoon of Parry's *soutenance,* along with Mr. and Mrs. Parry, the five jury members, and no doubt a few vagrant students or faculty, was at least one other scholar. His name was Matija Murko, a professor at the University of Prague, just then a guest at the Sorbonne. A sixty-seven-year-old Slovenian—years later, after the breakup of Yugoslavia, he'd wind up on a Slovenian postage stamp, sporting the luxuriant mustache he wore most of his life—he had studied and taught in many of the scholarly capitals of central and eastern Europe. Murko was a Slavicist, a student of Slavic culture and literature. Across three days the week before, he'd lectured on the epic poetry of Yugoslavia; Parry had noticed the poster for his lectures, but had interpreted their subject as far distant from his own. Yet now, at Antoine Meillet's behest, Professor Murko was on hand for Parry's thesis defense.

Meillet would describe not so much a hole in Parry's thesis as a door through which he might wish to step. What Parry had done at Cal, and now more definitively in Paris, showed that the *Odyssey* and the *Iliad* were the product of traditional cultures working, somehow, in traditional ways. But missing from Parry's formulation, Meillet held, was that this traditional style was probably the work of oral poets—oral poets like those who sang the Yugoslavian epic songs Professor Murko had long studied. Murko, no expert on Homer, was indeed an expert on the epic poetry of Serbia and the rest of what since 1922 had become the Kingdom of Yugoslavia.

So it was, with Murko in Salle Louis Liard with the others, that Meillet made a suggestion, delivered, as Parry recalled, "with his usual ease and clarity." It would stick in Parry's mind, stubbornly, through his brief remaining time in Paris, his travel back to the States, and across the next three years as he established himself as a professor and scholar:

The *Iliad* and the *Odyssey* had not been worked out, in all their length and complexity, on vellum, parchment, paper, or papyrus. Rather, they had taken shape in the minds, and on the voices, of singers and poets. And if Parry wanted to see for himself that this was true and, if so, how it worked, he needed to go where such singers and poets could still be found.

It might be possible to class all Meillet said as "criticism," representing gaps and missed intellectual opportunities. But alternatively— and more correctly, I think—Meillet's suggestion can be seen as fatherly guidance for the next phase of Parry's work: In response to the rich offering Parry had made to Homeric studies through his thesis, Meillet and the rest of the jury were giving him back their own reciprocal gift, a research program likely to engage him for years to come.

*

Nothing Antoine Meillet said that afternoon or that Aimé Puech wrote in his jury report could deprive Parry of all that was rightfully his: Noting "the effort expended, the originality and importance of the results, the elegance of exposition—particularly worthy of praise in a foreigner," Parry merited the highest honor, a *mention très honorable*. This the jury announced after brief deliberation and ratified that same day on a Université de Paris document to which they affixed their signatures— Meillet's minute and unreadable as always.

Marian didn't at first understand what these *mentions* meant. "I knew cum laude and magna cum laude and summa," the degree hierarchy back in the States, but not these French categories. She learned soon enough what a happy success Milman's *très honorable* represented.

The Parrys went off with friends to celebrate.

PART FOUR

Harvard

[1928–1933]

17

THE CALL

During the fraught weeks and months before his thesis defense, Parry had no job waiting for him once it was over, in America or anywhere else. He and Marian, uncertain of their future, frequented the cafés of Montparnasse, and fretted. Pedestrians observing the crowds seated at the little round sidewalk tables outside the Rotonde, the café they favored, might have seen in young Parry and his smartly dressed wife every outward sign of ease and well-being. But while Milman would soon get his doctorate, he was in one respect back where he was at Cal in late 1923, with a fine new academic credential and no job. "We didn't know what to do with ourselves," Marian would say, "waiting for some news."

Then the news came.

*

The previous spring, in Des Moines, Iowa, a small city in the American heartland, Charles Oscar Denny, head of Drake University's small Latin department, suffered a cerebral hemorrhage, reducing him, in the words of one account, to "almost helpless invalidism." Denny's roots at Drake went back almost to the founding of the university by a preacher and a retired Union general in 1881. An Ohio boy, born in 1860, Denny had come to Drake in the 1880s, became the university's teacher of Latin, and remained so for the rest of his life, except for two years at Harvard to get a master's. A devout Christian, he was devoted as well to Drake, which he so long served. Then suddenly, that day in spring 1927, he was cut down. His Drake colleague Mrs. F. I. Harriott, a Bryn Mawr graduate, was pressed into service as his replacement—"until," the university said, "a successor is found."

Sometime in the year after Denny's stroke, word of the vacancy reached George Calhoun, one of Parry's professors at Cal. What levers he pulled, or favors he called in, is uncertain, but, one morning in the spring of 1928, a long white envelope appeared under the Parry door at rue Marie-Davy. It was an offer from Drake to become professor of Latin and head up the department. At a time when fifteen cents bought you a quart of milk, Milman had a job paying $2,500 a year.

It must have been just days after this that Milman wrote Alfred Kroeber in Berkeley with news of his new position and a copy of his freshly printed doctoral thesis. The Cal anthropologist's ideas had flavored Milman's master's thesis, but he himself may have loomed as large

George Calhoun, one of Milman's professors at Cal, helped land the new Sorbonne graduate a job at Drake University, in Iowa. For young Milman, it was Paris in May, Des Moines in September.

to Milman as his ideas. Kroeber's whole life cut a romantic figure. He had befriended a northern California Indian and written a book about him and the lost world from which he'd come. Drawn to the teachings of Freud, he had signed on for psychoanalysis himself and then, over-lapping with his Berkeley professorial duties, had embarked on a brief parallel career as an analyst. He was in his midforties when Milman and Marian knew him, at the center of a circle of admirers and intel-lectual devotees, tall, with a trim goatee like Freud's. Milman's classics professors had filled his head with Greek, but it may have been Kroeber who helped turn him, then an impressionable twenty-year-old, toward a scholar's life.

On June 18, he wrote Kroeber:

I am sending you a copy of my doctor's thesis, for reasons per-sonal and not at all academic. Although if you should acciden-tally read the book; and should know of any related study in American Indian poetry, I should be glad to know of it.

Marian and myself, and our two children, are probably going to leave Paris at the end of this month, since I am now professor of Latin at Drake University, Des Moines—which is our present address.

Marian, he added, sent her love. He offered his own best regards. He signed the letter.

And then he went back to it—every detail of the original letter attests to it—adding something more, squeezing it into the line that said he was now a professor himself: "So the times change." I believe this small emendation may be understood to mean: *Back at Cal, you knew me as a very young man. But now I'm no longer a student, or a boy. I have earned a doctorate; here is my thesis. I hope you are proud of me.*

On June 30, in Le Havre, Parry and his family boarded the SS *Rochambeau* for New York, where they arrived on July 9. Marian took the children to Milwaukee to see her mother, who had sublet a house there for them for the summer. Milman, meanwhile, visited family in California. Along the way, a pair of late job offers materialized from Cal, one in French, the other in Latin. But neither was in Greek, which is what it would have taken to break Milman's pledge to Drake. According to Marian, Milman knew that returning to Berkeley was "the dream of my heart." Why, they'd even settled on the kind of dream house they wanted, "with a quadrangle, you know, and a court in the center." No wonder, then, that Milman "was afraid to tell me" that they could have returned to Berkeley.

In August, the *Oakland Tribune* carried word of the local boy's new position at Drake. In early September, Parry arrived in Des Moines, where someone from the local paper interviewed him. The article ran beside a photo of the dashing young classicist, still just twenty-six, emanating French savoir faire. Parry compared French to American coeds (the now archaic term for female students). He was quoted as saying the American educational system was more democratic, especially for young women, the French system more centralized and competitive. One of his several opinions was immortalized in the accompanying headline: "Parry Blames Teachers for Pupil's Failure." "We professors do not expect enough of students and consequently, the students, living up only to our expectations," achieve less than they might. Of course, the gap might be smaller for Greek and Latin students, whom he pictured as more "earnest and scholarly."

That was September 9. Parry's wife and children were to join him in Des Moines later that day; they'd be living in what Marian would recall as a "little bit of a house" on 51st Street, about three miles from campus. One day early in this, their brief midwestern moment, Milman came home "with what looked like a white cat," but wasn't. "It was a pure white collie dog and we loved him so much we had to get his sister. So we had two white collie dogs," which soon were rushing headlong through their little bungalow. "Adam was a baby and he'd be in his playpen and get so excited; he loved to see those dogs run."

It was a nice start. But as it turned out, the whole span of time Milman was fully *present* at Drake, in spirit as well as body, must be reckoned only in months. Early in December, he received a handwritten note from Herbert Weir Smyth, a seventy-one-year-old classical scholar at Harvard. Parry knew him from back at Cal, where, in the spring of 1923, Smyth had given that year's Sather Lecture, a series of talks on Aeschylus that later appeared as a book. Parry, then taking graduate courses, showed up for them and must have made an impression. Because now, a vacancy existing at Harvard, Smyth remembered him—in particular, the way Smyth's wife Eleanor told it later, how something in his questions "revealed a scholarly mind." Smyth may have also heard good things about him from Calhoun, or even Linforth. Parry's French thesis had already gotten generous notice from Paul Shorey in America, and the favorable opinions of Antoine Meillet and Pierre Chantraine in France may also have been known to him by now.

In his letter of December 2, 1928, Smyth veritably pounced on Parry, who was just completing his first semester at Drake: "Is there not a good chance of your attending the meeting of the American Philological Association held this year in New York after Christmas?" The letter reads more like a summons than a question: Work up a paper, show up in New York and present it; he'd get a chance to meet fellow scholars that way, introduce himself around. Smyth would be glad to nominate him for membership, and nomination would ensure selection. "Besides, I should like the opportunity of seeing you again and of learning more of your work abroad."

Smyth's letter came only a few weeks before the meeting, but Parry did as bidden, submitting a paper, if not an entirely finished one; even its title changed on its way into the association's *Transactions,* as "The Homeric Gloss: A Study in Word-sense." Parry was interested in certain unfamiliar words and expressions—"glosses," or *glottai,* as Aristotle called them—appearing in the Homeric epics. Roughly, these were obsolete, foreign, or otherwise forgotten words that begged explanation—which generations of scholars had attempted with little success to give them. The word *aigilips,* for example, had something to do with cliffs, but no one really knew what—just maybe, cliffs so steep even goats couldn't manage them. Probably even Homer didn't know what such words meant, yet used them, wrote Parry, because of their metrical convenience. They'd become so intimately linked to particular nouns, the two appearing as one, that their independent meaning didn't matter. Homer's listeners, too, might know nothing of what they meant, yet enjoy the mysterious poetic feeling they evoked. "One's style should be unlike that of ordinary language, for if it has the quality of remoteness," Parry quoted Aristotle, "it will cause wonder, and wonder is pleasant."

At a memorial service for Parry in 1935—the sort of event, it's true, where its subject is sure to be treated with consideration—a Harvard colleague spoke of

the impression he made in New York when, for the first time
in this country, he read the results of his researches in Homer
before the American Philological Association. Lucidity and precision marked his English diction; learning and imagination
illuminated his exposition of the poet's method. Several universities at once marked him for their own, but he chose to keep
his promise, and teach in a college which had had the wisdom
to call him early, before he would accept a place with us.

Nearer to what really happened is that, by the time Parry gave his
New York paper on December 28, he was all but Harvard's: A second
letter had gone out to Parry two weeks before the conference. That one,
typed on Harvard Department of the Classics letterhead, bore the signature of C. N. Jackson, the department chair. It was an offer to become,
beginning the following September, instructor in Greek and Latin and
tutor in the Division of Ancient Languages; this latter role, Jackson took
care to note, was "somewhat after the Oxford system," in which a tutor
works closely with students in ones and twos.

While Milman was in New York, Marian had stayed home with the
children. It was winter. "I was left then in the snow and ice with a can
opener; that was so I wouldn't starve. You know, if I couldn't get out."
That and the family's missed Christmas were her principal memories
of Milman's New York trip—along with his telegram from New York
informing her that he'd accepted Harvard's offer.

He seems not to have consulted her about it at all; nor did he likely
fret over it much himself. In Paris, Parry had absorbed values and sensibilities beside which, Harry Levin would write of him, "his return to
America contrasted unsatisfactorily. Parry was capable of meeting fully
civilized or definitely uncivilized people on their own ground"—the reference is to Parry's later Yugoslav adventures—but he could hardly be
expected to linger for long at a small midwestern college. He was not
about to spurn Harvard. Early in January, the President and Fellows of
Harvard University ratified the department's offer. When, the following
September, the Linguistic Society of America noted Parry's move in its
Notes and Personalia section, it did so in a single sentence: Parry had
accepted Harvard's "call."

So, less than three months after arriving in Des Moines as the new

Marian with the children, on the
steps of their bungalow in Des
Moines. For Milman, she'd say, it was
"a lost year"; for the two of them as a
couple, it was "about the low point of
our marriage."

head of the Drake University Latin department, he and his family having barely unpacked, Parry knew he wouldn't be around for long. He
had only to get through the rest of the year as a lame-duck professor,
which he did. He taught. He presided over the Latin department's offer-
ings. He built up the Classics library. But later that winter, when he and
Marian, along with other new faculty, were guests at Drake president
Daniel W. Morehouse's home on University Avenue, he must have felt
he was already gone.

Marian actually liked Des Moines, would have preferred to stay.
Theirs was a modest little place, their bungalow, set out on the flat-
horizoned edge of town; an artless snapshot of Marian sitting with the
children on the porch against a treeless winter landscape evokes the
bleakness of a *Waiting for Godot* set. But Marian, Midwest-born, fit right

in. "Iowa's very much like Wisconsin," she'd say, and less pressured than a Sorbonne or a Harvard. "I didn't have to put on any pretense." She'd be at home, wrapped in an apron, somebody would drop by, and so what? But for Milman, Drake was an agony, the atmosphere stultifying, its students impossible to find interesting, the very air puritanical, hostile to smoking and drinking. Marian didn't drink much herself—but not on principle: "I didn't want it in the house when I was alone all the time." They got out rarely. But one time, she told the story, they attended a party where they did meet a few interesting souls. Milman, who never got drunk, got drunk. The two of them had to be driven home.

For Milman, by her assessment, it was "a lost year." For the two of them as a couple, it was "about the low point of our marriage."

18

HIS CAT-LIKE SMILE

For Milman's first semester at Harvard, in the fall of 1929, he and Marian were installed in a house on Shepard Street, a few doors back from Massachusetts Avenue, the Cambridge main street that shot over the bridge from Boston, bisected the new MIT campus, and slipped around Harvard Yard on its way out to the suburbs. In their first year there, at least, Marian's mother lived in the same building on the same floor. With them, too, was Bridie Fitzgerald, whom the 1930 census records as servant. Milman made some of the furniture for their new place, including his desk. "It wasn't that he'd taken a course in carpentry or anything," said Marian. "He could just do things." They'd remain on Shepard Street, a ten-minute walk to campus, for three years.

At noon on Mondays, Wednesdays, and Fridays, Parry taught the *Iliad*. He also taught a course most faculty avoided if they could, Greek Prose Composition, which met on Tuesday afternoons. A note from the records of the Classics department from 1929–30 suggests Parry had not rid his classroom conduct of every last adolescent remnant; it reported "Parry looking out the window, apparently [with] lack of interest," that he was too given over to his Homeric epithets, even to selling copies of his Paris thesis. He was judged "a poor teacher but a great scholar."

Robert Fitzgerald, class of 1933, would also remember Parry looking out the window. Fitzgerald, who went on to considerable celebrity as a classical scholar and translator of Homer, recalled a class devoted to the Roman literary figures Horace and Plautus, over which presided a stooped young man in hard Donegal tweed who had piercing black eyes and a thin bony face with a slight mustache and goatee. My lesson from this man, Parry, came one day when I thought I could make my rendering of Horace more racy with slang. Parry usually spared himself at least the spectacle of recitations by keeping his gaze out the window. This time he let me finish and then swung around to fix his eyes fully on me while smiling a relishing smile. "An ignoble translation," he said to me with precision. I knew the word but had not in my time heard anyone use it; now I had had that privilege.

Parry had come to Harvard without the traditional German philological training many classicists boasted. But "if there was any suspicion of his ability, it vanished in the first month," recalled John B. Titchener, whose time at Harvard overlapped Parry's for a year before he left for Ohio State in 1930. "He was very shortly the Homer man of the department and recognized as that. By fairly tough critics. It is a little curious because there was no demonstration, no apparent evidence or proof; he simply was." Titchener recalled Parry as "slight, intense but never tense, friendly, reserved, never obtrusive or ostentatious, with his whole life devoted to one idea. He had his inspiration or theory or guess and he set out to prove it."

But, Titchener made it seem, Parry was in no hurry. He just plowed ahead. "He had no enemies so far as I know and few friends. Not that he rejected friendship; he did not need it. He had had his idea and he had deliberately prepared himself to follow it up, and this was his life."

Another of his students, Harry Levin, would tell of his own "good fortune" in meeting Parry early on. "The incisive impression that he left—the measured speech, the adventurous thought, the Parisianized tastes, the Californian energies—has proved ineradicable." Levin recalled his "exhilaration" as a freshman when,

after an anticipated routine of parsing and scanning, Parry would dismiss Terence and introduce Molière and Sacha Guitry, or further illustrations from comic supplements and burlesque shows. In those days there was still an aura of the Latin Quarter about him; it may have been the black hat, or the beard he wore for a while, or his collection of drawings by Marie Laurencin, or his relish for such unclassical poets as Laforgue, Apollinaire, Eliot, and Cummings.

Levin contrasted Parry with classicists apt to apologize for their subject, or who tried to sell it as a means "to attain the marks of [intellectual] caste." Parry never sank to that. "The study of Greek, he had found, is its own reward, and he never attempted to justify it on any but a personal and esthetic plane."

Another colleague, M. V. Anastos, who went on to a storied career as a Byzantine scholar, would call Parry "a charming and sympathetic sort of elder brother to me." He'd remember Parry's "bearded face—rare then—dark eyes behind glasses, a scholar's stoop, a beautiful voice with a precision of accent which seemed to carry reminiscences of his years in Paris. He was full of the men he had heard there. . . . To me he was always charming and I was very fond of him."

Of course, Parry was a little slapdash about his teaching responsibilities. Anastos and Mason Hammond, for example, were annoyed he didn't take his share of Ancient Authors papers. "We tutors were indignant," wrote Anastos, "because Milman would see a lad in September, suggest some reading, and add, 'Come and see me when you have this done.'" Perhaps it was left over from the French system that left you so much on your own. "Those were less earnest times," Anastos allowed from his perch of 1964. And Parry's approach "insured him much leisure for his own researches."

Indeed, at least in the glow of retrospect, with Parry dead and already a legendary figure, his colleagues could seem not all *that* annoyed with him; he was, after all, the department wunderkind. Senior faculty, wrote Anastos, "scolded us to bear the burden and heat of pedestrian duties" since, after all, they were not producing as much as he. Why, C. N. Jackson demanded of him, why wasn't he publishing the way Parry did?

A decade had passed since Parry's moment, literal or metaphorical, on the California beach, when Homer permanently arrested his attention. And now, in the early 1930s, it could seem, Parry was a happy man, at ease with himself. Fitzgerald would remember his "extraordinary intensity," but also his "cat-like smile." When Fitzgerald was set to graduate in 1933, Parry, who was only eight years his senior, asked him what he planned to do next. Why, head for New York and take up journalism, he replied. Parry "looked at me very closely and then he said, in that formal manner he had, 'You go to your destruction.'"

This story is fun to tell, whatever it means. But it was another moment with Parry that left the deeper imprint on Fitzgerald, a moment when, as he told it, Parry "forgot himself," when his measured demeanor fell away and the emotion beneath his work billowed up. Homer's diction, Fitzgerald recalled him saying, "reflected a way of life, a life completely different from our modern days, and he suddenly spoke with great intensity and enthusiasm, saying it was a life which was 'holy, and sweet, and wondrous.'"

Parry served on editorial boards, on department subcommittees. From his office in Kirkland House, he was one of the first nonresident tutors in Harvard's new "house" system. In the summer of 1930, he gave a summer course on Homer and Virgil. In December 1931, he was elevated to assistant professor. In 1932, he collaborated with a Harvard biologist to give an informal "Coffee Pot" presentation on the sciences versus the classics. He seemed to like being where he was at Harvard, and who he was. His colleagues respected him. The publication in 1930 of Cecil Bowra's *Tradition and Design in the Iliad* and, a little later, Martin Nilsson's *Homer and Mycenae,* which lauded Parry by name for his "able and sagacious work," left him feeling appreciated, surer than ever that he was on the right track. "The implications of his theory in those early days" of the early 1930s, former Harvard colleague Titchener would recall, "were staggering." He was on his way.

*

Parry's time at Harvard corresponded exactly with the worldwide economic depression, which took hold in the wake of the stock market crash of October 1929, then more painfully all through the 1930s; unemployment in the United States stayed above 18 percent all through the early and mid-1930s. There had probably never been a time in recent memory when the Common Man, seen as brutalized by an oppressive capitalist system, was viewed more sympathetically; or when the appeal of the Left, of socialism in its many shadings, was so strong. Some men and women of sense and conviction turned to the Communist Party as the best way to arrest the evils of the economic calamity that had destroyed so many lives and communities.

But social causes never much took with Parry; certainly the Left exerted little pull on him. He "was *not* a liberal in politics," Marian would report, even voting against a trade union at Harvard when the issue came up there. In 1964, Sterling Dow, summarizing what he thought he'd learned thus far about him, wrote of Parry that "he found nothing mystical and fascinating about the common man just because he is common." Parry was not a political animal, and not much of a social animal, either, often finding it a strain to be in crowds and groups.

The thirties were a time a little like France during the Dreyfus Affair, when those of some stature and distinction might be expected to speak out on the social tragedy playing out around them. But to the extent Parry held views on the issues of his time, it seemed to Marian, they aligned with the conventional and the conservative. Later, in Yugoslavia, Levin wrote of him, tellingly, "He respected the hierarchical nicety with which his hosts handed out the different cuts of meat. Their outlook seemed invested with an order" he missed in America, and admired.

He was, as should be plain by now, thoroughly traditional and conventional about women. In its division of responsibilities, authority, and control, their household diverged not a whit from the orthodox. He wanted Marian to look good; in Boston, once, he took her to a store where he apparently selected her wardrobe. He could be fiercely jealous. At one Harvard social function, Marian danced with a Classics colleague, Mason Hammond. Milman sent one of his students "to cut in so that I couldn't keep on dancing" with him. (And no, she'd insist, she'd not flirted with him in the least.) "That broke my heart because . . . really [the dancing] was such a pleasure," one Milman took care to deny her.

For the most part, Parry was happy to tend his own garden, live his own rich, interior, intellectually driven, comfortable life, and neither challenge nor trouble himself with the failings, frailties, and injustices of the world around him.

Rarely in his French thesis or in his other writing about the Homeric epics does Parry pay attention to their content, as stories of blood, struggle, and heartache; rather, he gives himself over to their language. "I wonder exactly what Papa thought of the Iliad as a whole," Adam would write to his mother in 1951, his father dead sixteen years. "He is always too busy speaking of the epic technique to say."

It happens that during the time Milman and Marian lived in Sceaux, numerous local streets had recently been renamed in memory of townspeople killed in the war. Out of a population of 5,000, 193 soldiers had died; in the busy commercial center of town along rue Heudon, crowds of shoppers would have included wounded and blinded men, most just a few years older than Milman. In 1921, a monument to Sceaux's war dead went up in the courtyard of the *mairie,* the town hall; later a book would give a page to each of the men, their families, how they fell, the honors they received. Several had grown up on rue de Fontenay, where the Parrys lived. At least one of the Sceaux dead was named Ulysse. Another was named Achille. Here were the real-life counterparts of the Homeric warriors who had fought at Troy. But almost never in Milman's papers and letters do we find mention of the Great War, its soldiers, or their sacrifices. Was this a testament to Parry's intellectual focus? Or else, seen through quite a different lens, to a deficit of feeling?

19

THE ORAL TURN

The Musée d'Orsay is the former Paris railway station transfigured in 1986 into a temple of art, home to one of the largest collections of impressionist and postimpressionist art in the world. Step into its great central court and at some point you come face-to-face with a great marble sculpture of the Roman poet Virgil.

Virgil, author of the *Aeneid,* scroll in one hand, stylus in the other.

Born in 71 BCE, Virgil was a contemporary of Julius Caesar and the emperor Augustus. His most celebrated work was the *Aeneid*, an epic myth-making evocation of the founding of Rome; an eighteenth-century painting shows him, scroll in his lap, reading it to Augustus. Written in Latin in dactylic hexameter, the *Aeneid* was inspired by the Homeric epics and can seem to use epithets much as Homer did in the *Odyssey* and the *Iliad*.

But as Aimé Puech realized from his review of Parry's thesis, Homer had to be judged from a perspective other "than that of a modern poet or even that of Virgil." Though closer in time to Homer than to, say, Shakespeare or Chaucer, Virgil had more in common with them than with Homer. For he was a writer, as Homer—whatever and whoever he was—was not. In the Musée d'Orsay marble, by nineteenth-century French sculptor Gabriel Thomas, Virgil is garbed in flowing robes and wears a laurel wreath, his right hand wrapped around his waist like the belt of a robe, supporting his left elbow. Scroll in one hand, stylus in the other, he seems poised in the middle of a thought, ready to seize on his next idea, scene, or verse and record it. He is the incarnation of what we think a writer ought to look like, clasping the tools of his craft, contemplating his next word, seeking his next inspiration. Save for his Roman dress, he could be a writer anywhere, of any era.

As Homer was not.

In introducing his father's papers, Adam Parry observed that ancient scholars sometimes showed "an awareness that Homer was not like later authors and that the Homeric poems had origins more mysterious and more complex than later poetic compositions." Back at Cal, Milman Parry had taken his first stab at highlighting this split—Homer in one camp, everyone else, including Virgil, in another. He'd compared Virgil's use of epithets to Homer's and found them quite different, though his judgment was based on thin tendrils of proof. Then, in the Paris thesis, he devoted a chapter to showing that Virgil's epithets, though they sounded like Homer, weren't really "ornamental," as Homer's were, but mostly served the action, just as they might in any modern work.

Now, in papers Parry turned out in his first years at Harvard— probably the ones Classics department chair Jackson held up as models of scholarly productivity—he told why: Homer's epics were the work of oral composition, not writing as we know it. They were breathed into existence by poets who had no scroll, no stylus, no paper, no papyrus, no alphabet, nothing written at all, but relied on an altogether different creative process—one far distant from Virgil's practice. The origins of the *Odyssey* and the *Iliad* were indeed, as Adam Parry had written, "more mysterious and more complex" than most had imagined.

In the three years after he returned from Paris, Parry wrote four substantial papers, none venturing far from Homer. And in the last three of them Parry finally took the Oral Turn. In it, his original notion of some shadowy "traditional" process to explain authorship of the epics came to seem merely a way station to another sort of insight entirely. This other way of poetry making would lie at the center of Milman Parry's study and thought for the rest of his life—and of Albert Lord's for the rest of his.

In his master's thesis, Parry at one point said that the traditional element in Homer "was essentially a part of an oral poetry, a poetry that was learned by the ear, not by the eye." But Parry dropped it there, with not another word. Besides, that Homeric poetry might be "learned by the ear," while tantalizing, wasn't the new idea. It was that it was *composed* orally—took flight, becoming itself, in the act of singing or speaking. Each song, across the years and centuries, until the epics were finally fixed on paper, was potentially fresh and unique. And each, in its way, was *good,* in and of itself, not some sad, feeble second best to a presumably more evolved written form (which, of course, didn't yet exist).

Well known long before Parry, all the way back to classical Greece in the fifth and fourth centuries BCE, was a class of singers known as rhapsodes—professional performers of songs they memorized, knew well, and sang for the pleasure of their audiences at festivals, feasts, and public events. Parry, however, was not referring to these rhapsodes now. For whatever they sang, however well they sang it, they got it from others, those closer, creatively, to its origins. They weren't composing anew, they were performing.

Parry held that the Homeric epics were the product of traditional cultures and were not the work of any one individual. In the French thesis, he'd so refined, massaged, and quantified this idea that many classicists would find it unassailable. Now he argued that what came down through such traditional cultures had its origins in song and speech. There *was* no conventional author, no one or several men or women who had battled with language and form, altering and reshaping, cudgeling from first drafts ever improved second drafts and third, finally yielding the "final" version of the text. Rather, it was truer to think of singers, many singers, who had brought the work, through all its variations, into existence, making up verses, then maybe doing it again a little differently, inspiring others who might next time sing the song, or something like it, with their own twists, deviations, additions, and ornamentations, some of which might stick in another singer's imagination, and so on. It wasn't that the epic poems *could be* sung; rather, that they had been sung, sung into being, yet by no one singer.

The first of Parry's papers after arriving at Harvard in 1929, "Enjambment in Homeric Verse," represented his earliest argument for oral composition of the Homeric epics. Enjambment refers to a poetic verse running over, across the end of a line, creating effects flowing from the hesitation, pause, or sense of incompleteness of the first line, resolved or enriched in the next:

> *April is the cruelest month, breeding*
> *Lilacs out of the dead land, mixing*
> *Memory and desire . . .*

This, from T. S. Eliot's *The Waste Land*, shows the first and second lines enjambed—"breeding . . . Lilacs," and "mixing . . . Memory and desire." There are many kinds of enjambment, of course, creating a great variety of poetic effects.

Setting up his ambitious article, which occupied twenty pages in the *Transactions of the American Philological Association*, Parry cited one of his Paris masters, Maurice Croiset: "Complicated groupings of ideas are absolutely unknown to Homeric poetry." That is, the reader more often experiences a straightforward sequence of scenes, speeches, or events. Odysseus tells his Phaeacian hosts in Book 7 that Calypso had released him from her island, and sent him

> *upon a well-bound wooden raft, equipped*
> *with food, sweet wine, and clothes as if for gods,*
> *and sent a fair warm wind. I sailed the sea*
> *for seventeen long days; on day eighteen,*

the murky mountains of your land appeared,
and I was overjoyed, but more bad luck
was hurled at me. Poseidon roused the winds
to block me, and he stirred the sea. I sobbed,
and clung there, going nowhere, till my raft
was smashed to pieces by the massive storm.

(WILSON *Odyssey,* 7, 264)

This heaping of fact and event, which rhetoricians term "parataxis," or arranging side by side, relies little on subordinate clauses, qualifiers, and grammatical niceties. It just piles up, its effects cumulative. "When, contrary to custom," Parry further quoted Croiset, a sentence does grow long, "the successive ideas join on to one another in the order that they occur to the mind." That is, not by dint of intricate and nuanced design, but from the natural play of sung or spoken word as it tumbles forth.

It was the strong paratactical basis of Homeric style that undergirded Parry's enjambment paper. Comparing the *Odyssey* and the *Iliad* to two later works, Apollonius's *Argonautica* and Virgil's *Aeneid,* through hundred-line passages of each, he found that Homer enjambed less. But when he did, he relied on one particular type of enjambment more than did later authors. Parry called it "unperiodic enjambment," though scholars since have preferred other, perhaps more apt terms for the same idea, such as "progressive" or "adding" enjambment: The end of a line approaches, can seem complete just as it is—no enjambment needed—yet the first words of the next line add something new, modifying or enriching it. In Book 11 of the *Odyssey:*

Moving back, I thrust my silver-studded sword
deep in its sheath . . .

Here, the first line doesn't *need* anything more to be a complete thought, yet the next line "deep in its sheath" comes along, adding, embellishing.

Parry showed that the Homeric singer mostly didn't enjamb, but when he did, he did so on the spot, moved presumably by something he wished to add as the thought crossed his mind, rather than being forced into it by the sense of the text. The two together—no enjambment or this additive enjambment—marked about 70 percent of Homeric verses, versus 50 percent of the two later text samples.

This was no trifling technical point, for it served and supported a larger claim: "Homer was ever pushed on to use unperiodic [additive] enjambment," and for the most natural of reasons—because "oral versemaking by its speed must be chiefly carried on in an adding style." Always adding—never deleting, never relying on refinement and qualification, never going back. The singer *can't* go back, because his last words have already taken flight, his listeners awaiting the next. Wrote Parry:

> The Singer has not time for the nice balances and contrasts of unhurried thought: he must order his words in such a way that they leave him much freedom to end the sentence or draw it out as the story and the needs of the verse demand.

The enjambment patterns he had identified showed just that. For Parry, these patterns were together like an archaeological artifact, unearthed from the soil of Homeric epic, evidence of its origins in speech and song.

*

In Parry's next two papers, which appeared in *Harvard Studies in Classical Philology* in 1930 and 1931, both bearing the subtitle "Studies in the Epic Technique of Oral Verse-Making," he set out what he would call a "new idea of poetic artistry." In these papers, the classicist Joseph Russo pictures Parry as now more comfortable simply asserting and affirming, abandoning some of "the scholarly caution" of the Paris thesis.

In previous work, Parry had shown how the epithet formulae helped to satisfy the stern strictures of the dactylic hexameter, and so made composition easier. Now, in his 1930 essay, he went further, insisting that they made composition *possible*.

> It must have been for some good reason that the poet, or poets, of the *Iliad* and the *Odyssey* kept to the formulae even when he, or they, had to use some of them very frequently. What was this constraint that thus set Homer apart from the poets of a later

time, and of our own time, whom we see in every phrase choosing those words which alone will match the color of their very own thought? The answer is not only the desire for an easy way of making verses, but the complete need of it.

Necessity compelled them,

> the necessity of making verses by the spoken word. This is a need which can be lifted from the poet only by writing, which alone allows the poet to leave his unfinished idea in the safe keeping of the paper which lies before him while with whole unhurried mind he seeks along the ranges of his thought for the new group of words which his idea calls for.

Not writing but rather singing or speaking, moving along in a never-ending rush, tale unwinding, audience attending, he needs ready access to the formulae, which "give him his phrases all made, and made in such a way that, at the slightest bidding of the poet, they will link themselves in an unbroken pattern that will fill his verses and make his sentences."

Just as "additive" enjambment served oral composition, so did the epithetic formulae.

Here was poetry, certainly, but made in a different way. And, in Parry's developing picture, its manifold differences from written poetry explained so much. "We shall find," wrote Parry, that classical scholarship's "failure to see the difference between written and oral verse was the greatest single obstacle to our understanding of Homer." That obstacle removed, he wrote (in cadences and emphasis reminiscent of Aimé Puech's jury report at his *soutenance*) "we shall cease to be puzzled by much, we shall no longer look for much that Homer would never have thought of saying, and above all, we shall find that many, if not most of the questions we were asking, were not the right ones to ask."

The Homeric Question represented, as we've seen, debate, discussion, confusion, and doubt occasioned by every sort of seeming contradiction in the *Iliad* and the *Odyssey*. Peculiar inconsistencies in plot. Odd repetitions. Variant dialects of ancient Greek—Achaean, Aeolic, and Ionic. Seeming omissions. Epithetic nonsense: "Blameless Aegisthus," for the seducer of Agamemnon's wife?!

But these were troubling, intrusive questions only so long as we imagined a writer, stylus in hand, who could delete, rub out what he wrote before, try something else, eliminate repetition, move toward faultless cohesion of style and theme. Why *wouldn't* he, in the normal course of refining and correcting his work, eradicate those mistakes, oddities, and anomalies that had so bedeviled generations of Homeric scholars? A real writer, as most had supposed Homer to be, might have been expected to do all that.

But the oral poet, wrote Parry, "unlike the poet who writes out his lines,—or even dictates them,—he cannot think without hurry about his next word, nor change what he has made, nor, before going on, read over what he has just written." That the epics were composed orally, as Parry had begun to assert in these papers, cleared away nagging problems about Homer that had beset scholars since time immemorial.

*

At Cal, Parry had begun his life's work set apart, almost haughtily so, from the line of scholars preceding him, relying almost solely on what he'd glimpsed from Homer himself. After Paris, however, he was better stitched into the intellectual fabric of his time. His papers were studded with new ideas, his judgments correspondingly enriched. The ones he wrote soon after his arrival at Harvard, son Adam would observe, were how most scholars first met with his ideas; the two in *Harvard Studies in Classical Philology,* 125 journal pages in all, were Milman Parry to the world—Parry of Harvard, Parry in English. Still, by 1931, he had not yet replied to voices lodged in his mind, whispering their truth, since Paris. These included, certainly, those of Antoine Meillet and Matija Murko, from that afternoon in Salle Louis Liard at his Sorbonne *soutenance.* But also that of a Jesuit priest of peculiar intellectual pedigree and eccentric cast of mind named Marcel Jousse.

This "renegade anthropologist," as he'd be called, was born in 1886 in a rural area southwest of Paris, Sarthe, into a largely illiterate peasant culture. His mother had gone to school for only a few winters and was mostly illiterate. Jousse would recall village gatherings, long evenings thick with song and story, among townspeople few of whom could read or write. Later, during the Great War, while briefly in the United States, he became interested in American Indians and their ways. Through popular lectures he gave in Paris (which Parry could have attended) he became something of a celebrity.

Jousse's 1925 book, *The Oral Style* (its subtitle all but untranslatable into English and little clearer in the original French), has been called "an idiosyncratic synthesis of philosophy, psychology, and secondhand field-work reports." It consisted in part of hundreds of quotations, a mishmash of insights that nonetheless, viewed through an encompassing enough lens, made a coherent argument about the power of gesture, movement, and voice in human communication. Parry would later assign it to his young student Albert Lord, who termed it an "early influence" on his mentor. To Adam Parry, Jousse's book "marks the change of emphasis in Parry's thought" toward the oral.

The weight scholars gave reading and writing, associating them with advanced civilizations, had blinded them to the fecund richness of illiterate cultures; Jousse set out to correct this bias. Men and women speaking, reciting, singing, gesturing, gesticulating, yelling, and whispering represented as full a field of study as words on paper. And, just maybe, they brought us closer to who we are as living beings than abstract squiggles on paper, scroll, and screen. To anyone who had spent his youth and young adulthood buried in books (like Parry), to slip inside the sensibilities of the unlettered and see them not as *lacking* the written, but *possessing* the oral, was a heretical idea, and an exhilarating one.

Books of prose and poetry come to life in the act of reading. Jousse saw power and beauty in communication never reduced to print, but expressed, rather, in the music, movement, gesture, and voice that figured so large in his boyhood. In 2014, Association Marcel Jousse, of Bordeaux, France, fashioned a one-hour documentary about its namesake. It included the usual talking heads, took the viewer to Jousse's boyhood home, quoted his words. It showed how memorization was aided by voice and movement. It told how prayerful Orthodox Jews gave themselves over to characteristic swaying motions. At several junctures, professors and others inspired by their master *performed*, by singing, dancing, and rhythmic rocking, their arms in free gestural flight, cheerfully clapping their way through children's songs like "Engine, engine, number nine."

In all this lay hints of an alternative oral truth, beyond words on paper, that now, in the late 1920s and early 1930s, Milman Parry had begun to absorb. He specifically credited Jousse in several papers; in one, the enjambment paper, he noted: "We may very well find that M. Marcel Jousse, from his study of various oral poetries, is right in believing that the order of ideas in oral verse is more closely suited to the inborn workings of the mind than it is in written style."

In Jousse's odd, confounding intellect resided something of the new world of oral culture into which Parry was taking his first steps. And Jousse's personal story conferred on him a kind of authenticity. He hadn't lived off the low-hanging fruit of an established academic discipline. He had created his own, inspired and enriched by his own experience of a largely oral world. Marcel Jousse, Parry must have sensed, had *street cred*. Whereas he, the superbly well-read assistant professor of classics at Harvard University, had none.

20

NOTHING ELSE TO DO

A year and a half into his time at Harvard, in April 1931, Parry wrote his sister Addison:

> Life here is unbelievably empty of any happenings which could be unusual enough to tell. Quite otherwise: the days are crowded with the details of teaching and studying—and I am hardly going to explain to you the importance of Greek composition, or the purpose of the classics, or the nature of Homeric verse.

He went on to tell of the children, normally Marian's province. The two did get out sometimes, most recently to see an early talkie, *Dishonored,* with Marlene Dietrich. Otherwise, all he and Marian did, declared the twenty-nine-year-old in his reliably flip persona, was get older. That, and have his teeth pulled, the "gruesome tales" of which, he reassured Addie, he would spare her. It was another of the light, ultimately unrevealing letters he often wrote home, except that he did have one morsel of real news:

> I am just now studying Serbian so that I can read Serbian epic poetry: then in two years or so I shall apply for a Guggenheim fellowship and spend a year in Jugoslavia to find the explanation of the Iliad and Odyssey.

To scholars who'd read his Paris theses or the papers he'd published since, it might seem he'd furnished plenty of "explanation." The Paris thesis had shown that the Homeric epics were the work of a traditional culture, not that of an individual author. His more recent work furnished evidence that they'd been composed orally. A new theory of considerable explanatory power was in place. What could he hope to find in Yugoslavia, of all places, to develop or enrich it?

After Paris, Parry would write, "I did not at once give myself up to the study of oral poetries." It was three years since he'd earned his degree and, he explained, "I found myself in the position of speaking about the nature of oral style, almost purely on the basis of a logical reasoning from the characteristics of Homeric style." *Found myself in the position*—as if he'd been caught with his hand in the cookie jar: He was all but calling himself an imposter, speaking of oral poetry, calling it the basis of the Homeric epics, yet with no direct, firsthand knowledge of it. What he knew of oral style was drawn from authors who, with the exception of Murko and a few others, he found "haphazard and fragmentary—and I could well fear, misleading." His own "logical reasoning" was not wrong, just insufficient. He did not really know what he thought he knew. He had never heard or met an oral poet. In 1932, Albert Lord would observe in a 1948 essay, Parry "had reached a crisis," though on the strength of his letter to Addie he was already there by 1931.

For Parry, according to Lord, "there was nothing else to do then but to learn Serbo-Croatian . . . have a recording apparatus built . . . and to go to Yugoslavia." In fact, there was plenty else Parry could do, lots of reasons he might never have gone. Many an artist, entrepreneur, or other dreamer gets an idea for some stupendous undertaking but lets the implacable tide of workaday life, the usual and the everyday, deflect him. Or else some other, maybe better, idea displaces it. One way or another, the idea just slips away. Indeed, for the three years since Paris, Parry, too, had been content to read, study, teach, write, do his job, be a responsible enough academic citizen. Conceivably, he could have gone on just as he had.

But other forces pushed Parry into this new adventure. After briefly considering Russia as a place to find modern-day epic singers, he soon settled on the Yugoslavia that Matija Murko had lectured about in Paris in 1928. Murko's Paris lectures were published in French the following year as a seventy-seven-page book, *La Poésie populaire épique en Yougoslavie au Début du XX Siècle,* which Parry certainly had in hand by 1931.

Murko's was an account of a remote, colorful place far from Paris, London, Vienna, and the other great centers of European culture. Yugoslavia was not Nepal or Patagonia, but there it was, remote enough, on the Balkan peninsula, the latest political entity to bear the tortured history of the region. Its people, as popular author John Gunther dared describe them to Americans in the 1937 edition of his book *Inside Europe,* were "rawboned, poor, hard-lipped, superb fighters, primitive."

Yugoslavia, which means "land of the South Slavs," stood at a fault line between East and West. It was bounded to the north by Austria, Hungary, and Romania; to the south by little Albania and, at the tip of the peninsula, Greece; to the west was the Adriatic Sea and, across its 150-mile blue breadth, Italy; to the east lay Bulgaria and beyond it, Turkey, which, as part of the vast Ottoman Empire, had ruled over the Balkan peninsula for five hundred years.

That, at least, was the current political map; the Balkans, wrote Gunther, were "a sort of hell paved with the bad intentions of the [larger European] powers . . . , an unstable pyramid of nationalist hatreds, and of minority hatreds within nations." As for Yugoslavia itself, no map's neat lines could convey much of the maddening jumble of entities that made it up. Politically, it was a young state, its capital Belgrade, astride the Danube. Formed from the wreckage of the Great War, the disharmonious result of postwar treaties, it had been known first as the Kingdom of Serbs, Croats, and Slovenes, then renamed Yugoslavia in 1929. But though about the size of Italy, it was populated by no people so relatively cohesive as the Italians. The regions making it up—Bosnia and Herzegovina, Montenegro, Serbia, Croatia, Macedonia, and Slovenia— were home to Muslims, Jews, Roman Catholics, and Eastern Orthodox Christians. Half a generation earlier, the assassination of Archduke Franz Ferdinand, in Sarajevo, Bosnia, had ignited the Great War. Half a generation later, the Germans and the Italians would carve up most of it. After World War II, it would become a Communist state under Tito that, expelled from the Soviet bloc, steered a defiant middle course between East and West. Its dissolution in the 1990s would unleash new waves of ethnic conflict, war, and genocide. It might be possible for a powerful intellect and strong political will to conceive of Yugoslavia as somehow one, with common ethnic and language roots. But it was easier and truer to see it as deeply riven, a ragged tapestry of ethnic sub-minorities, languages, religions, and long, long memories, where crossing a river or down through a mountain pass took you, uneasily, into a new and alien corner of the world. Yugoslavia embodied in itself much of what the word "balkanize" had already come to mean—*to divide into small, quarrelsome, ineffectual states.*

Still, there *was* a Yugoslavia at the time Murko wrote his little book, with its own king, Alexander I. And occasionally, Murko could report, the ancient divisions evaporated, likeness overcame difference, and sweet reason prevailed. He wrote of entering a café during Ramadan, the month of fasting for Muslims, where a Catholic was singing south Slavic epics for them. How could this be? Murko asked. "We live in harmony," came the reply. *"Onda bilo, sad se spominjalo"*: "All that once was—we evoke its memory now."

The languages spoken in Yugoslavia were, for the most part, mutually understandable; collectively they were known as Serbo-Croatian, though written in different alphabets. But because so much of the poetic heritage Murko studied came from the Muslims, who were neither Serb nor Croat, he declared the compass of his book to be all of Yugoslavia. In many areas, he reported, the old heroic songs had disappeared; no one sang them anymore, no one listened to them. But they remained popular in Bosnia and Herzegovina, and tiny, mountainous Montenegro (which, alone in the Balkans, had never fallen to the Turks) and parts of Serbia, especially in the hinterlands, far from the cities.

The singers Murko met on five trips between 1909 and 1927, he stressed, were not everywhere, and not everyone, but rather "certain gifted individuals" . . .

> There is no condition or profession one would find unrepresented among them. In the countryside the singers are for the most part farmers; in the towns they are artisans. In the mountainous regions they are mostly shepherds who delight in singing the epic songs, and these songs were naturally cultivated by the *hadjuks* [outlaws, or brigands]. . . . Among the singers were also found, and are still found today, the noblest Moslem lords, the beys, as well as priests of all faiths.

From time to time, Murko nodded to Homer and the Greek epics. He observed that likenesses between Homer and local epic tradition had been noted as early as the eighteenth century; that local blind singers had sometimes been compared to Homer; that the songs of Muslim singers especially tended to be long, sometimes needing two or three nights to sing, and that one of them filled forty-two pages of printed text—longer, he noted, than any one "book" (or chapter) of the *Iliad* or *Odyssey.*

If the variegated history, colorful folk cultures, and tantalizing nods to Homer in Murko's book failed to conjure up enough of the exotic to whet Parry's appetite, Murko's photos alone would have been enough. They showed ruggedly handsome men with deep, hooded eyes, strong and proud. They sported extravagant mustaches. They wore fezzes, vests, and leggings. They posed beside stone walls or in village squares with their gusles, the rude one-stringed instruments they played as they sang. Together, these oral verse makers stood for the untamed countryside in which they lived. Theirs was a poetry not of writers stuck in studios and garrets but of real men, mostly illiterate, their songs and stories telling of warriors, horses, and duels, gorgeous overblown hospitality, female grace, manly feats of bravery.

Parry's romantic streak left him susceptible. He had grown up with his father's stories of the sea and of Japan, a taste for the odd and the alien; one among the family's photos shows his father, in uniform, standing straight and tall beside a Japanese man in ceremonial kimono. In Berkeley, Alfred Kroeber and others among Marian's anthropologist friends helped legitimize intellectual work in exotic settings. At Harvard, where Parry was remembered for the beard and beret he wore for a time, Harry Levin would picture him as a "scholar-gypsy whom no amount of composition papers and committee meetings could tame," alive with wanderlust; certainly he was not one of those Americans who could journey abroad and come back as he had left, contemptuous of the world's wanton strangeness, sure that American ways were best. Parry would be remembered for his fascination with *Seven Pillars of Wisdom,* T. E. Lawrence's 1926 account of his part in helping the Arabs defeat the Turks during the Great War; indeed, Parry's interest in Lawrence of Arabia suggested to Mrs. Parry's interviewer Pamela Newhouse that maybe he was just "more comfortable in a primitive culture than in the civilized."

Victor Bérard had been troubled by Parry's determination to grasp the *Odyssey* through language alone. But now, Parry was cutting across old disciplinary lines; anthropological ideas and sensibilities were in the air and he breathed them in. His many anthropology courses at Cal led one scholar, Juan Garcia, to see Parry's turn to Yugoslavia as an entirely natural response to ideas he'd absorbed from Kroeber. In Paris, according to another scholar, Thérèse de Vet, he may have been influenced by Marcel Mauss, the pioneer French ethnologist; years before, as part of ethnographic research in French Indochina, Mauss had ordered fieldworkers to take special note of oral performance, including its characteristic repetitions and formulae. "Oral literature," Mauss had written, "obeys very different rules from those observed in written literature." What de Vet calls "Mauss's circle" in Paris, like Kroeber's in Berkeley at around the same time, may thus have helped nurture the anthropologist in Parry and make a long field trip to Yugoslavia seem natural, doable, and potentially fruitful.

But the most decisive impetus for Parry's trips to Yugoslavia may have been simple pride: He wrote and theorized about the work of oral poets, yet had never heard one. Murko's book had all those photos of guslars in Yugoslavia because he'd *been* there. Antoine Meillet, who had done some of his earliest research in Armenia, stressed getting away from books to immerse yourself in a new language. "Anyone wishing to hear how Indo-Europeans spoke," he was supposed to have said, "should come and listen to a Lithuanian peasant." Parry wanted to know, really know, orally composed poetry? He should meet those who composed it. That was Meillet's parting message to him in Paris.

Parry would make his first trip to Yugoslavia in the summer of 1933, a trip that, as David Bynum was to write, would have "remarkable consequences not only for his own field of Homeric studies, but also for the whole of humanistic science in the twentieth century." That trip was followed by a more extended one, of fifteen months, that began in the early summer of 1934.

21

A DARKNESS THERE

When Marian got wind of her husband's plans for his "expedition to Yugoslavia" we don't know what she said to him, but we do know how she felt about it: "I wasn't interested. . . . I mean I wasn't disinterested in it but I wasn't passionately involved in it in any way." It was yet another instance of common ground between them slipping away—as it had begun to do as early as 1923 when, as a young couple, Marian did not ask, and Milman did not volunteer, much about his master's thesis. In Paris, he'd imbibed something of the intellectual and literary vitality of the Latin Quarter, while she stayed home with their daughter out in the suburbs. Now, at Harvard, Milman's Yugoslav scheme may have pushed them yet further apart.

Marian was miserable at Harvard. For one thing, there was its sheer toxic anti-Semitism which, inevitably, she felt more acutely than he. One day back at Cal, the two of them walking up in the hills behind campus, talking about getting married, she announced, "Well, you know I'm Jewish." Milman laughed it off, saying "it was ridiculous, extraneous" to fret over that. But if it was extraneous in Berkeley, washed by the benign Pacific air, among people like themselves, it wasn't back east in Cambridge. There

> it was very far from extraneous. . . . [In that respect, it was] the worst place that we could possibly have come to. . . . There was so much unpleasantness about this, and this put me into a position that I didn't know how to deal with. Because I was taught that if anyone said anything unpleasant about Jewish people

she should speak up. But "I couldn't do that because of Milman's position."

As the Jewish wife of a gentile professor, Marian felt always the taint of differentness; to many of her new acquaintances, it seemed, the simple fact of her Jewishness loomed unnaturally large: "I wasn't there five minutes before I heard that the wife of one of the professors was Jewish." During summers in Cotuit, on Cape Cod, probably between 1930 and 1932, Harvard people of long New England lineage and otherwise impeccable manners would seem surprised when the Parrys, of all people, somehow knew people they weren't expected to know.

Among those Marian ranked as "terribly anti-Semitic" was Milman's friend John Finley, his colleague in Classics. Finley was two years younger than Parry, a Thucydides scholar, known for his wit and flair, who in later years, as master of Eliot House, would become a veritable icon of Harvard. "He thought nothing of saying unpleasant things"— nasty, blatantly anti-Semitic things, Marian makes clear. "So it was very hard for me to be friends" with him and, later, his wife.

And yet, the relationship between Finley and the Parrys couldn't be reduced to brute anti-Semitism; it was more shaded and complex than that. Years later, Adam Parry, pursuing his own career as a classical scholar, would take a class with Finley, recall him as "completely theatric and very brilliant," pacing back and forth, hands waving. Yet outside class, without the stage that was Finley's Harvard classroom, Adam found it "impossible to have a real conversation with him, he is so completely formal." From all he'd heard, Adam wrote his sister, Finley "had always liked Mother immensely, whereas he had been at once fascinated by Papa, and horrified by him, owing to his cruel treatment of Mother"—though in what way cruel he did not say.

Of course, when it came to Harvard anti-Semitism, it wasn't just Finley; the school's reputation went way back. Harry Levin would classify C. N. Jackson, head of Classics during this period, as a full-blown anti-Semite. "If a Jew entered the room," Levin told Sterling Dow, "Jackson left it." As a Jew bound for a prominent place in the Harvard firmament, Levin himself was such a rare bird that the writer Susanne Klingenstein made him a subject of her study of America's first generation of Jewish literary scholars, *Enlarging America*. During the 1920s, Jews were admitted to Harvard in substantial numbers, but their presence—especially those from eastern Europe, perceived as "too" Jewish—troubled many among Harvard's elite. In time, the college turned to numerical admissions quotas, which remained in force for many years. In 1934, as Harvard's new house system was getting under way, a memo on "Suggested Procedure for Assignment to Houses" advised house masters to see to it "that the total number of Jews does not exceed what 'the traffic will bear.'"

Though not himself attuned to anti-Semitism, Milman, just a few years out of the Oakland flats, did face other sides of Harvard elitism. "He felt that he had to make his way," make a name for himself, said Marian, "because after all we didn't come from the east and we didn't have the same backgrounds as these people did." Competition was fierce: "Out of all this sea of instructors" in Milman's cohort, Marian would remember, "only one or two would be promoted." Promoted, that is, to tenure which, once granted, left its recipient with a prized lifetime position. But it was denied more often than not, and many able young scholars were left to flounder about for years.

Still, for Milman, his already strong scholarly reputation helped him fit in. In Marian's telling, some in the department "were not enthralled" by his arrival, one of them presumably out to sabotage his prospects: "They were afraid of him. Because he published articles every year." His drive was ferocious. "Milman was a terrific worker," said Marian. "I don't think I've ever known anyone so single-minded."

So Milman thrived, felt proud to be part of what he esteemed "the finest university in the world." It was not so much the faculty, though he thought highly of some of them, Marian noted, as "the fabulous students. He called them 'the lads.'" In 1931, he was elevated from his first entry-level position to a one-year term as instructor and tutor, and beginning in 1932 to the rank of assistant professor, now for a three-year term. His salary for 1932–33, in the middle of the Depression, was $4,000 a year, almost double what he'd started at.

But Milman's blooming prospects did nothing to warm Marian's life. She had few friends, most of them unaffiliated with Harvard, and found the university's social calendar distasteful. "On Sunday you were supposed to go to these at-homes of the full professors; you couldn't be a full professor unless you had a samovar and served tea." So Sundays were dreadful. Better were Friday evening get-togethers at the apartment, no faculty, just a few students, for cucumber sandwiches, grape juice, and conversation. She was included, but at the periphery. It was nothing like the rich social life, with lots of friends their own age, that Marian remembered her parents enjoying in Milwaukee. Still, "it was a sort of life."

At one point, what she conceived of as her chronic bodily frailty, a relic of her Wisconsin childhood, kicked in. Her mother gave her money for a maid, but their Shepard Street place, "an absolutely awful house," was just too much for her. "It had so many flights of stairs and I was going up and down like a mountain goat." Milman turned a deaf ear, so Marion decided she "couldn't do this anymore because I was having palpitations of the heart." Resolve overtook her one day while out on the Cape with her mother. Marian went back alone to Boston and found a house for them in Belmont, a suburb west of Cambridge. It was a modern house, one she could tend without a maid. (Of course, it was far enough out that it hobbled her already thin social life.)

Marian accepted the day-to-day running of the household as her job. "Milman was very, very orderly and liked order," she'd say, but that, at least, was no issue between them. "I kept the house the way he liked it without . . . forcing myself to. I liked it that way, too." So they had that in common. But not much else. He was quick to thank her for a good meal. He'd take her into Boston to see a movie; they saw the edgy and controversial *Mädchen in Uniform,* about girls in a Prussian boarding school, three times. But more often, the daily round of their lives left them divided and distant. At one point in December 1981, after listening to Marian talk about her life with Milman, Newhouse all but threw up her hands, lamenting that Milman seemed so remote and unknowable. His Harvard colleagues seemed to think he was easy enough to appreciate and enjoy, at least up to a point. But generally, Marian would say, Milman wasn't very social. It was "easier for him to work than to go to parties . . . unless they were talking about something that he was interested in." He didn't like groups. "It made him miserable to be on the subway" with its crowds. He was most at home within himself.

We have in Marian, through her letters, through her long, winding interview with Newhouse and the impressions of her children later, a picture of a vigorously chatty woman, riffing on every passing thought, repeating herself, stopping short, changing direction, saying things in new ways. All this adds up to something like a recognizable human picture. With Milman we have nothing of the sort. Listening to Mrs. Parry across three days, Newhouse was forced to conclude that Milman's "opacity remains intact." Writing to her later, she offered up this verdict—that Milman "didn't confide in you nearly enough to enable you, forty-five years later, to be an authority on the machinations of his carefully concealed inner life."

In Greece, in 1925, when he was twenty-three, Milman took to recording what he saw on his bike trip through the Peloponnesus, his sometimes disjointed notes amounting to a crude travelogue. At one point, he wakes up in a hostel or guesthouse after a "sleepless guesting of bedbug, flea and louse."

> "You slept well?" gesturingly asks the hostess, of Spartan fierceness and a browbeaten youngmother daughter.
>
> "Most well," for complaint is beyond my knowledge of Romaic [the Greek vernacular language].
>
> Then something expecting a no answer.
>
> So, "No."
>
> Proudly, "At other hotels you know," and full gestures of removing single vermin after single vermin between thumb and forefinger.

Especially with the trip to Greece coming, as it probably did, just after Victor Bérard's rebuff, we wish we had more of what must have been a memorable journey, how Milman felt about the Greece he saw before him, what he fretted over, what moved him. But here is one of only a few times where the author surfaces at all. Otherwise, for page on page, it's mostly a topographic and geological portrait of that summer's Greece:

> A mile from the rocked river and I come to the acropolis of Sparta. It is not bad in this cool dawn, having drunk the last of the watermelon, in spite of a small from time to time taste as of sulfur water from it, to go over the ground with the Guide Bleu. A little temple in porous stone, early. I see a few square

stone blocks. Then go on up the hill, all planted in silvered green
olives, with dry wheat stubble beneath where a shepherd guards
his blackedfaced tinkling herd.

Bits of this are charming. But mostly, it's tedious, certainly in this uned-
ited form, for it goes on and on—up one hill or rocky slope and down
the next, a low mound of olives and wheat, a steep hill of red shale—but
missing a human face, certainly Milman's.

Likewise ten years later, as we'll see, in Yugoslavia: Bad weather and
snow-choked winter roads keep Milman from venturing into the interior, leaving him stuck in Dubrovnik. So he hauls out his dictaphone
and, day after day, talks into it about what he's experienced thus far
in Yugoslavia, singers he's met, what he's learned, his developing ideas,
problems he's encountered. Later, Lord transcribes them. The result is
a useful record, but one that gives little sense of Parry himself, except
insofar as it reveals the play of his intellect. Parry remains a shadowy
presence. "He was not the kind of person to intrude with confidences,"
John B. Titchener, his Harvard colleague for a time, would say of him.
He was not inclined to chatty letters, Albert Lord would report. He pos-
sessed, as a close colleague of Lord's concluded from their many conversations about Parry, "an impermeable steadfastness in keeping his own
counsel." For biographer and reader alike, it troubles us not to know
him better.

Of course, in one sense, we *do* know him. Milman Parry doesn't
tell us, doesn't reveal, keeps to himself, doesn't write those chatty letters, doesn't intrude with confidences, shares little with his wife. And
yet, he stands ever before us: We know him by his acts, which serve his
interests and ideas. Here—no guesswork required—is the largest part of
Parry, more than any morsel of raw human personality we might wish to
extract from him. He is a man given over to his ideas, fed by his work,
his unanswered questions, his great subject.

At home in the evening—not at Kirkland House, where he was nonresident tutor—Milman would read or study, he and Marian not talking
much. But he wanted her around, Marian recalls, just to *be* around.
One night, she'd recount, "I went over to see this French friend who
lived quite close by and Milman didn't like that. He wanted me there
although we weren't talking." They were riven by so much, even in their

relations with their children: "Milman was devoted to Marian. And I was devoted to Adam." One time back in Des Moines, they'd been on a picnic, Adam just learning to walk, Marian enjoying every minute of it. "Why?" Milman sneered. "You think it's wonderful just because he can walk?"

In the end, a cloud of uncertainty and surmise shrouds the Parry marriage—as, from the outside, it does most every couple's marriage. Plainly enough, though, Milman never felt with Marian the pleasure, the sometimes silly adolescent ease, he'd enjoyed with his family growing up. Could some of that owe to their earliest days together, in 1923, when Marian announced she was pregnant? This new life, he cruelly told Marian then, meant the end of his. In conventional terms, he did the "right thing," by marrying her. But, cast into a family life for which, at twenty-one, he wasn't ready, he may have borne a grudge.

This is rank speculation. Less in doubt is that a certain toxicity afflicted their marriage. "In the first two great periods of her life, [first] when she lived with her mother and [then] when Papa was alive," Adam wrote sister Marian fourteen years after their father's death, in one of several letters in which the siblings psychologically dissect their parents, "Mother was as it were crippled; she was made wholly dependent. But if Nana [Marian's mother, Mildred] made her unable to take care of herself, Papa created in her the necessity of living for someone else."

Of the Parry marriage, Professor Anastos wrote Sterling Dow, "I have always felt a darkness there."

*

In February 1933, Hitler became chancellor of Germany, almost immediately assumed total power, and began rearming the Reich. A few weeks later, Franklin Roosevelt took the oath of office as president of the United States. The world was lining up for its deadly reckoning. Meanwhile, the international economic depression left millions of people miserable and desperate. In Cambridge, Harvard faculty (even Milman Parry) pitched in for the relief of those less fortunate.

On the whole, however, Harvard seemed largely insulated from the worst of the world's evils. On two successive evenings in March, around the time of Roosevelt's inauguration, audiences of more than two hundred gathered in Lowell House for the Harvard Classical Club production of *Philoctetes,* a Sophoclean tragedy about Odysseus's efforts to bring the wounded Philoctetes back to Troy from the desert island where he lived and so, with his legendarily formidable bow, defeat the Trojans.

Playing Philoctetes was Robert Fitzgerald, the future translator, who would graduate later that year; as he would tell the story later, he had to memorize more than six hundred lines of ancient Greek. The composer Elliott Carter, just then in Paris studying with Nadia Boulanger, was commissioned to write incidental music. The director was Milman Parry. The production featured a chamber orchestra and chorus, which Parry's friend Finley helped coach. The budget for this college play was the equivalent today of about $8,000, which went toward costumes, wigs, and masks, fees for the musicians, posters, programs, and publicity—all the trappings of a professional production. The only potential blemish to this pretty picture, as the evening of the first performance on March 15 approached, was Harry Levin, who played Odysseus. Levin knew scarcely a word of Greek.

It seems that the student originally supposed to play the epic hero dropped out at the last minute. Parry turned to Levin, whose prodigious powers of memory were legendary around campus. Determined to salvage the production, he all but locked Levin in a room to memorize his lines—which he had to do, under Parry's coaching, by sound and intonation alone. The effort cost him two weeks of missed classes. But apparently he swept the audience along with him, leaving it unaware that he had scant idea what he was saying.

The experience left an enduring mark on Levin. In a draft chapter devoted to him in her book, Susanne Klingenstein asserted that the relationship Levin developed with the poet T. S. Eliot, visiting Harvard that year, was the highlight of Levin's senior year. Not so, Levin wrote Klingenstein on seeing the draft, the highlight of the year was that fevered last-minute working-up of his Odysseus lines with Milman Parry.

Much later, in 1976, Robert Fitzgerald gave a talk on that memorable production; Mrs. Parry attended the talk, as she had the performance itself forty years earlier. In a letter to her granddaughter Laura, she recalled Fitzgerald's memory of Parry, sitting at the back of the hall, "laughing at the abominable acting."

Close to Milman at Harvard, clockwise from upper left: Fellow classics professor John Finley; student Robert Fitzgerald, bound for a celebrated career as a translator of Homer; another student, Harry Levin, who would recollect "the measured speech, the adventurous thought, the Parisianized tastes, [and] the Californian energies" of his teacher.

*

Three months after the final performance of *Philoctetes,* Milman and his family arrived at Commonwealth Pier, Boston, to board the Italian Line ship *Vulcania.* They were bound across the Atlantic, first for Lisbon and Gibraltar, then across the Mediterranean to Palermo and Naples, and finally, in the footsteps of Matija Murko, to Yugoslavia.

PART FIVE

Yugoslavia

[1933–1935]

22

RECONNAISSANCE

Parry wasn't in Yugoslavia long before he heard the tale of Prince Marko and the outlaw Musa. At a tavern, drinking, Musa grumbles that he's worked nine years for the emperor in Stamboul, but has nothing to show for it. He resolves to go down to the coast road and build a *kula*—a fortified stone house, or tower, three or four stories tall, a fixture in the Balkans—from which to plunder passing merchants. "What Musa said he would do when drunk," the song continues, "he proceeded to do when sober." The emperor sends crack troops to capture and kill him, but none return to Stamboul alive.

One of the emperor's viziers reminds him that the royal prison holds a man the equal of Musa. This is Marko Kraljević, Prince Marko, a mainstay of Balkan lore whose folkloric incarnations go back to a real fourteenth-century figure. For a year, Marko has been rotting in jail. "He had become as dusky as the grey rock, for the dank from the prison stones had destroyed him; his hair hung down to the ground and his fingernails were like ploughshares." Just now, he's hardly prepared to take on Musa. But, he tells the emperor, install him in a comfortable inn for a month, "and I shall tell you when I'm fit to fight."

After a month, the emperor asks if he is ready. Bring him a specimen of cornel-wood, cured for nine years, Marko requests. It's delivered to him. He squeezes this extremely tough, dense wood—but not hard enough, as "no drop of water came out." It's not time yet.

A month later, the test is reprised, but this time, yielding to his strengthened grip, the wood spurts three drops of water. Marko is ready.

He approaches Novak, master blacksmith, for a new saber. Is it the best he's ever made? Marko asks. No, Novak admits, "I have forged a better one . . . , and for a better man"—for Musa, the outlaw. Enraged, Marko attacks Novak, cutting off his arm, and hands him a hundred ducats. "Take this, Novak, and buy yourself some wine."

Reunited with his beloved horse, Šarac, Marko gallops off in search of Musa, finding him at last near Kachanik Castle. They fight. "When both had broken their sabers, they dismounted from their good horses and grappled each other. Thus they fought till high noon of a summer's day. Foam formed on the mouth of each, Marko's white, and laced with blood."

Exhausted, Marko appeals to a *vila,* a Slavic mountain nymph. "Have I not told you, Marko," she answers him from the clouds, "not to do combat on a Sunday!'"

Musa the Brigand casts his eyes up to the *vila,* too. In that instant of inattention, Marko whips out a knife and slices him open "from his navel to his lily-white throat." Within Musa's bared, bloody chest cavity, he discovers three vipers, now awake. "'Say a prayer of thanks to God, Marko Kraljević!'" says one of them. "'Had I not been sound asleep, I would have done you to death this day!'"

Marko brings Musa's head to the emperor, leaves with treasure, and returns home to his castle and his loving mother.

*

This was one of hundreds of songs Milman Parry would bring back to America over the next two years—tales of heroes, flashing sabers, lavish wedding parties, intrigue, pride, nobility of spirit, and bloody gore; in this last respect, "Marko and Musa," as it is known in the inventory of Parry's Yugoslav work, is typical. The ready killing that runs through it and most other "heroic" songs echoes the tragic threnody of blood that sounds through Balkan history.

In Yugoslavia, Parry also gathered "women's songs," ballads, bawdy songs, lullabies, and love songs sung by men as well as women for their own delight, for the singing as much as the song. But he was chiefly interested in those poems of larger-than-life heroism he saw as reminiscent of Homer. He had studied the work of the early-nineteenth-century philologist known as Vuk—Vuk Stefanović Karadžić—revered for his recovery, study, and classification of the old songs and stories. But Parry was less interested in the stories themselves than in the language patterns among them, their uncanny likenesses, their telling peculiarities. And, especially, for just how their singers, typically illiterate, had learned them; for how songs changed in the singing; for how the same song, sung by many a singer, or even the same singer, was never the same song after all.

*

The synopsis, above, of "Marko and Musa" is drawn from a translation from the Serbo-Croatian by Albert Lord, and inevitably loses much from the original. Like virtually all the other heroic songs Parry gathered, it was sung in the Balkan lands by singers known as guslars, who accompanied themselves on the distinctive stringed instrument of the region, known as the gusle.

A gusle was a single string of horsehair stretched across a frame of white maple culminating in a hollowed-out bowl, covered, drum-like, by sheep or rabbit skin. Albert Lord would tell how once, when a singer's gusle needed a new string, "someone went out, pulled some hair out of a horse's tail, and brought it in. It was cured in hot water before being strung onto the instrument." Played with a rude bow, a gusle could be rustic and plain or ornate, its carved neck perhaps surmounted by the figure of a goat's head, or a falcon's claws. It could seem like "nothing more than a mere musician's trinket," Beatrice L. Stevenson wrote of it in 1915, almost twenty years before Parry's trip, "but found in many a Serbian home, [it vividly recalled] centuries of poetic outpouring of artistic impulses as well as many a living picture of the guslar singers themselves." Not just in Serbia, but Bosnia, Herzegovina, Montenegro, and all through what, in Parry's time, was still Yugoslavia.

To an ear bred on English ballads, American pop songs, or French *chansons,* the gusle's uneasy, monotonous croak could mightily offend. Yet, a lone singer's voice set to its rhythm could hypnotize, too. The Serbian-American poet Charles Simic, born in Yugoslavia on the eve of World War II, would recall his first experience of the gusle when he was about ten.

I suppose I expected the old instrument to sound beautiful, the singing to be inspiring as our history books told us was the case. *Gusle,* however, can hardly be heard in a large room. The sound of that one string is faint, rasping, screechy, tentative. The chanting that goes with it is toneless, monotonous, and unrelieved by vocal flourishes of any kind. The singer simply doesn't show off. There's nothing to do but pay close attention to the words which the *guslar* enunciates with great emphasis and clarity. We heard *The Death of the Mother of the Jugovići* that day and a couple of others. After a while, the poem and the archaic, other-worldly-sounding instrument began to get to me and everybody else. Our anonymous ancestor poet knew what he was doing. This stubborn drone combined with the sublime lyricism of the poem touched the rawest spot in our psyche. The old wounds were reopened.

The gusle was the national instrument of Serbia and the chief means for telling the legends and recalling the cultures of the Balkans generally. And those who played it, the guslars, the subject of Matija Murko's lectures in Paris the week before Milman Parry's *soutenance,* and of Murko's later published book, were the men Parry had gone to Yugoslavia to meet and hear.

It was true, Murko wrote, that in his native Slovenia there was little left of the guslars and their epic poetry. Likewise in southwest Croatia. But

> where the national epic poetry is very well conserved is in Bosnia, and better yet in Herzegovina and Montenegro, chiefly on the ancient border between these latter two provinces, where Christians and Moslems did not cease from continuous battles until the occupation of Bosnia-Herzegovina in 1878.
>
> . . .
>
> [These regions were] inhabited by the people of the Dinaric Alps—strong, heroic, and at the same time possessed of a delicate sensibility and endowed with a natural rapport between imagination and intelligence, as well as with a sense of language and form.

Through his travels, Murko wrote, he'd hoped to learn how "folk epic poetry lives; who the singers are; for whom, when, and how they sing; whether folk songs are still being created; and why the folk poetry is disappearing and dying."

From Parry's perspective, though, Murko's work suffered from one maddening lapse: "I did not seek new songs," Murko wrote, "and I did not transcribe any, except in fragments." Recording was difficult at best, and at harvest time impossible. Parry, arriving in Dubrovnik in July 1933, was out to do all Murko had not—gather songs, record them, and transcribe them; he needed intimate and sustained contact with the guslars, from whom he was determined to learn how they learned what they learned, and sang what they sang.

*

Parry's trips to Yugoslavia over the next two years took him into landlocked mountain country with rugged, rocky vistas, insular, cut off,

The Parrys, bound for Yugoslavia. Here, their passport photograph.

primitive. But Dubrovnik, his base of operations for most of this time, home to his wife and children, was different. It was everything Gacko, Glamoc, Kalinovik, and the dozens of other little places he'd visit were not. Until 1808 the seat of its own 580-square-mile republic, the city was a small one, yet cosmopolitan, more West than East, with a history of maritime power and influence. It had become Dubrovnik only recently, just after the Great War; early-twentieth-century postcards still called it Ragusa, its traditional name (not to be confused with a Sicilian town of the same name). Even in Parry's day, it was a tourist draw. In *Black Lamb and Grey Falcon,* her chronicle of 1930s Yugoslavia, author Rebecca West records her husband telling her as they arrive, "Dubrovnik is perhaps the most exquisite town I have ever seen." Exquisite, in large part thanks to its Old City, with its thick-walled defenses that, across five centuries, had never been breached; its ramparts and towers; its tight grid of narrow streets; its crenellations and tile roofs. The whole perfect little pocket of it was tucked between the mountains and the sea on a slim sliver of Dalmatian coast, views from every window and castle rampart affording vistas of ocean, stone, and sky.

Dubrovnik was not itself guslar country but, rather, butted up against it. Once you surmounted the range of peaks that rose over the castle walls of its Adriatic site, you were suddenly within range: Bosnia and Herzegovina, where Murko had met so many guslars, were almost within commuting distance. Montenegro was just down the coast and a turn inland from Kotor. Parry's choice of Dubrovnik as home base bubbled up naturally from Murko's *Poesie populaire,* for Parry a kind of *Guide Bleu,* or newcomer's guide, to the region. So concluded David Bynum, a classicist and Balkan scholar who absorbed something of Lord's knowledge and understanding of Parry's Yugoslav venture through long conversations with him on five later trips to the Balkans. If Parry wanted entrée to the guslar-rich regions of Yugoslavia as well as a safe, comfortable place for his wife and children, "there simply wasn't any realistic alternative to Dubrovnik."

*

For the Parrys, their first month in Dubrovnik seems to have been pleasant and low key, as much holiday as work. "This is a lovely vacation-place when not too hot," Marian wrote Addison Parry on August 2. "Mountains go right down to the sea all along the coast." Their hotel, the Pension Viktoria, stood "on the side of a long rather low mountain, all gray rock and fuzzy green above us and a terraced garden going down to the rocks from which we take our morning swim." The Old City, about a mile away, stood out against the sea, "so that we can [see] its gray stone walls and red-tiled roofs while we have our breakfast of rolls and coffee outdoors. Our day is very lazy and simple"—though more so for her than for Milman, who "spends all morning taking Serbian lessons."

A few days after arriving in Dubrovnik and settling in, Parry met Ilija Kutuzov, a young man of about his own age who'd emigrated from Russia in 1920 and had studied literature in Belgrade. Just now, fresh from earning his PhD at the Sorbonne, he was in Dubrovnik working as a grammar school teacher—and feeling, we may guess, underemployed. Kutuzov agreed to give Parry lessons in Serbo-Croatian.

At one point, the Russian took him to a nearby *kafana,* a local place for coffee, wine, and song, ubiquitous in the Balkans. This one was located in the heart of the Old City, near the Rector's Palace, in a plaza familiarly known as the Italian Market. It was frequented by laborers from across the provincial border in Herzegovina looking for work, and was one of only a few places in Dubrovnik where a guslar could sometimes be heard. Its proprietor, Pero Arbulić—well-off, with a big house down the spiny Dalmatian coast south of the city—had agreed to ask a local guslar to sing for them that evening.

Arbulić's promised man was there, drinking wine and setting his instrument in order, when Kutuzov and Parry arrived. His name was Nikola Vujnović. A man in his midthirties, a stonemason by trade, he came from a village near Stolac, about sixty miles north in Herzegovina. That evening he sang for them. Dubrovnik's tourists and more citified residents could be hard on a rude, rustic guslar, the songs he sang and the music he played, sometimes making noisy fun of him. But not tonight. Tonight, a few weeks after leaving Harvard and America, Parry got his first taste of a guslar, this young man singing his old song, sawing away with his bow on his peculiar instrument.

A few days later, Parry and Kutuzov were back with Nikola at Arbulić's. Parry offered Nikola a glass of wine. Nikola at first declined, saying he could pay for his own, thank you, but then accepted. Parry,

At Arbulić's *kafana* in Dubrovnik's Old City, early in Parry's Yugoslav adventure.
Nikola Vujnović, who would become a trusted assistant, sings and plays the gusle;
Parry's Russian acquaintance Ilija Kutuzov in the chair beside him; Pero Arbulić
behind the counter.

almost certainly through Kutuzov, interrogated him. Did he know the
old songs, particularly those of Kosovo? No, Catholics like him in Herzegovina wouldn't know such as those. Instead, Nikola sang a song he
had learned from his Uncle Vlaho, and soon was drawing them into the
culture that had produced him: Uncle Vlaho was one of five brothers,
two of whom played and sang, and from whom Nikola had learned his
repertoire; they lived right next to his father's house, so he heard them all
the time growing up. One uncle, the better of the two, would sing while
making himself a pair of *opanke,* the local rustic shoe. Nikola's father
was "altogether indifferent to the songs," Parry would recall, and when
young Nikola bought a gusle with eighteen dinars of his own money, he
made known his displeasure.

Two nights later, they all returned to the *kafana.* Nikola sang them
the beginning of "Marko and Musa." But amid the clamor of the Saturday night crowd, Nikola grew self-conscious and had to stop. Well,
suggested Parry, why not simply write down the poem he had started?
Nikola was as literate as a few years in school could make him, enough

that, two nights later, he was able to give Parry his version of the song, all written out.

A week later they were back and Nikola, now more at ease, sang for them again. Sometimes, when he paused to rest, other workmen borrowed the gusle from him and sang, one of them quite ably, with his own distinct style. Nikola, Parry reported, "was piqued by all this," but on subsequent nights became more relaxed.

Some time later, Parry asked Nikola to again sing "Marko and Musa." He and Kutuzov had a typed copy of Nikola's version from before and Parry, from all he'd gleaned from Murko, suspected the two versions might differ. This, he wrote later, "Kutuzov would not believe," though the Russian did agree to record any variations that did crop up. Nikola began—and almost immediately Kutuzov was swamped. "He could scribble only a small part of them," Parry wrote, and "lost the place for a while and finally gave up the attempt." Even Nikola was surprised by the many discrepancies. But its departure from the original—or rather, we must now take care to say, from the *earlier* one, for who is to say which, if any, was the original?—represented for Parry a kind of data point in his quest to understand the origins of the Homeric epics.

*

The Parrys had come to Dubrovnik on July 5. They were scheduled to return home to Cambridge on September 4, in time for the start of classes. But by mid-August, the barest handful of mediocre singers from Arbulić's was about all Parry had to show for his time.

Earlier that month, he had taken a ten-day trip to Belgrade and Zagreb, probably by train, to buy texts of printed songs and, more urgently, a sound-recording device. It was one thing to have a guslar dictate a song for you; another to have him sing it; a third altogether to record it for posterity. Lamenting the loss of native cultures in California, Parry's anthropology professor at Cal, Alfred Kroeber, had made, even before World War I, early recordings of Ishi, the California Indian he had befriended and studied; Kroeber went on to record numerous myths and tales in various Native American languages. Now Parry hoped to do something like this in Yugoslavia. He "had steeped himself in the methods of the anthropologists," Albert Lord would write of him in 1949, "and it was to their methods that he turned when he began his own field work." Parry returned from Belgrade with a Parlograph, a heavy, black, pre-electronic lug of a dictating machine, originally developed in America by Thomas Edison, that recorded sound on wax cylinders, as Kroeber had done.

But for him it didn't work, or not well, anyway. One day in mid-August, Nikola and a friend of his, also a stonemason, returned with Parry to Pension Viktoria to try it out. The target song was "The Wedding of Theodore of Zadar." But the screech of the gusle drowned out Nikola's singing. So he was asked to lay aside the instrument and sing without it. But this time, without its rhythmic constraint, he sang faster, too fast, in time unintelligibly so. The following morning, Parry tried something new: Nikola should simply recite the song, not sing it, into the dictaphone. This, though, Nikola found awkward and unnatural. Later that day Kutuzov, "with great difficulty and patience," transcribed the first two-thirds of another Nikola song, "John of Sibinj and Little Marianus." But, Parry would write, "the gaps which it was necessary to leave in certain lines, and the complete uncertainty of others, forced us to give up hope of obtaining much by means of the dictaphone." Simply recording a song out in the field, which in a few years would become easy, routine, and cheap, was just now fettered by a technology that lagged way behind Parry's ambitions.

Most songs Parry collected that first summer, then, were simply dictated and written down. In one Herzegovinian village, Parry snapped a picture of a guslar named Šepan Prkačin who would dictate ten songs for him: The singer and his amanuensis, Kutuzov, sit at a small table outside, in what looks like a small courtyard. Prkačin recites each verse as Kutuzov, hunched over pencil and paper, writes it down. While Kutuzov earnestly scribbles, the singer pauses, then takes up the song again a moment later. Line by line for one hundred lines or one thousand: It was one step removed from an original guslar performance, but it was intelligible, as the dictaphone mostly was not, and it came straight from the singer.

On Monday, August 21, Parry, Nikola, and Kutuzov set off for Stolac, bound first by train to Mostar, the town a hundred miles north of Dubrovnik later made infamous by the destruction of its picturesque stone-arched bridge during the wars of the 1990s. From Mostar they were driven south by car—through valleys flanked by hills, circling round the sides of mountains, up steep grades, engine grinding—finally reaching Stolac. In a village outside town, a boy was sent to fetch a singer Nikola knew. Before he arrived someone in the gathering crowd borrowed the *kafana*'s own gusle and sang—"in a voice whose lack of beauty" Parry could never quite extinguish from his memory. Fortunately, Nikola's acquaintance, Petar Vedić, soon arrived, downed a glass of *rakija* "to clear his throat," and sang more successfully "Marko and Nina of Kostun."

Vedić's Marko was a version of the same protean and legendary figure we met earlier. This time we first encounter him while drinking wine with his mother, sister, and wife. They may never see him again, he tells them; he is to join the sultan's army for a nine-year term. He leaves for the court of the sultan and enlists, surrendering sword and horse, to be returned only at the end of his service.

In time, Marko receives word from his mother that his *kula,* or tower house, has been captured by the cruel Nina, who has insulted her and taken his wife captive. Marko informs the sultan, asks for the return of his horse and sword, as well as a contingent of the sultan's soldiers, with which to find, attack, and slay Nina.

He and his men, well disguised as monks, come upon twelve women at a spring, washing clothes. One of them is his wife. She does not recognize him (though she does recognize his horse, Šarac, with its distinctive splotched coat). Marko informs her that her husband is dead, that Nina should be told she would now be married off to him, and that they would all arrive that evening.

Marko and his men are welcomed by Nina. Marko's wife serves them wine. Marko asks permission to dance, which Nina grants. So vigorous is his dancing that the whole *kula* shakes. Why, he's never seen anything like it, exclaims Nina. Of course not, ripostes his guest, because Nina has never seen the likes of *him*—Prince Marko. He reaches for his sword, cuts off Nina's head, kills many of his men. More bloodletting ensues. Marko erects a monument to his victims, and takes his wife off with him.

Vedić told this story in 154 ten-syllable lines.

A year later, Parry, this time with a better recording device, returned to Stolac, tracked down Vedić, and asked him to sing the same song. He obliged, now taking 279 lines to do it.

The same day, he dictated a third version, which needed 234 lines. In the second version, Marko worries, before it happens, that Nina will capture his *kula* and steal his wife. And Marko later meets his wife not at the spring but at Nina's tower, where she calls down to him in the courtyard.

In yet another version, when the monks at first refuse to give Marko and his men their clothes, Marko slaughters them.

Do these and other variations make the song different? Or does it remain, despite them, essentially the same?

More than in the particulars of Marko's bravery or vengefulness, Parry was interested in how songs come to be, how singers sing them, how they evolve, what it even means to call them the same song, and what this and other experiments—for that is what they were—might say about the origins of epic poetry.

*

Petar Vedić's subsequent renditions of the song came on Parry's *second* visit to Yugoslavia. To future generations of scholars, his two Yugoslav trips together made for a landmark in the study of oral poetry. The number of songs gathered; the sheer physical weight of the recordings he brought back to America; his constant experimentation; the energy, focus, and intelligence it represented, would project an aura of well-worked plans and formidable competence. Adam Parry, who could be critical of his father's work, would write approvingly of "the care and the scholarly control which Parry exerted over his interviews and his fieldwork generally. . . . The desire in some manner to relive the world of Homer [in Yugoslavia] did not detract from the sobriety of his scholarly judgment."

But if triumph attaches to the whole Yugoslav venture, it owes mostly to the second year. In this first trip, Parry's judgment was not always so sober, and uncertainty, inexperience, and ignorance dogged his time there. It was only late that summer, when it was practically time to leave, that Parry finally reached prime guslar country—Stolac, Nevesinje, and Gacko, near the Montenegrin border. In those places, over a span of just ten days, old men, as most of them were, dictated a few songs for him, like "Marko Recognizes His Father's Sword," and "Mustajbey and Janković Stojan." In Gacko, within half an hour of his arrival in town,

Parry was told of a guslar named Ilija Vuković, proffered a showy picture postcard of him, advised of the extraordinary ornateness of his gusle, and made to listen "to an admiring account of the cash value of his costume." Parry didn't always know what to make of what he saw and heard.

His ignorance extended to Serbo-Croatian, the language. In 1931, Parry had written his sister that he'd begun the study of it. But back at Harvard, Mrs. Parry would report, "he didn't have very much time to study the language because he was teaching"; short stretches in the evening were about all he could give it. In Dubrovnik, in 1933, he took up with Kutuzov—from whom, as Mrs. Parry would put it, he "got the rudiments of it." And rudiments were all they were at first. Years later Kutuzov's son would encounter Parry's daughter—little Marian, now all grown up—on a train to Paris. Once they got to talking, introduced themselves, and realized who the other was, the Kutuzov boy took plain delight in pointing up the great Milman Parry's weakness in the language and reliance on his own father's gifts. He was more right than not. In the summer of 1933, certainly, Parry didn't know much of the language, didn't know much of Balkan ways, had to rely heavily on Kutuzov and Vujnović.

"There were no rules laid down for Parry's investigation," Adam Parry would write; his father needed to find his own way. Viewed more severely by David Bynum, Lord's longtime colleague, Parry came to South Slavic studies "as a complete outsider and novice. . . . From any conceivable late twentieth-century point of view, as a South Slavicist he was . . . a complete *ingénu*." Bynum pictures him as sometimes too tamely embracing the views of Murko and other established South Slavic experts; and of reaching premature conclusions about what he saw and heard himself. For example, Parry misinterpreted the tendency of some singers to stress the vowels and obscure the consonants of their songs as a strength, not an affectation of weaker singers, which it was.

At the end of his first trip to Yugoslavia, Parry had interpretations to revise, mistakes to correct, and much to learn.

*

Once home in America, Parry wrote a report looking back to the previous summer and ahead to what he hoped would be a year of greater progress. He did have some accomplishments to crow about: He was "the first person of any sort who has ever come to Stolac for the poetry." To Nevesinje, only Murko had preceded him. Nikola's version of "The Captivity of Janković Stojan," well known to the South Slavic scholarly community, was according to Parry "longer and finer" than anyone else's. Another poem he'd collected, "The Illness of Daničič Đuro," had never before been reduced to print. All told, he had 55,000 lines of new texts. "The number of excellent poems to be obtained from [the following year's more] abundant recording should be very great."

But, if his readers needed reminding, as they probably did, Parry emphasized that he was not collecting South Slavic poems to serve South Slavic scholarship:

> My Homeric studies have from the beginning shown me that Homeric poetry, and indeed all early Greek poetry, is oral, and so can be properly understood, criticized, and edited only when we have a complete knowledge of the processes of oral poetry.

And those processes differed greatly from those of written poetry: If you write, you know the alphabet, have learned to form words from letters, how to set them down on paper or equivalent. You sit for a while, think, scribble and scrawl, erase or cross out, maybe write it all out again, probably through several iterations. And so, with due allowance for individual intellects, temperaments, genres, and writing technologies, you have writing. But what was its counterpart, the equivalent body of practice, for oral composition? What did the singer do, and how did he do it? *This* was the new territory Parry was so determined to explore.

Parry laid out the goals for his second Yugoslav trip: He wanted to learn how much the oral poet depended on the particular tradition out of which he came; how much a poem remained the same in successive recitations by a given singer; how it changed with time, and as it passed from one region to another; how a "heroic cycle"—a series of poems of similar theme and characters—was created, how it grew and declined; how the would-be events of such a cycle correlated, if at all, with historical events. And, "so on and so on"—that, of course, being Parry to a T: His Paris thesis showed the inexhaustibly varied perspectives from which he could analyze the same thing.

It was, to be sure, something of a quixotic quest—to better understand what few had ever thought much about at all, a variant species of poetic artistry, one granting backdoor access, through modern Yugoslavia, to the Homer of three millenniums before.

*

Parry was already back in Cambridge with his family when, early in October 1933, he received in the mail a song from a guslar he'd met in Nevesinje, Milovan Vojičić. It was called "The Song of Milman Parry," and began:

> *Dear God, praise to Thee for all!*
> *What I shall sing is the straight truth.*
> *In one thousand, nine hundred*
> *And thirty three,*
> *A gray falcon flew*
> *From the beautiful land of America*
> *He flew over lands and cities,*
> *Until he came to the shore of the sea,*
> *There a steel ship awaited him,*
> *And the falcon flew onto the ship,*
> *And rested his heroic wings,*
> *The name of the ship is Saturnia,*
> *And it is as swift as a mountain vila.*
> *That was not a gray falcon,*
> *But Professor Milman Parry the glorious!*

The song continues in like fashion across 150 lines. Harry Levin would picture it as a fond farewell to Parry after his first round of field research.

Of course, if the English translation conveys anything of the Serbo-Croatian original, it reminds us that a native guslar need not be a brilliant poet. Nor an accurate one: Many of the odd contemporary particulars in Vojičić's poem are, at least in a drearily literal sense, untrue. Parry didn't go over on the *Saturnia*, but its sister ship, the *Vulcania*. We may wish to chalk up such lapses to poetic license.

In the end, any interest it might have for us lies very little in its own poetic virtues or failings, but rather in the charming irony of Parry, student of Serbo-Croatian poetry, becoming, this once, its subject.

23

KIRKLAND HOUSE

Parry, back at Harvard for the fall semester of 1933, taught the *Iliad* three days a week at noon and Greek Prose Composition Tuesday afternoons at three. He also taught Latin—a course on Horace, Persius, and Juvenal—three days a week. Yet while dutifully performing his job, he may sometimes have seemed detached during those ten months from September to the following June. Even before Yugoslavia, he could seem distracted in class, his gaze disconcertingly directed out the window. Now, inevitably, his thoughts would sometimes return to the previous summer in Yugoslavia, or race ahead to the coming year there. In November, he gave a talk at Kirkland House on "Travels in Yugoslavia." In the spring, for a talk in the Eliot House senior common room, he spoke on "The Oral Poetry of the Serbian Peasants and Its Connection with Early Greek Poetry." A week later, he gave a lantern-slide lecture on similar themes for the Linguistic Society of America.

That fall Parry wrote his first paper rooted in the Balkan project. It was called "Whole Formulaic Verses in Greek and Southslavic Heroic Song." In it, as Adam Parry would distill it, he all but removed Homer from "the conventional context of 'Greek Literature,' and placed him in company with singers of other lands who tell of the heroic way of life," like the Yugoslavian singers of the previous summer. Wrote Milman Parry:

> When one hears the Southern Slavs sing their tales he has the overwhelming feeling that, in some way, he is hearing Homer.

This is no mere sentimental feeling that comes from his seeing a way of life and a cast of thought which are strange to him, nor from the fact that the man who is singing to the four notes of a horsehair string calls himself a *singer—pjesnik,* as the blind poet of the *Hymn to Apollo* calls himself an *aoidos,* and that he calls his songs *heroic songs—junacke pjesme.*

Rather, for Parry the link was more precise, even technical—and visible, for example, in the "whole formulaic verses" of his article's title. Here Parry referred to instances in which a whole line of a poem tracked a character's movements, or introduced a speech.

For example, Homer repeatedly uses this formulaic verse: "And addressing him he spoke winged words." A similar South Slavic formula is: "And quietly she began to speak to him."

Or, then again, to show the passage of time: For Homer, "the sun set, and all the ways grew dark." In the South Slavic, the parallel is, "The day passed, the somber night came on."

The previous summer, noted Parry, he'd met Mićo Savić, an eighty-two-year old Gacko singer who sometimes sported an old silver flint-lock pistol tucked into his belt and a black band in his cap to mourn the Serb defeat at Kosovo in 1389. One of his songs told of an uprising against the Turks half a century before in which he himself had taken part.

> Dvije pas bismo i ubismo
> *Two pashas we fought and overcame*

Parry had encountered the almost identical phase in a compendium of South Slavic poetry:

> Tri je pase bio i ubio
> *Three pashas he fought and overcame.*

To Parry, this revealed how old Savić conceived his life: The verse was not one he had made, but "came down to him from the past. For the people as a whole who created the verse and kept it, it is an ideal; for this man it has become a boast."

Savić, then, sees himself as the living expression of the old ideals and the old ways. And he says so, in the old ways.

*

During the fall after his return, Parry completed his American Council of Learned Societies proposal to help fund the coming year in Yugoslavia. He had made only modest progress on the first trip, but now he had a good feel for what he'd need for the second: Fifteen months and $11,000, equivalent today to perhaps $200,000. He'd need a Remington typewriter with Cyrillic-language keyboard, $64. He'd need to pay typists, at "10 dinars (23 cents) an hour, eight hours a day, for 200 days," or $368. He'd need his car to get from village to village and to pay for

Mićo Savić, one of the scores of Yugoslavians who sang for Parry, his voice captured on aluminum discs now at the Milman Parry Collection at Harvard.

shipping it from the States, as well as an allowance for "transportation by horse in regions without roads." He had to buy songbooks; he already had a sizeable collection, but needed some from the 1800s, which were harder to come by. And he had to pay the singers: "It is necessary to keep them in spirits with wine, rakija, Turkish coffee, and cigarettes. On a fairly lavish entertainment depends in no small measure the prestige of the recorder and the willingness of the singers to give their best efforts." Six dollars a day should do it.

And he needed to pay an assistant.

The previous summer, in Mostar, Parry had snapped a picture of Nikola Vujnović and Ilija Kutuzov. Kutuzov, his dark hair memorably mussed, briefcase nestled against his body, looks warily at the camera. Nikola, as if brought in reluctantly to complete the tableau, stands to the side, tall and upright, the early morning sun raking his chiseled face. They wear jackets and white shirts, dress shoes coated with a light sheen of dust. They carry briefcases and satchels. They look like part of the little research team they actually were. But Kutuzov, Sorbonne educated and perhaps not wholly at home in the rude peasant world of guslars that Parry hoped to penetrate, would soon leave Parry and Dubrovnik for Belgrade, the Serbian capital. Nikola, on the other hand, would remain the sure, steady constant of the whole Yugoslav enterprise.

"The greater part of what success I had this summer was due to the aid of Nikola Vujnović," Parry wrote in his ACLS proposal. "That he was of the region and knew the people and their ways," together with his uncanny understanding of Parry's needs, "went a long way towards making the people accept me." He was a blond, muscled man of mixed Serb and Croatian heritage, with high cheekbones and bright blue eyes. He was honest. He made sure Parry wasn't overcharged. He managed what Parry called "the ticklish business" of paying each singer according to his local reputation. "I thus propose to take him into my service for the entire period of my study." He'd pay Nikola the 60 dinars a day he normally earned as a mason, about $1.30 in Depression-era dollars, plus another dollar a day for living and traveling expenses. Nikola became Parry's chief assistant, mediator, and interpreter, on long drives, Parry would recall, sometimes "singing to himself beneath his breath parts of certain of the heroic songs we had heard." When, the following summer, they began to interview singers about their lives, it was Nikola who asked the questions, Parry occasionally piping up from the sidelines. And this able, adaptable man, Parry was sure, could learn to work the new sound-recording instrument he had in mind for the following year.

In her interview with Pamela Newhouse, Mrs. Parry would several times refer to her husband's ease in the mechanical world. He was a photographer, comfortable with cameras, at home with technology generally. He was the first professor at Harvard to have a lecture broadcast— "direct for the first time from the classroom!"—over the local Yankee Network, as he did in February 1934 with a talk on Sophocles from Emerson Hall. Now, for his second tour in Yugoslavia, he was determined to equip himself with a recording contrivance better than the one so disappointing to him the year before.

The new one, which worked something like a modern record player only in reverse, replaced the wax cylinders of 1933 with twelve-inch aluminum discs: A microphone picked up the singer's voice, transforming it into an electrical signal that, through an electromagnetically driven cutting head, lightly embossed the spinning blank disc with squiggly grooves embodying the original sound; the song could be "played back" on the same apparatus. In those days of radios and phonographs in most American homes, sound quality could be expected to be good, and was.

But it was not alone fidelity to the moaning chant of the singer and the whine of the gusle that mattered to Parry. He had an additional need, one arising from the original premise of the Yugoslav venture itself: Epic song—whether in Greece three thousand years ago or Yugoslavia in 1934—was almost by definition *long*. It went on and on; you needed hours and hours to hear the whole *Iliad*, and, if it was some Balkan *Iliad* you hoped to find, *that* might go on for hours as well. So for Parry, the ability to record some sweet snippet of song or brief dramatic speech, however purely and distinctly, was not enough. Take, for example, the previous summer's dictaphone, with its wax cylinders: After a few minutes, the first cylinder fills up. So the singer stops, midsong. The cylinder is extracted. A new one is introduced. Finally, the recording is taken up again and the singing resumes. This would never do, not if it was a Balkan *Iliad* you wanted to capture. The same applied to the 78 rpm records of the day. Years later the LP, or long-playing record, could hold twenty-five minutes per side; the 78s of Parry's era were good for only four or five.

Whether the apparatus he took to Yugoslavia that second year was Parry's idea or that of the engineers and technicians who, at his behest, built it, is unclear. The machine itself is lost, but its overall design does come down to us: Imagine two turntables and two recording heads, controlled by a single toggle switch that, stopping one turntable, starts the other. Flip the toggle and the disc situated on turntable A stops recording, while the one on turntable B begins. Remove the just-recorded disc from turntable A, replace it with a fresh one, and, long before the B disc fills up, you're ready to flip the toggle and continue. The guslar never stops singing. In this way, songs of any length could be recorded without interruption. A little skill was required to throw the toggle at just the right instant, such as at the end of a verse, so as to make any break in the recording indiscernible.

There was nothing high-tech here. It didn't push the electronics of the day. In principle, any backyard tinkerer might have come up with it. Its manufacturer was a Waterbury, Connecticut, company, Sound Specialties, Inc., founded in 1932 by a bright young Worcester Tech grad named Lincoln Thompson. "Every part that goes into a SoundScriber machine is rugged and made for years of service," the company brochure boasted. "The whole construction is characterized by ruggedness, simplicity, and precision."

"I made a couple of trips with Parry to Waterbury to see the equipment and to bring it to Cambridge," wrote Albert Lord later.

*

Born in 1912, Albert Bates Lord grew up in a house in Allston, a Boston neighborhood virtually in the shadow of Harvard, just across the Charles River. On brisk fall days back in the 1920s, the streets around his house on Franklin Street would be thronged with alums, bundled up in fur coats, laden with blankets and banners, for Harvard football games played at the nearby stadium. But Lord was a townie, with a strong Boston accent to prove it, and Harvard, he'd write, "was a remote world to me," however close to home it was.

He came from an old New England family that now, in the wake of the Depression, had fallen on hard times; his father's business—Lord's Candy Co., Specialty Manufacturers, Boston, Mass.—which Lord's children recall as a purveyor of those sweet slabs of hard taffy known as Mary Janes, flirted with bankruptcy. Lord attended Boston Latin School, a prestigious public school, first and oldest in the United States, going back to 1635, which had a long tradition of feeding top students to Harvard. In 1930, Lord was one of them; he applied nowhere else. At Latin, it was all language all the time for him; two years of German, three of French, three of English, four of Latin. He knew he'd study classics at Harvard, and did.

In the spring semester of his first year, he wound up in an advanced Latin course taught by Milman Parry. Later, he took another with Parry, Greek Composition. It's likely, however, that any affinity developing between the two did so less in class than within the cluster of brick buildings off Dunster Street recently conjoined, socially and administratively, as Kirkland House. There, after his freshman year in a Harvard Yard dorm, Lord lived for three years. Parry was among its first generation of nonresident tutors.

Of all the exemplars of the new Harvard "house system," Kirkland House was the smallest, with about two hundred residents. It had been cobbled together from existing dormitories and the old Hicks House, quarters for George Washington's officers during the Revolutionary War. Moved to its new location, Hicks House became Kirkland's own cozy library, laced with reading rooms spread across three floors, fireplaces, easy chairs, and ten thousand books—including, it was said, a facsimile of the Ellesmere Chaucer and a choice collection of erotica. Kirkland had its own kitchen, high-ceilinged dining hall, social life, and budding traditions. Sunday evenings brought in faculty for Kirkland's "Coffee Pot" series, introduced in November 1931; talks, the conceit went, were to be ten and a half minutes long, on any subject, be it "whimsies, scholarly essays, indeed anything that might be found in a coffee pot," burdened by "no hopes, no past, no ideas, no platform," all followed by vital, engaging discussion. In such ways, within the tidy residential communities of the new system, reminiscent of the colleges of Oxford and Cambridge universities in England, bonds between professors and undergraduates were supposed to flower.

In Parry's Kirkland House office, off stairway H, on the ground floor, just beside an arched portal from the street, he could meet with students or do his own work. It was a modestly sized room, maybe twelve feet by fifteen, a fireplace on one wall, the windows opposite looking out on a handsome courtyard, warmed by a fine rug. It was very comfortable— perhaps "too" comfortable, in that Parry was always there. "As time went on," his Classics colleague M. V. Anastos would report, "he lost himself more and more in his great subject. Never, I think, much of a family man, he took to spending many nights in his Kirkland House tutor's suite." Years later Parry's daughter, Marian, would assert that there, in his Kirkland digs, he entertained women. Of course, she was probably too young at the time to know any such thing. And she told me this in very old age, when she had begun a gradual slide into dementia. What seems safer to conclude is that Parry escaped to Kirkland in part to relieve tensions and dissatisfaction at home. Mrs. Parry would tell of her husband frequenting Kirkland poker sessions, of only rarely inviting her to social events there; he wanted to shield her, she has him earnestly explain, from "the slurring things they said about Jewish people."

Kirkland's house master was Edward A. Whitney, who at the time of Parry's death would speak of his "unbounded admiration for Milman." As for Whitney's wife, Mrs. Parry would remember her as "a very good-looking woman, and a perfect goose," who'd prattle on about the fine carriages her prominent family once kept. To Marian Thanhouser Parry of Milwaukee, never at ease in Harvard's cloistered precincts, this did not go down well. In any case, Kirkland House was another locus of split and separation between her and Milman.

"Nineteen Thirty-Four was the first Harvard class to enjoy three full years in the new Houses," wrote Lord a few years after graduation. "We were, so to speak, the guinea pigs of a new experiment." For him it was a successful one, in part for drawing him into Parry's orbit. Parry infused him, he would write, "with an interest in his Homeric research," though it's unclear whether this interest predated Yugoslavia. Beginning with Lord's junior year, Parry was his assigned tutor. Parry monitored his progress, signed off on his academic plans. "If I am not mistaken," Parry would write in the spring of 1935, while Lord was with him in Yugoslavia, "he was well liked in the [Kirkland] house, and my good opinion of his ability and his person has been altogether confirmed by the work he has done for me this year." But he writes more measuredly than if they'd already become close at Harvard. Years later, recalling those among Parry's students they'd have over to their place in Cambridge, Mrs. Parry would speak fondly of Dan Margolies, later part of the team of prosecutors at the Nuremberg war crimes trial, and Harry Levin and others. But not Lord: "I can't remember ever having him for dinner at Harvard." Nor was Lord part of the *Philoctetes* production of the previous spring.

If, as seems likely, it was early in 1934 that Lord arranged to join Parry in Yugoslavia, the terms of the arrangement remain indistinct. By David Bynum's reckoning, Lord had no idea what he would do after graduation. His original hopes for a full-fledged Grand Tour had been defeated by the Depression; Yugoslavia would be a fallback. Lord's situation, Bynum would observe, "was the sort of upset in undergraduates' personal affairs Parry was known for wisely counseling." Here, he more than counseled: Parry, Lord would write, "was good enough to allow me to go with him," at Lord's own expense. Or rather, that of his Depression-ravaged family. By Bynum's account, only a modest cache of savings coming down through Lord's mother made it possible. Lord would pepper his letters home from Yugoslavia with expressions of gratitude for his parents' sacrifices, along with attestations of his own frugality.

In the months before the expedition, Parry made trips to Waterbury, Connecticut, to monitor progress on the new recording equipment, and to Hoboken, New Jersey, to test it on a Yugoslav singer; Lord apparently accompanied him at least twice. He may also have been the unnamed student Parry paid, as he wrote in a report, to help him "with preparations during the last days" before the trip. In any case, as Bynum would have it, "the bargain was struck": Lord would spend the summer in Europe and later join Parry in Yugoslavia—though in what role, and under what conditions, may not have been specified.

In March, Lord sat with the other forty-three Kirkland House members of the class of 1934 for a group photographic portrait. There, cross-legged in the front row, hands set comfortably on his lap, face set in an easy welcoming smile, he seems more genial, less haughty, than some of his housemates. Academically, though, he was quite the star, graduating magna cum laude and Phi Beta Kappa. His passport was issued on June 5. He gave over his last days in Boston to securing visas for the coming trip—France on June 8, Germany on the ninth, Yugoslavia on the fourteenth.

24

THE ACTUAL PROCEDURE OF WORK

Whatever want of enthusiasm Mrs. Parry had about Yugoslavia, she stifled it enough to accompany her husband, along with the children, on both trips there. The first was easy enough; in the negotiating from which no marriage is exempt, Milman may have billed it as a superb vacation opportunity more than a research trip crucial to his work; and Marian may have bought into the idea.

The second trip—viewed all along as spanning more than a year—was the bigger problem. Marian didn't want to go, nor did her widowed mother want her to go. But Marian's great-aunt, a woman Marian liked and with whom her mother lived at the time, all but looked her straight in the eye and declared, "You must go with your husband. . . . It's your duty to go." Marian yielded, signing on for the Yugoslav venture, telling her mother she'd send for her later. She didn't. It could never have worked, she'd tell Newhouse, apparently still trying to justify herself, "living as we did way up on the side of the mountain."

For most of their time in Dubrovnik, they were indeed up on the side of a mountain, Mount Srd. Sprouting up from the city late in the nineteenth century were small suburban enclaves, several of which grew up north of the Old City on steep ground rising toward a fort built by the French in 1810 during the Napoleonic Wars: Stone walkways marched up the hill, flanked by houses with walled courtyards, vines and flowers overspreading the walls, the broad width of each house affording fine views of the Old City and the Adriatic below. The Parrys lived in one of them.

Little Marian, ten years old the summer of the second trip, kept her

own girlish diary of the year, for which she'd have lifelong happy memories. On June 4, their first full day out of Boston, aboard the *Vulcania,*
the same ship they'd taken to Yugoslavia the previous summer, "Papa
gave us a dinar for sleeping," about two cents. "I was to write a poem or
a story a page long every day."

By June 9, they were across the Atlantic in Gibraltar, the British
enclave at the southern tip of Spain, whose streets they took time to wan-
der. "We saw Spanish women and Turks, bobbies and tommies, besides
the other population." On the way back from the Moorish Castle, they
saw "a Turk who had made a pilgrimage to Mecca. We could tell he had
done this because of his turban."

In Naples, after a day spent touring the city and its museums, they
returned to the ship to find it uncomfortably crowded with Germans—
"very impolite. 'The lowest class of people,'" her mother called them.

Finally, on June 16, in the middle of a driving rain, they reached
Dubrovnik, checking in once more to the Pension Viktoria.

Young Marian's entries trailed off soon after their arrival, but in July
she recorded: "We moved into our own house"—this would be the one
on the slope of Mount Srd—"and papa began to take trips." One of the
first, on July 14, was to Stolac.

*

"A little town with a river running through it, a mosque with a shop
with a good cook, and a castle on a hill in back," little Marian, when
she saw it later that summer, would call Stolac. Pronounced *sto-latz,*
Stolac means "seat" or "throne"; during Ottoman times the village was
the seat of the local Turkish military governor. But its history went back
long before that. The area had been settled for fifteen thousand years.
Fine third-century mosaics unearthed from Roman ruins nearby, now in
the National Museum in Sarajevo, include portraits of stylishly coiffed
women and large geometric designs of formidable artistry. At one end of
town, a little back from the river, perched on the lower slopes of a hill,
stood a *kula,* the stone defensive tower mentioned in some of the songs;
from it, one might survey approaches to the town or look to the cliffs
across the river with their muscular stone outcroppings. Rising behind
it was a castle, the Vidoski fort, going back to before the Ottoman con-

quest in 1465, much altered over the centuries, but by Parry's time mostly a splendid ruin. From among its turrets, stone stairways, and ramparts, the fort could seem to preside protectively over the town at its base, with its Orthodox and Catholic churches, its mosques and minarets, the crowded Islamic streets around them, and the Bergrava, a calm rivulet of lime-etched blue-green water, flowing sedately through it.

Parry had visited Stolac briefly the previous summer, and would return three times during the second trip. It was a little jewel of a place, and it's hard to imagine Parry oblivious to its charms. But in his writings he doesn't acknowledge them. We hear from him nothing of Yugoslavia's mountainous beauty, no passing expressions of awe. He is all scholarly discipline, firmly resistant to getting drawn away from his subject. He knows why he is in Stolac. He is there for Ibro Bašić, Nikola's uncle Vlaho, Lazar Papac, Halil Rajgorić, and the others among the two dozen guslars he'd meet, hear, and record there over the next year.

After Stolac, it was two days in Bare, a tiny village where Hajdar Đozo dictated one song, "The Wedding of Orlovac Alija," and sang into Parry's new recorder another, "Alagić Alija and Velagić Ibrahim."

Then Vlasotina; then, two days in Novi Pazar, to which Parry would return for long visits later; then, in August, Gacko, Trebinje, Budya, Podgorica: substantial towns, or small villages comprising a few rude houses, some barely on the map at all, a blur of alien spelling and sound that together counted for stories, songs, and traditions that cities known better in the West—the Sarajevos, Belgrades and Zagrebs—had lost. In those villages, in their mountain fastness, many of them whose homes, ethnic identities, and even names would be swept away in the cruel wars of the ensuing century, Parry found his singers.

"The actual procedure of work in the field is simple," Parry would write.

> Along the road we question whomever we pass, where he is from, are there singers in his village, who is the best, what is his name; or we go to a Christian or Moslem cafe for the information. . . . On the whole we have found it best in a new locality to arrive in the place where we intend to work in the latter part of the afternoon and spend the evening in obtaining singers who will sing the next morning.

On September 22 Parry drove the car he'd had shipped over from the States, a boxy black 1932 Ford, into Kijevo, a town on the Croatian side of the border with Bosnia, accompanied by Nikola and, probably, Kutuzov. Said to be the best guslar in those parts, a regular at weddings and other celebrations, was a man named Ante Cicvarić. "Sugo," they called him locally; villagers from nearby towns were known to arrive on horseback in the middle of the night to beg him to entertain. He was fifty-one years old, Roman Catholic, the father of four, lived in a simple hut; kept sheep, a cow, and a donkey; and was illiterate. At Nikola's behest, Sugo was brought from his own fields to a nearby threshing floor. He was dressed as he'd been at his work, his trousers rolled up, and barefoot. Asked if he knew how to sing to the gusle, he replied in the traditional formula, "As many days as there are in a year, each day I can play a new song."

It was a hot, late September day. Sugo planted himself in a shady spot near the door of a local man's hut. Children gathered, along with a few local shepherds; a guslar's performance was commonplace, a foreigner's interest in one rare. The equipment was set up and Sugo began to sing—songs that by sound, subject, and theme by now probably didn't sound quite so alien to Parry: "Omer and Ajkuna"; "The Wedding of Marko." The first time one of the songs was played back—the toggle flipped, the record set to turning, the curls and swells of its cut grooves pushing sound back through the primitive electronics and into the speaker—stunned the assembled villagers. How could this machine "sing just like our Sugo"?

Parry's sound recording device was doing its job. It preserved sound which, transcribed and reduced to print, could be used for the scholarly analysis to which Parry planned to later subject it. But such moments as were enacted in Kijevo added up to more than that. For they offered, in the plainest, most direct way, not a *description* of the oral-poetic processes Parry sought to understand—not just more words, not at one remove—but something close to the thing itself. It was something of Yugoslavia, and by extension ancient Greece, brought back to Harvard through sound. It was Marcel Jousse's ideas made manifest, in sound. It was the Oral Style, direct to one's ears. One Harvard classicist, Peter McMurray, has suggested that the nascent academic discipline of sound studies could be thought to have begun with Parry himself, who "heard what others could only see, transmuting a textual genre back into its original state of sonic liveliness."

Sugo played for the children, the shepherds, and the scholars almost a century ago, when disembodied sound was still new on the scale of human history, even for Parry. The villagers, we may be sure, were not the only ones moved by the words and music billowing up from his machine.

*

The singers and the songs accumulated, slowly. Much time had gone into "the mere organization of the work," Parry would write in a report at the end of October. In it, he again stressed the pivotal role of Nikola, who worked with the singers, answered questions from the typists, transcribed recorded songs often speckled with words left over from the centuries-long Turkish occupation. Nikola was irreplaceable, often working from seven in the morning to late at night.

Parry devoted much of his report to comparing funds spent so far versus those budgeted, and establishing a grand total for expenses projected for the following September, down to the last penny, namely $14,089.98. But it *wasn't* a grand total. Because he then put in an additional request: "I should wish to add further $250, for the following purpose . . . ," and so first mentioned the name of Albert Lord.

With this addendum, it becomes plain that Parry had not, up to then, provided for Lord in any tangible sense. His proposal from the previous fall made specific room for Nikola. But it never mentioned Lord, who at that time may not have figured in Parry's plans at all. Lord had left the States on June 28 and for much of the summer enjoyed his truncated version of a Grand Tour, some of it in Nazi Germany. In early September he entered Italy, where he spent ten days. Then, on September 22, he arrived in Split, the old Dalmatian town on the Adriatic whose roots went back to the Roman Empire. On September 27, Lord finally reached Dubrovnik, where Parry and his family had been since mid-June.

Lord had come to Dubrovnik, Parry wrote now, "to study Southslavic popular poetry with me"—not, it seems, to take on a promised job. But in recent weeks, circumstances had changed. Parry had talked with him about helping him on the project, and Lord had agreed. His duties? To take "complete charge of the numbering, labeling, and cataloguing of the manuscripts and discs." These, some months into the second trip, stood at five hundred and counting; there would be thousands more to come. "The mere keeping in order of the material, keeping accounts of expenditures, of payments, and countless other little tasks of keeping things going, has taken a very great deal of my time which would have been much better spent on the study of my material." Administratively, Parry was drowning. "My records of the trips are still in notes, and my knowledge of my material is in my head. The organization of the work, the trips, the necessary reading, my study of the language, have left me no leisure."

Lord witnessed the scale of Parry's operation soon after arriving at what he called "Parry's headquarters" in their rented house above the Old City. Living room was now workroom, for transcribing the aluminum discs. Mrs. Bandur and Vjekoslav Monopoli typed the texts as they came from the transcriber, Nikola. Like many a quasi-military operation before it, Parry's risked degenerating into a logistical nightmare. Lord was to help straighten things out.

But with the onset of Lord's new job, "Parry-Lord"—the vastly influential line of thinking about oral poetry later linked to both men— did not abruptly spring into being. Lord was barely out of his last undergraduate classroom. He had no previous work experience. Mrs. Parry, who was not unfailingly generous in her recollections of him, would rank him much below Nikola in his importance to the project, referring to him as "a jack of all trades"; her husband had kindly "made a place for him." Parry proposed to pay him, as his clerk, typist, and general assistant, just what he paid his Yugoslav typists, 1,000 dinars, or $21.86 per month. "I trust," wrote Parry, "that this request will not be misunderstood as a desire to obtain funds for a deserving student." His own needs, as director of a project that risked spiraling out of control, "lead me to ask with the greatest earnestness for this sum."

Parry's resolve to absorb this new expense reflected his dealings with Lord over the past few weeks—probably the most time he'd spent with him in the three years he'd known him. Their first trip together, in the Ford with Nikola, began on October 7 and, Lord would write, it was "a memorable one." Parry came back from it, it seems plain, trusting in Lord's abilities and temperament.

They first stopped briefly at Gacko, in eastern Herzegovina, to visit Miĉo Savić, one of Parry's singers from the previous summer, "whom we found, as usual, in the bar." Then, Nevesinje, to visit Milovan Vojičić, the guslar who'd celebrated Parry in song. Lord scrawled notes, in pencil and in pen, of whatever he saw and heard around him: Sheep's cheese and bread for 16 dinars in Bileka. Good wine in Gacko. Men working in the mountain passes said to earn just 2.75 dinars a day. In the car, Nikola snoring loudly or talking in his sleep.

Near the top of a mountain, set in a landscape of rocky hollows and chalky outcroppings, snow-capped higher peaks in the distance, they reached Kalinovik. From a large *kafana* there, they made known that they sought local singers—paying 25 dinars if they showed up to sing with their own gusle, 15 if they had to borrow one. Business was brisk; they had no time to eat that rainy evening, so busy did the singers keep them. One was Hasan Kajimović, whose song, "Halil and Orlanović Rescue Zlata," would become number 546 in the catalogue of the Milman Parry Collection. Number 547 was Ago Sabljica's "Mujo and Kostreš Harambaša."

The *kafana* was smoky, crowded, thick with flies. Its customers, Lord would write, showed "more interest in the foreigner and his apparatus than in the singer and the song," freely interrupting him. No more, Parry resolved after Kalinovik, would they try to compete with unruly customers. Instead, after having local boys or village hangers-on summon likely singers, they'd set up a studio in a local inn; Lord would preside over the apparatus in one room, Parry and Nikola remain with the singer in the other, the two of them serving as a small but appreciative audience. The singer would be offered refreshments and, as Lord wrote later, after "a decent interval of . . . polite conversation" the singing would commence. This became established practice.

The night after their interminably long day in Kalinovik, they drove down the mountain through rain and mud, and then fifty miles to Sarajevo. A couple of days later they stopped again in Bare, where Hajdar Đozo, in his house by the side of the road, sang for them "The Sultan Attacks Baghdad"; then they spent the night in the nearest sizeable town, Gorazde. It was there, Lord wrote, "while Parry was attempting to repair the recording apparatus . . . that we received news of the assassination."

Alexander, king of Yugoslavia, had been shot and killed in Marseilles, on a state visit. Early that morning, Parry showed up at Lord's room with the news. They needed to get out of there fast, and back to Dubrovnik; the assassin was said to be a foreigner, maybe Italian, and Parry's international license plates bore Italian markings. By 8:30, all three of them, including Nikola, were on the road—all three of them, by David Bynum's account, "thoroughly frightened," Parry especially so for his family in Dubrovnik. It was in Sarajevo, the city they'd just left, that, twenty years before, the Austrian archduke and his wife had been assassinated, setting Europe on fire. Now, *again,* the Balkan tinderbox? Lord noted the crowds outside churches, the demonstrations everywhere, heard rumors of impending war with Italy, of movements of the French and English fleets. Cars that failed to display a black flag of mourning, police advised Parry and his anxious contingent, risked the wrath of angry crowds. In Sarajevo, two officers rode the car's running boards, assuring the crowds they were innocent Americans. Late that night, the city quiet under a full moon, they reached Dubrovnik.

Parry's daughter, Marian, had heard about the assassination that morning as she came downstairs, from Marija, their maid. "All morning long the bells rang. . . . Everybody spoke in an undertone except the roosters and my brother." Mrs. Kutuzov, wife of Parry's language teacher, called to say goodbye; she and her husband were leaving, for Belgrade. Mrs. Parry took one of Milman's academic robes, folded back part of it to hide its band of bright color, and made a black flag of it to hang outside the house.

Alexander was no mere figurehead, but a substantial presence. "In pictures," an uninhibited John Gunther could write of him a few years later, he "resembled a small-town dentist." In fact, he went on, Alexander was "industrious, cruel, charming, capable of almost inexplicable sudden flights of worry, temperament, and fury, yet disciplined and shrewd—a complex character." It was Alexander who, in 1929, had made Yugoslavia into a monarchy. His murder stirred sadness, and bitterness, all across the stricken country. For two months, public singing was banned; Parry and Co.'s trips in search of song stopped. Mostly, they were stuck in Dubrovnik.

About the farthest they got in the weeks after the assassination was a car trip, one rainy day, to the Arbulić house in Konevala, just south of the city. Little Marian sat in the front between Lord and Pero Arbulić, proprietor of the *kafana* where Parry had first met Nikola. Lord would remember the Arbulić home for its "huge chimney . . . large enough for a great fire to be made inside, with benches along the walls for dishes, and for people to sit on." The food was good, but he was already homesick, yearning for "real American pies" (which Mrs. Parry promised to make). On the way back to Dubrovnik, "we had to have a black flag on the car. There were services in the church, processions, moments when the whole populace were on their knees in the streets."

It was a time of great political instability across Europe. In what became known as the Night of the Long Knives, Hitler had brutally purged his enemies within the Nazi movement. Just recently there'd been an attempted putsch in Austria. Would Parry and his family have to leave the country, his whole project upended? It was a time to lie low. Parry used the enforced hiatus to write the report requesting $250 for Lord; during that worrisome week after the assassination, it seems, Lord had proved himself. "Unflappable," young Marian would call him years later.

Around this time, too, Parry wrote C. N. Jackson, chair of Classics, outlining his plans to return to Harvard the following fall. In Yugoslavia, "I have found once more that complete lack of distraction from my studies which I have not known since the years in Paris." Happily spoiled by his scholarly freedom—no classes, no students, no dreary administrative chores—he all but pleaded for relief from the ordinary course load when he returned and that he be permitted to build a new graduate course around his Yugoslav work.

*

By mid-November, Parry was on the road again, back into the familiar pattern of his research. And there *was* a pattern: Load up the car, drive along miles of rutted roads to the next town, repair flat tires, solicit singers, set up the recording apparatus, collect songs, return after a few days or a few weeks to Dubrovnik for supplies, good food, and clean sheets. Marian the younger would remember:

> Every few weeks he would come back from a field trip, his car covered with brown mud and filled with records and other objects; we would rush out to the yard entrance and be overwhelmed with the unloading of hundreds of records—until the

car was so weighted down that it could hardly negotiate the mud roads—and for us presents, toys, pottery, embroideries and even on one occasion, as a special gift for my mother, 24 chickens and a white rooster.

Marija, the maid, cut their heads off.

The children would look back warmly on the Yugoslav trips of their childhood. When, years later, Adam, by then a young father himself, living in London, wrote his mother at Christmas, he'd report finding a good tree, "which we shall decorate with candles, as we used to do in Jugoslavia." The big house on the hill overlooking the Old City and the sea filled their childhood memories; Adam was going on eight that last summer, Marian twelve. "My brother and I enjoyed tremendously every minute," Marian told a Harvard audience in 2010. Dubrovnik was "another world, a remarkably beautiful place," with its oleander orchards, each a different color, pinks and whites, all throwing off "a wonderful perfume." She'd remember a neighbor's overgrown garden, with many insects she'd never see again, beetles of every size, description, and color. Her room was on the third floor; from the window, she could look out and see "different shades of blue depending on the ocean currents, astonishing colors." She'd sit and watch for hours, wondering how the ocean could yield so rich a palette.

The children would remember, too, Papa's stories, many of which pitted a reliably villainous version of Winnie-the-Pooh, bent on world domination, against the great and good Mickey Mouse. In one story, Mickey captures two of Pooh's henchmen, warns them that should they refuse to reveal their secrets he'll dispatch them on the spot. The two grin at the absurdity of it: *Mickey, the ever noble Mickey Mouse—kill them? Impossible!* They say nothing. Mickey counts to ten, and shoots one of them. The other promptly reveals all, leaving their master, Pooh, bested once more.

Adam and Marian met larger-than-life local characters, such as a Turkish man their father was having to the house for dinner one evening. He was, as Adam reports their father alerting them, " 'a real hero,' a man of great strength and ferocity, whose hands were 'as large as dinner plates.'" Did he ever kill anyone? Marian wanted to know. Oh, many times, said their father. He was "anticipated with fearful excitement and

Mrs. Parry and the children, around 1935.

actually turned out to be tall, but stoop-shouldered and exceedingly gentle, with a scraggly black moustache."

For him and his sister, Adam would write, "the sojourn in Jugoslavia (even if the milk did have to be boiled in a great blue pot, and thus rendered unpalatable, and ginger ale was hard to come by) was a great adventure," enriched by their father's taste for all things heroic. "Papa's feeling that Homer was still alive and that one could still be an Homeric hero," Adam wrote his sister in 1949, made Yugoslavia wonderful to them. "Would it not be absolutely marvelous," he went on, as if in reverie, to go back there?

For their mother, who turned thirty-six that second summer, Yugoslavia was another, not so happy, story. "Mother was quite lonesome, and didn't enjoy it as much as we did," young Marian would say. In her conversations with Pamela Newhouse later, Mrs. Parry allowed that her husband left her alone a good deal. And she'd sound regretful, as in Paris, of opportunities neglected, experiences missed. There was, for example, a certain Dr. Orlich who'd sometimes drop by the house. "I could have had . . . all sorts of funny little adventures if I'd wanted to," she told Newhouse. There was also a Turkish gentleman, who presided over his elegant shop and its beautiful things, and was "absolutely the most handsome man I had ever seen." She and the maid, Marija, liked to compare notes on him. Of course, with that blond English girlfriend of his, he probably wouldn't have been interested in her. But Milman took no chances: "He just froze that Turk. . . . Somehow he made it impossible for me to ever have a moment to speak with the Turk. I've often wondered what became of him during the war."

Milman was well aware, wasn't he, asked Newhouse, "that you really could be susceptible . . ."

"Well," replied Marian, "that I was human."

But, as in Paris, Marian just soldiered on. "I think he had the better of the whole thing . . . all these adventures. It was much more interesting for him." The kids weren't in school, so she had them "to entertain." And she had the cooking—"because Marija didn't cook. And then I served these people that were doing the transcribing, sandwiches, something in the middle of the morning and something in the afternoon. I think I rather spoiled them. I wasn't interested in them at all, but I did that because I thought it would keep them working better."

*

Saturday, November 9, was "an ordinary day," little Marian noted in her diary, given to chores, arithmetic, French. That evening they went to the movies, where they saw *Chandu the Magician,* an early talkie, along with a newsreel, *The Burial of King Alexander.* The day's entry ended, "Papa is going to Novi Pazzaar tomorrow."

When, in 1954, Albert Lord published the initial volume of *Serbocroatian Heroic Songs,* the first book-length recouping of Parry's Yugoslav investment of twenty years before, he built it around their work in Novi Pazar. Set in a valley along the river Raška, flanked by mountains, "New Bazaar" had for centuries been in the middle of things. Some reckoned it the birthplace of Serbia. From the end of the fourteenth century it was part of the Turkish empire. Albanians and Muslim refugees from wars with neighboring Christian powers had settled there. After the Balkan wars of 1912–13, it was returned to Serbia, then became part of the new

Yugoslavia. In Parry's time, it was a melting pot of ethnic identities in some ways mirroring Yugoslavia as a whole. Its older generation, wrote Lord in "Songs From Novi Pazar," his introduction to the volume, "was born and brought up under Turkish rule, but at a time when the Turkish Empire was . . . in its death throes." Matija Murko had visited after the Great War, encountering in Novi Pazar "a patriarchal way of life that was truly epic, extremely curious, but very hard." And so it had entered Parry's list of potential research sites.

He had stopped there briefly in July, before Lord arrived, and would have gone there again but for Alexander's assassination. Now, in November, with Lord and Nikola, he arrived for a ten-day visit. While there, Lord would write, Parry "first came to realize the importance of the Moslem tradition"; their songs were longer, more embellished than those of the Christian singers—in part, Lord held, because, for so long the ruling class, they'd simply enjoyed the leisure to listen.

"Where we sit, let us make merry, so that God may bring us . . . merriment and good entertainment, and that he may grant us a better lot, both here in this place and in all others!" So began Salih Ugljanin, one of Parry's premier singers, in "The Captivity of Đulić Ibrahim," a "tale of what happened in times long past"—and a tale, inevitably, with echoes of other Serbo-Croatian songs:

After twelve years in a Christian dungeon, Đulić learns from a new inmate that while his true love has resisted marriage all these years, now, with Đulić reported to her as dead, she has been promised to another.

With his comrades, Đulić has suffered greatly. "When I arrived at the bottom of the dungeon," he says, "you should have seen the horror of the icy prison! The reeds grew waist high, and there was cold water up to our knees. . . . The snakes bite us and the scorpions drink our blood. We sing and talk with them for entertainment." Now, though, his pain is immeasurably worse: "Since my love has been betrothed, I shall scream from my white throat!"

Đulić's cry reverberates through the *kula,* in whose dungeon he is imprisoned, frightening the twin children of the *ban,* the prince or viceroy, of Zadar. In a long, disturbing speech, his wife begs him to learn what lies behind Đulić's blood-curdling scream and do something about it. "Either release him, or cut off his head! Dispose of Đulić in some way!"

The *ban* descends to the dungeon himself, hears Đulić's story, and agrees to send him off on a journey to his own country, Udbina: He is to bring back with him Halil, the man who is to wed his love in fifteen days. "You will bring him alive, that I may inflict great torture on him, so that he will not ravage the earth."

At first Đulić cannot go: "Into what a sorry state had Đulić fallen!" His clothes were rotted away. "His hair was so long that he could gird himself with it, and his nails were like plowshares." Finally, though, he sets off. At Đulić's own *kula* in Udbina he is reunited with his mother and, in the stable, his cherished horse: "My chestnut horse, my falcon's wing! Do you not recognize your master!" The horse looked upon Đulić, "and let tears fall."

In the end, Đulić makes short work of "thirty captains and all twenty dukes" among his enemies, slices off the heads of three generals and, finally, that of the *ban* of Zadar himself. The Christian and Muslim armies clash. "When the two forces met, sabers flashed and blood flowed. Men's heads rolled, and dead limbs twitched." Corpses litter the plain, the surrounding hills with heads set on stakes.

In its casual bloodletting, this was about par for Serbo-Croatian epics.

Ugljanin's song was recorded at Novi Pazar on November 24, 1934. We have already encountered its name, "The Captivity of Đulić Ibrahim." But Parry found several songs, by several singers, of the same title and subject. And this very multiplicity, this curious terrain of muddled authorship, was the basis for what Lord would call one of Parry's field experiments: How does a song change from one performance to another? How does it change when it passes from one singer to another, or with the passing of months and years, or when it is spoken rather than sung?

Ugljanin recited the song onto a disc on November 20. He dictated it on November 23. He sang it on the twenty-fourth. They were altogether the same and yet different. Reviewing the differences between two of these versions later, Lord would list seventeen notable variations. In one, Đulić's original capture is described at length; in the other it is omitted altogether. In one, Đulić asks a single long question to which he gets a long, faceted reply; in the other he asks three distinct questions, eliciting three distinct replies. In one, it's the *ban*'s wife who hears

Đulić's screams from the dungeon, not her children. Through just such tangled and disparate oral pathways, Parry's life's work argued, the *Iliad* and the *Odyssey* may have come to be, and probably did.

In Novi Pazar, Parry began to record conversations with the guslars. Their songs were not the sole object of interest now, but they themselves, as creators of song. For each, Parry wanted to know how he had learned, from whom, his tastes in song and singing, his "day job" as farmer or mason. The songs *were* the singers. "By this almost revolutionary idea," wrote Lord a quarter century later, "the camera's eye was shifted to the singer as a composer, and to his problems as such," the singer as object of almost anthropological interest. In the spirit of Ernest Renan, whom he so often quoted, Parry hoped to step into "the moral and intimate life of a people."

Through Nikola he could do so—Nikola, the crucial intermediary and emissary between him and the singers. So central was his role that at least one scholar, Slavica Ranković, came to view Nikola, more than Parry, as the "author" of these crucial conversations. "Managing the 'Boss,'" Ranković entitled her dissection of these delicate three-way interactions. With old Salih Ugljanin, for example, Nikola kids him along, using ingratiating nicknames and "patriarchal terms of deference and endearment . . . , placing himself in the position of instant familiarity, as a curious, loving grandson hungry for his grandfather's stories."

NIKOLA: Which story shall we pick, grandpa?
SALIH: Eh, which? Then you're going to laugh.
NIKOLA: Good! Let it be a bit funny.
SALIH: Well, funny it'll be, but true as well.

Parry remains outside this cozy little bubble. And when he breaks in, he can seem intrusive. At one point, Nikola is drawn away on an errand (to secure an exemption from the ban on singing after Alexander's assassination) and Parry tries recording without him. But "his attempts to imitate Nikola's manner of address are detected by the singer," who, Ranković writes, "finds the collector's requests funny," even desperate; Parry's tone is commanding, but his accent is foreign, his attempts at levity feeble. "While Parry may be the boss," she concludes, "it is Nikola who holds the authority and the singer's confidence." (Of course, as Mrs. Parry would insist, it was her husband with the ability to "pick out a Nikola" in the first place.)

One way or another, the turntables turned and lives were set down on the discs. Like that of Đemail Zogić, thirty-eight, photographed in fez, vest, and the wide ornamented belt of the district, who kept a coffee-house in town—and two wives as well. "They both live with me in Novi Pazar; only we have two apartments," one for each. He had two daughters, one with each wife. "I stay a week with each one. That's the way we live. It's a fine life."

During Ramadan, he recounted, the town's coffee shops, like his, stayed open all night. "There we gather as soon as we have had supper," after dusk. "We gather where there are singers," remaining until *sufur,* the breakfast consumed just before dawn. In the weeks before the Islamic holy month, Zogić recruited singers, offered advances—sometimes a hundred dinars each—to singers most apt to pull in sizeable crowds. And not only to Muslims; some Orthodox Christians came, too. "They order coffee and sit by the singer and like to listen to what happened in the old days, to what the heroes did."

One particularly rich conversation was with the eighty-five-year-old singer of "Đulić Ibrahim," Salih Ugljanin, whose pointy white beard reminded Lord of Greek vase paintings. "His rags do not become the hero poet that he is. Put a sword in his hands and he will brandish it with skill born of long experience."

He was born in Ugao, a village of seventy houses, eight hours on foot from Novi Pazar, a good place to raise cattle. But if it was such a good place, asked Nikola, why leave?

"We quarreled among ourselves and fought and could not find any peace, so I left there and came here. . . . Anger came, and then killing, and afterwards repentance, and there was no good in it. . . ."

The old man had seen his share of warfare. "How many heads have you cut off?" asked Nikola. "Tell me truly, on your honor."

Two or three, replied Salih, two in Montenegro, one in Greece.

"Why did you cut off their heads, Salih?"

"They wanted to cut off mine. . . . We were at war, and they wanted to kill us, and I met their attack and cut them down, by Allah."

And there was one best way to do it, too, Salih added, just the right place for your sword to slice: "Three fingers of hair above the nape of the neck. Then it jumps off like a cap."

It was from Salih that Parry learned of a singer legendary in those parts named Ćor Huso Husein, Blind Huso. "What was his trade?" Nikola asked Salih. "Nothing, he had no trade, nothing but his horse and his arms, and he went about the world. He was blind in one eye and his clothes and arms were of the finest. And he went thus from town to town and sang to everybody to the gusle."

"Nothing more?" asked Nikola.

"He went from kingdom to kingdom and learned and sang."

"Was he a good singer?"

"There could not have been a better."

To Parry, Lord would write, Ćor Huso "symbolized the Yugoslav traditional singer . . . [much as] Homer was the Greek singer of tales par excellence." Some of the best songs Parry collected in Novi Pazar were from singers who had themselves heard, or learned from, Huso.

Or so it was said. As befits so legendary a figure, some would claim that Ćor Huso was just another singer, one who gathered to himself more than his share of story and lore. Or else that he'd never existed at all.

*

In early January, Parry wrote Addison that the winter's snows had blocked roads into the interior; the backcountry towns, rich with native singers, were for now unreachable, so "I must stay a few weeks here at home on the coast." His life slipped into a slower track. He wrote to family. He read some Dickens. In December he had begun to look back upon his work thus far. Now, all through January, putting the logistically straitjacketed moment to good use, he kept at it, dictating his ideas into the Parlograph; the dictaphone he'd used the previous year was little good for scratchy-throated guslars and their whining instruments but fine for ordinary speech. Lord would type them up.

This new project, which Parry foresaw as one day occupying "volumes," never got much beyond pages of notes tied to a brief personal foreword. "Being notes only," Adam apologized for his father, "they have not the refinement of thought we find everywhere in Parry's published work; and as a record of his investigations in the field, they certainly contain much that he would later have modified." As with any first draft, they were hobbled by awkwardness and overstatement. But they plainly mattered to Milman Parry. He gave the nascent work a name, one nodding to the legendary singer he'd learned about through Salih Ugljanin, and so endowed it with a tincture of the heroic. He called it "Ćor Huso: A Study of Southslavic Song."

25

AVDO

In his foreword to "Ćor Huso," Parry looked back on his own scholarly life. He told how, in Paris, Antoine Meillet had observed how gaps in his thesis's edifice of proof might best be breached by an understanding of "a still living oral poetry"; and how Matija Murko, the Slovenian scholar invited to Parry's *soutenance* as an observer, had described a place where it did still live—Yugoslavia.

That is, Parry hadn't gone to Yugoslavia—as to the casual eye it might seem—simply to gather songs, however lively a contribution they might make to folklorists or other scholars. He was there to corroborate his big idea, his life's understanding of how the Homeric epics had come to be. In Yugoslavia he hoped to find something close to proof that "Homer" was what he, Parry, said Homer was; that the epic poetry of Yugoslavia was composed orally in a way that, by analogy and extension, the *Iliad* and the *Odyssey* might be as well; and that he'd be able to see it happen close up in places like Stolac and Novi Pazar.

But before the summer of 1935, a year into his second trip and just two months before heading back to America, Parry didn't have all he wanted. Overall, he had much to show for the year. By the time he was writing "Ćor Huso," certainly, he had grown more tuned to the complex guslaric world around him, his sensibilities more doubting and refined. "No statement made by any singer," he would categorically declare, "can be simply taken at its face value." He looked back to his early days in Dubrovnik, when Pero Arbulić had welcomed him to his home in Konavle, where he had been introduced to Niko Skurić.

"A small man with a large sense of importance," Skurić was a regular at guslar competitions, public events laden with big shots and politicians. These drew competitors, Parry would write, "with operatic voices and a stupendous style of song," making them much "removed from the older life which produced the poems as a natural thing." By the winter of 1935, Parry could see that Skurić and his ilk were empty and inauthentic, indeed, "one of the final stages in the disappearance of the tradition of oral song." He was seeing through new eyes.

A little later, in March, when it was time to write his latest "Report on Work in Yugoslavia," Parry had much to say about his trips in Novi Pazar, Herzegovina, and Bosnia. "The material which we have obtained is excellent both for the purposes of my own conclusions"—that is, the Yugoslav analogy in support of his ideas about Homer—as well as for "its absolute artistic value." He'd return with "a collection of the finest material available in the region of Southslavic song. . . . I believe that I shall bring back to America a collection of manuscripts and discs which is unique in the world for the study of the functioning and life of an oral narrative poetry." He already had more than a thousand recorded discs, almost two thousand texts, of both songs and conversations.

Still, costs had billowed up higher, and this latest report could be seen as one long appeal for money, or patience, or both. He ran a substantial operation, with a team of assistants, five in all—Nikola, Albert Lord, two typists, and a Herzegovinian guslar who transcribed some of the recorded discs. The American Council of Learned Societies had turned him down for an additional grant. The five months remaining on the project had begun to feel urgent and crimped, and he didn't want to waste time courting new grants, writing new applications. Bynum pictures Parry as "in a palpable near-panic that his expedition might fail for want of presentable results to show his financial benefactors." By this harsh reading, "Ćor Huso" could be seen as an effort to milk all he could from the relatively little he'd thus far gathered. Certainly some want of confidence *can* be discerned in Parry's late March appeal: "It is generally felt at home that I have already asked for more money for the present expedition than it is worth. However, my own opinion of the matter may be to the contrary."

Don't cut him short, he begged. "The work of the expedition is now in full swing."

*

Back in the States, Parry had gone to much trouble to secure the best sound-recording equipment he could find. But still it gave him problems, especially its electrical static—a crackle and hiss in the recording that was getting worse. The recorder required 300 volts, fed by a motor-generator set, a sure recipe for static; the design's condensers (capacitors in today's parlance) were supposed to address the problem but didn't, or didn't fully. Parry was forever diddling with the setup and finally threw up his hands, resolving to take it to the Bell Edison works in Zagreb, Croatia's largest city, 350 miles north. In January, they tried to get there, but couldn't get through the snowed-in mountain passes. "In his characteristic headlong way," Bynum would write, "Parry had not foreseen and reckoned with the inevitable winter doldrums of 1934–35. There is nothing accommodatingly gentle about winters in the Dinaric uplands, and the roads into them from anywhere on the Dalmatian coast were totally impassable."

The following month, Parry and Lord undertook a twenty-mile trip by horseback through steep mountain terrain to an ancient fortress mentioned in poetry they'd collected; the horses and guides for the day cost them ninety cents American. After a brief stay in Dubrovnik, they went to Gacko, one of their prime collecting sites, this time with Mrs. Parry, whose feminine presence helped get them into a Turkish home. They saw local women close up, "in their native costumes, both ancient and modern," Lord wrote his parents, "a privilege rarely granted, I can assure you." Then, finally, in late February, through mud and lingering snow, they reached Zagreb.

They'd grown used to paying twenty dinars for a night's lodging in the villages where they stayed, about fifty cents American. But in Zagreb costs ran double that, a substantial load on their strained budget. "So we landed in a flop house near the railroad," Lord wrote home on March 2. "Since then we have spent some time in book-shops, [and] at the Edison laboratories here."

The Edison technicians dispensed with the troublesome motor-generators altogether, replacing them with a battery pack. The result? Static gone and only the voices of the guslars and their instruments reaching the disc—their best recordings yet. On the other hand, success strained their budget. In a letter home on March 7, Lord worried about his job. "I am terribly afraid that Mr. Parry may have to discontinue my salary because of the terrific expense of the new apparatus"—three hundred dollars, more by far than Lord's total salary for the year. Parry was "pretty well discouraged and in a bad state of mind yesterday." Lord thought some more money might be coming in, but "if that is refused, God knows what we shall do." In any case, they'd be off to Bihać, in northernmost Bosnia, in the next day or two.

The songs they collected there that April could sound like so many others they'd recorded previously, for the good and simple reason that they mostly welled up from the same broad epic tradition; it was like Agamemnon or Athena appearing, and reappearing, in one Greek play after another. "I like to think," Lord would write later, "that in 'The Captivity of Sarac Mehmedaga' and in other similar songs in the South Slavic tradition, one is hearing the *Odyssey,* or ancient songs like it, still alive on the lips of men, ever new, yet ever the same."

It bears repeating that the content of these songs, as stories, was not the point, as edifying, inspiring, bloodthirsty, or amusing as they sometimes were. Rather, as Parry wrote in "Ćor Huso" that winter, what he sought in Yugoslavia was what "could be carried over to the Homeric poems." Through close study of South Slavic poetry,

> we can go much further than is possible in the case of the *Iliad* and the *Odyssey,* or of any of the other early poetries of Europe: the actual practice of the poetry itself suggests the hypothesis. . . . We can learn not only how the singer puts together his words, and then his phrases, and then his verses, but also his passages and themes, and we can see how the whole poem lives from one man to another, from one age to another, and passes over plains and mountains and the barriers of speech,—more, we can see how a whole oral poetry lives and dies.

In May, the expedition was back in Bihać for a week, followed by stays in Gacko and Stolac. Then, after returning to Dubrovnik, they were off again, the backseat of the car heaped with recording equipment, driving down the coast through Kotor and its bay, striking inland through "a region of gray rocks and small stone villages," as Lord would recount, and thence across Montenegro, to Podgorica, a substantial town. But "Podgorica yielded nothing of great interest. It is too civilized a place."

After making their way along the vertiginous Morača River canyon, on a road that clung precariously to mountain faces, through tunnels and along switchbacks, the blue-green river hundreds of meters below, Parry and Lord reached Kolašin, reputed to be the native place of Ćor Huso himself. There "we sought eagerly for every trace of his tradition," Lord would write. "What was he like? How did he sing? How did he make his living? How did he die?"

Spread across a valley set in a wide bowl of mountains, Kolašin bore the outward signs of an unremarkable Balkan town surrounded by dairy-farming villages and hamlets; its houses square-sectioned, with high-peaked roofs; its town center boasting a modern hotel, complete with restaurant and sidewalk terrace. Such appearances, however, belied its tortured history. Kolašin had for centuries been the site of battles to free Montenegro from the Ottomans; by the time Parry arrived, few Turks were left. Most of its residents now were Orthodox Christians— "picturesque representatives," Lord called them, "of the heroic tradition which fought for centuries against Islam." Sometimes they still brandished pistols in their broad leather belts, clutched each other as in the old poems—where, as Lord quoted one of them, heroes "stretch forth their arms and embrace between their black eyes, where the gray falcons kiss." "These Montenegrins," a friend lamented to Rebecca West, just arrived in Kolašin later in the 1930s, "they are all heroes, they are boastful imbeciles, like the Homeric heroes."

Parry and his team recorded ten singers and dozens of their songs in Kolašin, including another version of "Marko and Musa" and "The Battle of Kolašin." Their best singer, by Lord's reckoning, was a hollow-cheeked old man with a bristling white mustache named Stanko Pižurica, a reformed bandit.

Then, after ten days, they were off to Bijelo Polje, about thirty miles away, a largely Muslim town of some few thousand set beside the river Lim.

And there, right from the start, it was plain they'd stumbled on treasure. If earlier they might have forgotten just what they were looking for in Yugoslavia, in Bijelo Polje they could not help but remember.

*

It was market day, a sleepy afternoon in late June 1935. The broad plaza, flanked by low tile-roofed buildings, was crowded with hundreds of people, mostly men, wearing small white caps, the *takkiyah,* standing or squatting around bags, baskets, and rude tables of local wares. You could buy anything there, Lord would report, "from a pipe with which the shepherd boys beguile their lonely hours to homemade woolen rugs of intricate and colorful design."

Parry and Lord checked in to a small hotel. Then, looking for singers, they dropped by a two-story *kafana* abutting the plaza and ordered coffee. On a bench near them lounged a tall, lean Turk who held his cigarette in an antique silver holder. Yes, he replied to their query, he did know some local singers. The best of them was a local farmer, living about an hour away, a man in his sixties, Avdo Međedović.

Avdo was sent for. When he arrived, they set him to singing Salih Ugljanin's favorite song, about Baghdad in the days of Sultan Selim. Asked what other epic songs he knew, he recounted his whole repertory. It came to fifty-eight songs.

They arranged to record him the next day, on the second floor of the hotel, which stood beside the plaza. The large room where Parry and Lord slept got the recording apparatus; in a smaller room across the hall, they established a simple studio, with a place for Avdo to sit, a microphone tilted away from the gusle, toward his mouth. A rug was suspended from a rope to dampen echoes from the plaster walls. Wrote Lord:

> We listened with increasing interest to this short homely farmer, whose throat was disfigured by a large goiter. He sat cross-legged on the bench, sawing the gusle, swaying in rhythm with the music. He sang very fast, sometimes deserting the melody, and while the bow went lightly back and forth over the string, he recited the verses at top speed. A crowd gathered. A card game, played by some of the modern young men of the town, noisily kept on, but was finally broken up.
>
> The next few days were a revelation.

On June 27, having arrived in town that morning from Kolašin, Lord had begun a letter to his mother that, several times put aside and resumed, would span several days. By now, after nine months in the field, he sounded like an old Balkan hand. He wrote of his clothes, so tattered and worn he planned to leave them behind. He indulged in a light taxonomic riff on local bugs: Cockroaches wouldn't bother you, fleas were a harmless nuisance, bedbugs demanded a thorough dose of Flit, lice were dangerous, as carriers of typhus: "Everything is drenched with chloroform. We bathe carefully."

Resuming the letter two days later, Lord reported that the morning before, they'd found their beds full of lice and bedbugs. Still, they were staying where they were, "because we found very good material."

Then, the following day: "In fact it's splendid material." He meant Avdo, and his songs.

Over the next six weeks, Avdo Međedović sang nine songs for Parry's much-tinkered-with recording apparatus and dictated four others. Seventeen other singers were recorded in Bijelo Polje. Like eighty-year-old Mustafa Čelebić, who was said to have learned songs from Ćor Huso himself. And Šećo Kolić, just out of prison after serving a term for murder. But it was Avdo who fired Parry's imagination. He had Nikola question him at length about his life. Their conversations filled 180 aluminum discs.

In recent years, Avdo told Nikola, he'd struggled to scrape out a living from his own meager bit of land. Once, though, things had been better. He'd inherited some money from his father and grandfather, and had his own butcher's shop in town. His easy-mannered, "orderly" son, he'd expected, would grow up to run it, leaving him able to comfortably retire. "But it didn't turn out that way," he told Nikola. "No, sir; he turned out to be just a bum and a good-for-nothing," through drinking, gambling, and women, that familiar troika of a young man's dissipation. And no one had whispered to him a word of his son's misdoings. Avdo himself had always had good credit; local merchants would front him money without even an IOU. But then, once his son got his hands on the family business, no one would loan him a dinar. Two years later, the boy left to join the army and Avdo hadn't seen him since.

As a young man, Avdo said, he had himself served in the army, for nine years. In one of the many Balkan conflicts, while serving "on the other side of the mountains, over toward Kolašin," a bullet ripped into his side, then into his arm, shattering it. His account breathed a certain

"We listened with increasing interest," Albert Lord wrote of Avdo Međedović, "to this short homely farmer, whose throat was disfigured by a large goiter. He sat cross-legged on the bench, sawing the gusle, swaying in rhythm with the music."

epic fabulism—on horseback night and day to Sjenica; "a doctor who didn't dare look me in the face" so awful was the wound; teams of four doctors here, a dozen there; finally, shipped by train to Salonika, where surgeons extracted from him a lump of lead. But another remained in his bone, leaving him unable since to raise his left arm. For all that, Avdo reckoned his army years as good ones. Especially for the food, those big tureens of meat and bean stew. The pay wasn't bad, either, enough to save something on. And he learned Turkish. He was twenty-seven when he got out, twenty-nine when he married, to a girl he'd never laid eyes on, the match arranged within the village.

At Parry's behest, Avdo served up this account of his life in late July and early August 1935. Earlier, he had stunned them with the longest epic poem Parry or anyone else had heard in Yugoslavia. The song he sang was based on a much shorter one originally read to him from a published songbook by his friend Hifzo, a fellow butcher; Avdo himself could neither read nor write. "When," as he told Nikola, "the meat gave out"—that is, when he had no butchering to do—"I used to go round and say: 'Hifzo, read me some of that song now, will you?'"

But Hifzo's was the barest skeleton of a song; Avdo gave it flesh, made it into a living thing, with fire, soul, and humanity. For two hours each morning and two in the afternoon, with breaks every half hour for coffee or drink, Avdo sang for Parry and Nikola that one song. And when finally, after a week, his voice broke down, it still wasn't finished. Only after another week's rest could he resume. Avdo and the other singers didn't normally entitle their songs, identifying them simply by subject, hero, or first lines. This one went down in Parry's records as "Osmanbey and Pavičević Luka." At more than thirteen thousand lines, it would be reckoned "the longest complete and continuous oral epic text . . . recorded anywhere in the modern world," almost as long as the *Odyssey*.

Before Avdo, nothing of such scale, grandeur, and goodness had been collected from the more than one hundred singers they'd met in Yugoslavia. Their songs were all worth gathering, yielding important clues about oral composition; "the tradition" depended as much on mediocre singers as on gifted ones. But it was, after all, Homer who had driven Parry to Yugoslavia, in search of songs comparable to those of the master. But no Homer, nothing like a Homer, had yet materialized. Not the previous summer. Not over the past year.

And now, in Bijelo Polje, it had. Or so Albert Lord would maintain all his life.

It is possible that Avdo came to loom even larger in Lord's mind's eye than in Parry's; something like hero worship bubbles through his many writings about him. On the gusle, Avdo's "singing ran ahead of his fingers . . . ; thoughts and words rushed to his mind for expression." Lord would write of his "amazing sensitivity to the feelings of other human beings, sprung from within the singer himself." He was not merely "'preserving the traditional'; Avdo was the tradition." In 1951, Lord would return to Bijelo Polje, renew his acquaintance with Avdo, and have him sing once more the songs he had sung first for Parry in 1935. "He was straining to prove himself," Lord wrote, "but most of all, I believe, he sang it for Milman Parry and Nikola Vujnović, in memory of a peaceful, sunny day so many years before." A photo taken that summer of 1951 in the yard of Avdo's house in Obrov, across the river from Bijelo Polje, shows old Avdo, with his dark eyes and great white mustache, leaning back onto a rock, one knee slung easily over the other, squarely facing the camera. Lord, wearing a white-collared, Western-style shirt, squats beside him, perched, somehow, on his left heel, looking earnestly across the frame of the photo to Avdo—a boy at the old man's elbow, ever the acolyte.

In 1935, barely a year out of college, still Parry's clerk-typist, Lord might be expected to embrace the notions of his mentor. And yet, what *exactly* did Parry think? Except at one remove, through Lord, we can't say for sure. Because three months after Avdo's voice and the twang of his gusle had been set down on aluminum discs, not yet transcribed or translated, Parry was dead. None of what little Parry wrote in the last months of his life speaks of Avdo. "Ćor Huso" offers nothing; it was the product of a moment in the expedition six months earlier. His progress reports likewise all came long before he met Avdo.

But Lord gives us reason to think Avdo Međedović really was Parry's Chosen. In Avdo, Lord would write, "Parry found what he had searched for throughout the country, a singer of tales who could produce songs as long as the *Iliad* and the *Odyssey*." Parry made much of Avdo, expected much from him. He encouraged him, Lord reports, "to rest whenever necessary, and to sing as long a song as he could." And, indeed, it was to plumb Avdo's seemingly preternatural talent that Parry concocted one of his more intriguing experiments.

Another singer he'd recorded in Bijelo Polje was Mumin Vlahovljak, whose claimed repertory of songs included a substantial one, "Bećiragić Meho," of several thousand lines. Parry established that Avdo had never heard it and had Vlahovljak sing it while Avdo listened. When Vlahovljak was done, Parry turned to Avdo. Could he sing it now? Maybe even better than Mumin?

Having heard it precisely once, Avdo did just that.

In Avdo's version, the original story was all there, but now, much enriched, there was more to it, winding up three times as long. "The ornamentation and richness accumulated, and the human touches of character," wrote Lord, "imparted a depth of feeling that had been missing in Mumin's version." Of the song's unhappy hero, Avdo sings that "his heart was wilted like a rose in the hands of a rude bachelor."

It was a song rich with a hero's sufferings. "To those who have ears to hear," wrote Lord, it was reminiscent "of Odysseus in the court of Alcinous, recounting his wanderings and . . . misfortunes."

*

About forty years after Parry's trip to Yugoslavia, a song called "The Wedding of Smailagić Meho" would be published by Harvard University Press in two volumes—in Serbo-Croatian as Avdo recited it in 1935 and in English translation by Albert Lord. This was the song, of all those in Avdo's repertoire, and of all those Parry had heard in Yugoslavia, that came closest to validating, at one stroke, Parry's claims for the roots of the *Odyssey* and the *Iliad*.

After a brief introduction, or *pripjev,* Avdo's "Meho" begins:

> Now to you, sirs, who are gathered here I wish to sing the measures of a song, that we may be merry. It is a song of the olden time, of the deeds of the great men of old and the heroes on both sides in the time when Sulejman the Magnificent held empire. Then was the empire of the Turks at its highest. Three hundred and sixty provinces it had, and Bosnia was its lock, its lock it was and its golden keys, and a place of all good trust against the foe.

The song, as we take it in through Albert Lord's translation, tells of young Meho, favored son of Smail, who enjoys all riches but by age twenty has achieved nothing of note and remains unmarried. The story begins at a gathering of local royalty and leaders—"thirty beys, the chief men of all the city of Kanidža, and four and twenty of the sultan's agas"—their weapons and finery sumptuously on display, all at their ease, proud and happy, save for Meho.

> Meho, the hadji's son, was unhappy. His fair face was saddened, his black eyes downcast. He looked as though he had just buried his father or his uncle, Cifric Hasan. His hands were thrust into his sash. He looked as if he were dying. He drank neither wine nor brandy, nor did he draw upon his pipe, or say a single word.

All around him have much to crow about. One

> boasts how he has broadened the border, another, my son, of taking a captive. One boasts how well he has wed, another how he shall wed. One boasts of his son, another of his daughter or his sister or his brother's daughter. All are merry, not one is sad. But you, my star, why are you so sorrowful?

This litany of ritualistic boasting is just the problem: Meho has nothing to contribute. "I have known nothing of raiding or campaigning, not to mention single combat. The broadening of borders is unknown to me. I do not even know where the border is." He likens himself to a woman, rebukes his father and uncle for failing to instruct him in the arts of war. His shame and self-reproach are painful to listen to.

In the wake of this sad scene, Meho's father is persuaded that the time has come to pass command from his own weakening grip to his son's. Meho must travel to Buda—on the Danube's west bank, today's Budapest—to see the vizier, thought to be loyal to the sultan. But the vizier is anything but. He is the vilest of villains, master of deceit, in league with the Christians.

There is much more to it. As Lord deftly distills the rest of the long, richly ornamented story, full of Machiavellian intrigue, Meho becomes a worthy hero: "He kills the treacherous vizier and the vizier's henchmen; he saves a maiden; he restores law and order in Budapest, and brings exiles back from Persia."

That an illiterate Muslim singer, a butcher by trade, could sit down and recite thousands of lines of verse, forming a colorful and substantial work that might reasonably be compared with Homer, helped corroborate Parry's ideas about the origins of Homer and, more broadly, about the legitimacy and worth of orally composed poetry.

Even before the 1934–35 expedition, Parry had discerned parallels between the Yugoslav epics and those of Homer, as he had pointed out in his "Whole Formulaic Verses" paper the year before. But after that first summer, his "Yugoslav analogy" was still based mostly on written texts, especially those collected by Vuk Karadžić a century before, and hardly at all from what he'd gathered from his own first trip.

The second trip changed all that. After fifteen months in Yugoslavia and the accumulation of great troves of material, and especially in his discovery and appreciation of Avdo Međedović as a latter-day Homer, Parry could stake his claim for a far stronger Yugoslav analogy. As we'll see, by the time he and his family, bound for home, boarded the Italian Line ship *Conte Grande* in September 1935, the elements were in place for the extension and expansion of this one slice of Homeric studies into a new humanistic discipline.

PART SIX

Memorial

26

AT THE PALMS HOTEL

When the Parrys arrived back in Cambridge, Marian's mother wasn't there to meet them. She was in Los Angeles now, living on Whitley Terrace, in a stunning, Mediterranean-styled house once home to the French actor Maurice Chevalier, perched on a verdant hillside across the valley from the Hollywood Bowl. She was living beyond her means, and she needed help. *Please come, immediately,* she all but begged her daughter. A friend counseled Marian: "I wouldn't go just because she said you should." But after arranging for someone to take care of the children in Cambridge, Marian headed for L.A.

Marian's relationship with her mother, we've seen, had always figured large in her life, and still did. When she was twelve, Marian helped hand out her mother's suffragist pamphlets. A few years after Marion's father died in 1916, Mildred had shepherded her to Berkeley, where they attended classes and lived together. Later, when Marian gave birth, her mother returned to California to help care for her and the baby. When the Parrys got back from France, Milman traveled to California, while Marian went to Milwaukee; her mother had sublet a house for her and the children for the summer. "My mother, you see, really was awfully good to me," she'd tell Newhouse.

Now, in fall 1935, with her mother in financial distress, Marian headed out to the coast—November 12 is the best guess—to help her. On the sixteenth, Milman wrote Addison in Berkeley a note reporting that "Marian is now in Lost [*sic*] Angeles—address 6680 Whitley Terrace, Hollywood. You should write her and find out when she is coming up to Berkeley. I should like to get out to California next summer, but I fear it must be the Albanians for me," a reference to what promised to be the next phase of his Balkans research. That is, he didn't expect to get out to California even by the following summer, eight months hence.

But in fact, he was in California a few days later.

*

The trip to California ended with Parry's death. "No one could go very far in studying Parry's life without some thought about the strange aspects of his death," Sterling Dow would observe in the 1960s. In all the years since, rumor, legend, and surmise about the last days of Milman Parry have never abated.

The day after he wrote Addison from Cambridge, Parry was to give a talk about Yugoslav folk songs in the Kirkland House common room. The next day, November 18, he wrote a Classics colleague, Arthur Stanley Pease, about his impression of a student's paper, probably a thesis in progress. It had far to go, he said, but "I believe we can let him go ahead without feeling any uneasiness." On the twenty-second, he was supposed to give a lecture. He was also said to be at work on a paper he planned to give at an American Philological Society meeting in New York in late December. In short, academic business as usual.

Then Parry vanished. "Suddenly and unexpectedly," in the words of one account, he was gone from Cambridge, and off for California. Asked later about it, John Finley said he "did not know the reason for the hurried trip across the continent." Others didn't realize he was gone at all. "I had sent a message [that] I wanted Milman to come to Los Angeles," Marian would say later, "because I felt my mother's situation wasn't good." Not good because Mildred had managed to wreck her personal finances and now faced a crisis.

Her granddaughter, the younger Marian, would remember Mildred, mostly from a later period, as "a good-natured, pig-headed, weak-minded lady . . . , fat and friendly and diffuse, easily taken in." Mildred had grown up in substantial wealth but, according to Mrs. Parry, had by now blown much of it. She'd bought second mortgages on houses in Chicago she'd never even seen, Mrs. Parry reported in wonder to Newhouse; then, with the Depression, people couldn't pay and Mildred refused to foreclose on them. Now, by the fall of 1935, perhaps com-pounded by illness, her situation had worsened. "She started spending her money in a very wild way," said Marian: " 'Well,' she'd say, 'I have to live.'" And now, Parry family lore converges to suggest, some breed of L.A. lowlife was after what remained of her wealth. According to Mil-man's granddaughter, Laura Feld, the aim of the Los Angeles trip was to remove Mildred "from the clutches of those crooks." According to Laura's brother, Andrew, Milman may have packed a handgun for his trip west, as protection against, or intimidation of, them. Closer to the events, in the 1960s, Harry Levin told Sterling Dow of some "quack," or other unsavory, underworld character, intent on cleaning her out and that, in Dow's summary, "it was to end this menace" that Milman and Marian went to Los Angeles.

So, Marian urgently wrote Milman: *Come.* And he did—though exactly when, and by what means and by which route, remains unclear. The train, which could get you across the country in three or four days, is the most likely candidate. But Parry completed a later leg of the same trip, from San Francisco to L.A., by air, and conceivably he traveled from Cambridge across the country the same (expensive) way. Air travel was not yet routine but was finally beyond its commercial infancy; the airline industry carried 6,000 passengers in 1930, but more than 450,000 by 1934, on its way to more than a million by 1938. Two airports served the Los Angeles area, one the forebear of LAX, one in Burbank. Early propeller-driven planes, like the Boeing 247, the company's showcase exhibit at the 1933 Chicago World's Fair, or the fourteen-passenger Doug-las DC-2, were noisy, slow, and cold. Still, they were reliable enough that Parry might have gotten across the country, with refueling stops about every eight hundred miles, in a few days, reaching the coast as early as, say, November 24.

One scenario that fits much of the incomplete and contradictory evidence of the last two weeks of Parry's life is that Milman traveled straight from Boston to L.A., joining Marian there, perhaps seeing Mil-dred at the Whitley Terrace house, if she was still there; or at an apart-ment house on Ocean View Avenue, cited in a later document, to which they might have moved her, or planned to move her, to help ease her financial problems. "We had said good-bye to Mother," Marian would say. "She didn't know that this plan of arranging for someone to take care of her affairs was afoot at all." By this scenario, after three or four days, perhaps around the twenty-eighth, Milman and Marian together went up to San Francisco.

While in suddenly leaving Cambridge for the coast Milman can seem to have responded in the spirit of Marian's sense of urgency, his actions weren't entirely precipitate; he did, apparently, request a brief leave of absence from Harvard for a week or two—in order, it was said, to visit an ill family member. And he devoted much of the next two weeks not to Mildred in Los Angeles but to personal and professional interests in the Bay Area. Around November 30, Parry saw his sister Addison, who remembered him, in her relentlessly upbeat way, fairly "bubbling over with joy," as he regaled her with stories about sipping coffee with Turks in the Balkans. Their father lived in San Francisco, and Parry likely saw him, too. The Philological Association of the Pacific Coast was meeting at Stanford University from November 29 to 30, and Parry's former professor at Cal George Calhoun was giving its presidential address; conceivably, Parry attended that. And Parry certainly did visit another of his old professors, Ivan Linforth. They met at Linforth's house in Berkeley, talked in the garden. In Dow's clipped summary, Linforth reported that Parry "seemed happy, quiet, composed."

Seven years after dispatching to him a fresh copy of his Paris thesis, with its telling accompanying note, Parry also saw Alfred Kroeber. "We came up to Berkeley to see our old friends," Marian would report, "and Milman made the point of going to see Kroeber," with whom he talked extensively. He had "a very definite reason" for seeing him—but, maddeningly, she doesn't say what it was. In her rambling interviews with Pamela Newhouse, Marian did not always follow the most direct pathways of memory into the past, but here she left little doubt that in Kroeber her husband found intellectual or professional communion.

All this played out five hundred miles up the coast from L.A., in San Francisco and environs, never far from the little houses in the Oakland flats where Parry had grown up. At some point early in the California trip, Milman telegraphed word home, to James R. Ware, a Harvard lecturer and friend, that they might not be back until December 17, apparently a date beyond which he had first planned.

On Monday, December 2, Milman and Marian left San Francisco by plane for Los Angeles. If the promised seventeenth date for their return controlled their schedule, that allowed them two weeks for completing their business in Southern California and getting back to Cambridge. They may have briefly seen Mildred again, but just now they were actually bound for San Diego, to visit Milman's sister Lucile and her family; in 1930, Lucile had married Ramiel Youngjohn and settled on a citrus farm in El Cajon, outside San Diego.

The facts coming down to us don't supply irrefutable validation to all these details of the last two weeks of Parry's life. What is certain, however, is that now, on the afternoon of December third, Milman and Marian were in Los Angeles, staying at a hotel on South Alvarado Street, dressing for their trip to San Diego later that day.

*

The hotel in which Milman Parry died, the Palms, changed much across the twentieth and early-twenty-first centuries. It started out in the early 1920s as a pretty, modestly scaled four-story hotel designed by a University of Pennsylvania–trained architect better known for the big Westlake Theater a few doors down from the hotel. By the 1940s and '50s, it had morphed into the larger, grander Palms-Wilshire. During a grim period in the 1970s it fell from grace, becoming a decrepit, single-room-occupancy hotel, part of the city's "Skid Row West," a little out of downtown. Then, some years into the new century, it was gutted, neatly refurbished as a home for local indigents, and renamed Parkview-on-the-Park. All the while, a few constants held. One was the distinctive arch that marked the building's entrance on South Alvarado Street. Another was the recurring, apparently irresistible aesthetic or promotional urge to photograph the hotel framed by the palm trees of Westlake Park, today's MacArthur Park, across the street.

Around 1925, the original hotel at 622 South Alvarado, the Park Vista, was doubled in size, an all but identical sister structure grafted onto it. That became the Palms, at 626, a mirror-image duplicate. So around the time Milman and Marian checked in on the morning of December 2, it was actually two connected hotels, a hidden alley running between them. The double-winged blond brick structure fronted about one hundred feet on Alvarado and reached back almost twice that far from the street—room after room, two hundred in all, each going

The Palms Hotel on South Alvarado Street in Los Angeles, where Milman Parry died of a gunshot wound.

for two or three dollars a day, lined up along the halls of each wing. Banks of fire escapes and iron balconies draped down the front of the building. A spacious lobby, all mirrors, carpets, and drapes, the check-in desk toward the back, greeted one's entry from the busy street. The result, thanks to the park, with its tall palm trees, set in a green hollow across the street, was almost worthy of its advertised boast as "a bit of the country in the heart of town." The Palms was never one of the grande dames of the Los Angeles hotel world. But if it enjoyed anything like a heyday, it was probably about now, when Mr. and Mrs. Parry, needing a room after getting off the plane from San Francisco and bound for San Diego, checked in.

*

As they were dressing, early in the afternoon of Tuesday, December 3, Milman called to his wife in the next room, asking where an article of his clothing, apparently his underwear, was. She told him.

Rummaging through his luggage, Milman, naked above the waist, jostled a handgun wrapped among his clothes.

The gun went off.

A bullet struck him in the heart.

He died a little while later.

This represents the official version of what happened, a distillation or adaptation of which went out in many, otherwise often inconsistent, news stories the next day. It was incorporated into the Los Angeles Coroner's report the day after that. "Homicide" and "suicide"—both physically inked out—were rejected as possibilities.

It may have happened just this way. But it may not have.

At 1:45 p.m., Marian called the hotel desk; according to a later report, hotel staff first supposed that she had killed him. At 2:30, the police were called. Two detective lieutenants, both seasoned homicide professionals, responded. One was B. L. Jones, LAPD badge 374. The other was beefy-faced Eddie Romero, badge 276, probably the senior man; Romero came from a family of LAPD cops, and from time to time found his picture in the paper, at a murder trial or crime scene. They talked with Mrs. Parry. They examined the evidence. They concluded Parry's death was an accident. By 3:30—just an hour after the police were called—Parry's body was at the morgue. No autopsy was performed. He was cremated on December 5.

From the beginning, inconsistencies and contradictions dogged reports of the incident. By one account, the pistol discharged when it fell from the suitcase. In another, detectives found it still in Parry's luggage, within its holster, wrapped in a shirt that bore evidence of powder burns. In a third it was a revolver that went off, in a fourth an "automatic," meaning a semiautomatic pistol, somewhat more liable to accidental discharge. In one report, Mrs. Parry, in the bathroom, didn't even hear the gun go off, being alerted to the accident only by the "groans" of her husband a few moments later. In another, a "muffled report" alerted her.

Haphazard, deadline-driven news reporting can be blamed for some of these inconsistencies. But that Parry could die in such a lamentable, entirely unheroic way cried out for surer explanation. So sad and stupid a death. For a scholar of Homer who had ventured into the mountains of Yugoslavia for the sake of knowledge, who held up the epics for their nobility and grandeur, to die like this?

"Most people who know anything about him," wrote Sterling Dow of Parry three decades after his death, "believe, without adequate basis, that he committed suicide. What is known of the circumstances encourages this notion without establishing it as true." When Dow took up the torch of sorting out Parry's death in 1964, and again when he spoke with Pamela Newhouse in 1981, it was suicide with which he seemed preoccupied. It had become, he said, the prevailing theory, built on the supposition that Parry had been denied a permanent slot at Harvard, fallen into suicidal depression, and thus been moved to take his own life. Today, as then, suicide is sometimes bruited about as fact, without qualification.

At Harvard, Parry had occupied the position of instructor from 1929 to 1932, then been named assistant professor of Greek and Latin in 1932 for a three-year term, his colleagues in the Classics department reporting to the dean that Parry "richly deserves this promotion." At Harvard, he'd hardly been put upon, but if anything had been a little coddled. He'd enjoyed a rare full-year leave in Yugoslavia, a venture that had worked out successfully in the end and that promised rich fruits of knowledge in the coming years. As we've seen, he published regularly, more than most of his colleagues. When Parry died, Harvard president James Conant noted that "by his death, the University loses one of its most promising younger scholars." A colleague, Charles Gulick, called him "one of the most brilliant scholars we have ever had here." At a meeting of the senior members of the Department of Classics on October 16, 1935, six weeks before his death, the vote was 8–0 in favor of granting Parry a second three-year term.

But could anything from this chorus of approval be heard as a dark note, reason for him to be depressed?

Only, I think, from one exceedingly narrow, sharply defined standpoint—that in December 1935 Parry did not yet have the perfect security of a permanent job; promotion to associate professor would have amounted to tenure, a lifetime appointment, and he did not yet have that. No matter that he was only age thirty-three; that even at the end of this second three-year term, he'd still be just thirty-six. Dow reports hearing from Harry Levin that the department was "likely to have acted favorably" in the end. But the bare, brute residue of job insecurity might, conceivably, have been cause for disappointment.

In 1964, Dow devoted several pages of notes to the possibility of Parry's suicide, at one point methodically laying out reasons for and against. In the former category, Dow included Parry's situation at Harvard. And he cited a rumor of homosexuality, from some unnamed Yugoslav "informant"; conceivably the revelation of such a shameful truth in Los Angeles—this is Dow's imagined scenario, for which he offers no evidence—might have led Milman to take his life. Then again, maybe Parry suffered from a classic Lawrence of Arabia syndrome, with death at an early age, at the top of one's form, seen as somehow fitting. Above all, there was the bare *fact* of Parry's sudden death; that is, as Dow wrote later, "The very circumstances of the death, without hints from anyone, suggested suicide."

In 1971, a reviewer of Parry's collected works referred, in the British journal *New Statesman,* to Parry's "somewhat mysterious early death in 1935." Adam and sister Marian wrote the editor, specifically referring to the "widely inferred" conclusion that their father's death was a suicide, though

> no one has, to our knowledge, suggested a plausible motive for suicide. We (his son and daughter) have at the time of the misfortune many years ago, and more recently, considered seriously

both Milman Parry's character and the specific circumstances of his death, and have concluded with a reasonable degree of certainty that that death was in fact an accident.

None among those Dow contacted in 1964 imagined Parry killing himself or saw in him any hint of depression—not Linforth, not Addison Parry, Harry Levin, or Lord. Lord told Dow that Parry gave no sign of having suffered disappointment at Harvard's hands. Addison told Dow, "He was too fond of living, always eager to see what would come next." The prospect "seemed so ridiculous, it hasn't ever troubled us." Another of Dow's informants, John B. Titchener, wrote: "I know of no man who had less reason—to my knowledge—to commit suicide."

Indeed, that seems to me the least likely way to explain what happened at the Palms that December afternoon.

In 1964, when he was Sather Professor at Cal, six months after having first discovered Parry's master's thesis and becoming interested in the circumstances of Parry's death, Sterling Dow asked a colleague of his at UCLA, Albert Travis, for a favor: "It would be a service to the history of American scholarship," he wrote Travis, whose PhD was from Harvard, "to have the facts [surrounding Parry's death] carefully recorded for the future. At present there is only ignorance and gossip." It occurred to him that he, Travis, "a Classicist, a person of standing in the community, and an officer of the University, might be in a unique position" to do so.

Travis did his best to oblige. He tracked down the coroner's report and gathered much other information, but was forced to report that the police department's records of the investigation from almost thirty years before no longer existed, and that both Romero and Jones, the two investigating officers, were dead. The police had presumably sifted the evidence, they had reached a conclusion: Parry had died in a tragic accident, case closed.

But then again—and he chose to lavish on this single, telling observation its own separate paragraph—Travis added:

There may be an insurmountable obstacle of tact [to his saying so], but it would seem to me that the historian's essential informant turns out to be identical with that of the police, Marian Parry.

That is, the world's understanding of what happened at the Palms that day—as told first to the police, working its way into news reports over the ensuing days, and finally forming the basis of the historical record—rested on the assertions of Mrs. Parry and, it seems, hers almost alone.

A photograph of her, taken soon after Parry's death by an Acme News photographer, was accompanied by this caption:

WIDOWED BY CHANCE SHOT

Mrs. Milman Parry, who was widowed in Los Angeles, recently, when her husband, in a tragic example of professorial absent-mindedness, accidentally shot himself to death. The accident occurred, apparently, when Professor Parry forgot that the safety catch on a revolver in his suit case was released, and that the revolver had been wrapped in a shirt.

This, of course, sheds no light on what actually happened except that the cliché of the absent-minded professor was ready at hand, like a Homeric formula.

Mrs. Parry seems to have been caught unawares, her attention momentarily drawn to the camera, when the flashbulb illuminates her in its white glare and the shutter clicks. She wears a small cloche-like hat, perched at an angle, brim drawn down over one eye, in the style of the time, and what seems to be a heavy, dark winter coat; the photo is dated December 7; she may already be back in New England. Her lips are pursed. Her hair peeks out from under her hat in disarray. Her eyes, peering at us sideways, reluctantly, speak distrust, or fear. Read one way, she looks guilty as hell. Read another, she simply looks grim.

Errors, contradictions, and variations in emphasis pepper the news accounts of Parry's death. But one detail makes its way, almost without exception, into every account—that Marian had been in another room when it happened, she rushing in to find her husband on the floor, dead or dying. The *Los Angeles Times* said that. So did that the *Los Angeles Examiner*. So did the wire services. Of course, Dow would write, Mrs. Parry could hardly be conceived as a credible suspect: She was "questioned at length by the police. No one, I think, could suspect her; the choice is between suicide and accident. . . ."

Mrs. Parry, caught in the glare of a news photographer's flashbulb, a few days after her husband's death.

But someone *could* suspect her, and did. Right from the start the universe of possibility had been wider than it seemed to Dow, and included murder: Milman Youngjohn, son of Milman's sister Lucile, reports his mother telling him that "police came storming into the room, wanted to arrest Marian, saying, 'You murdered him,'" resolving otherwise only later. "But they originally thought that Marian had done it." When in his notes Dow again referred to the possibility, he dismissed it out of hand: "It would be hard anyway to believe she would [kill her husband]. She is not, one feels, that sort of person"—though, he allowed, there was some "estrangement" between husband and wife.

In her interviews with Mrs. Parry in 1981, Pamela Newhouse developed a fascination with the Parry marriage; she could hardly have not, as Marian herself returns to their marriage repeatedly. At one point she tells Newhouse: "Before this happened, before he died, I was thinking that, you know, he just meant everything to me. . . . He fulfilled all these different roles of husband and companion and father and just everything. And I was much more at that time in love with him, I think, than possibly he was with me."

But this is the exception: Mrs. Parry never frames her memories of Milman as criticism, yet they usually come out that way. Again and again, across those three days, bubbling up from the free and seemingly uninhibited flow of her thought, Milman emerges as coldly single-minded, distant and unmoved, heedless of her needs, interests, or happiness. Whether in Paris, Cambridge, or Dubrovnik, Marian is left to feel lonely and ignored.

In her conversation with Newhouse, Marian periodically *realizes,* as if surprising even herself, how it sounds: She drifts into reverie, hears her insistent criticisms as they surface, catches herself, vows to rebalance her portrait of her husband, but never quite manages: On page 32 of the transcript, remembering where the interview had broken off the day before, she says, "I wanted to tell you some nice things about our marriage but it's really terrible the way I made it sound, so awful."

On page 55, having referred to Milman's seeming lack of attention to her problems on Shepard Street: "I'm awfully afraid that maybe I've said so many bad things."

On page 57: "I'm so scared that now I've told you these things in such a terrible way that maybe this will discourage you"—that is, discourage Newhouse from pursuing Milman's biography. Plainly, their

marriage had been troubled, Marian often left unhappy and, at some
level, surely, angry.

Angry enough to kill her husband?

Among the Parry children, eleven and seven at the time of his death,
that their mother might have killed Milman was, at least in later years,
taken seriously; this despite their joint letter to the editor of *New Statesman* in 1971. Young Marian, her relationship with her mother twisted by
a lifetime's enmity, held to this conviction all her life. Her son, Andrew,
grew up hearing her many times assert as much and, over the course of
years, give reasons for it. There was, first of all, the pain of the women
Milman presumably saw in Paris, Mrs. Parry being stashed away in the
suburbs with their little girl to make his liaisons easier. And his promise
to help her return to school to get the degree that their marriage, and
his studies, had frustrated; it never happened. "You don't actually miss
him, do you?" Mrs. Parry is said to have once sneered at her daughter,
who was crying for the loss of her father. As for the "accident" that was
supposed to have killed him, she didn't believe it for a second. Milman,
so adept with technical gear, would pack a gun, *loaded, the safety off,* in
his luggage, then forget about it?

Of course, if Marian did kill her husband, it need not have emerged
from plot or plan, but, conceivably, in a sudden fit of fury. At least
in later years, children and grandchildren would attest, Mrs. Parry was
capable of terrible rages, erupting sometimes with no apparent provo-
cation. From what he'd heard of these eruptions from his mother, says
Andrew Feld, they were "literally insane, where she would have no
memory of having been in that state," in which she would "scream and
beat our mother."

Letters years later between Adam and Marian the younger, now
grown, draw a picture of their mother as frustrated, paranoid, unbal-
anced, and prone to just such fits of uncontrollable anger. In one letter,
Marian pictures her as "trembling with anguish" over the ups and downs
of a stock she owned:

> She started out talking to me in a fairly friendly fashion but as
> the conversation went along I could hear that the sound of my
> voice was activating the old loathing. There is a curiously invol-
> untary quality to her hatred of me; it's like a spirit which enters
> & possesses her & and over which she has not control.

Stephen Parry, Adam's son, tells of dinner at Mrs. Parry's house in Berkeley when he was a teenager. Stephen rather liked his grandmother, found her quirky, clever, and warm, appreciated that she indulged his interests and enthusiasms. And yet, he adds, "there was a nasty side to her personality." At dinner this time, at some adolescent breach of etiquette—he apparently took too sizeable a portion of lamb to suit her—Marian abruptly raged at him, literally threw him out of the house, leaving him to find a place to sleep that night on his own; he never saw her again. Could she have killed her husband? "I don't think that's entirely implausible," he says.

There is no direct evidence to suggest this happened. Two experienced LAPD detectives, at the scene of Milman's death, with an opportunity to talk with Mrs. Parry themselves, at least briefly, did not consider her culpable. Moreover, the seeming improbability of the accident—jostled luggage setting off a revolver whose safety had not been set, its barrel just happening to precisely align with Milman Parry's heart—doesn't prove homicide; many stranger accidental handgun deaths have happened. On the other hand, the possibility cannot be discounted. Conceivably, they argued over something, perhaps over her mother, perhaps over a lifetime of heaped-up marital disharmony, and things got out of hand, Milman's suitcase with its holstered gun looming open before them, Marian getting her hands on it first.

In considering Parry's possible suicide, Sterling Dow at one point wonders whether, issues of insurance or unwelcome publicity at stake, Mrs. Parry could have "persuaded the officers it was an accident." The question, of course, grants Mrs. Parry agency—as someone who, at a stressful moment, her husband lying dead, the police grilling her, could have put her rhetorical and feminine powers to work against a ruling of suicide. But if she could do that, as Dow for the moment entertains, could she not as well have done so in her own defense, artfully deflecting attention from herself?

So maybe it was an accident. But if not, that Marian killed Milman Parry seems far more likely than that he killed himself.

*

Christine Henry, the daughter of Milman's sister Lucile and older sister of Milman Parry Youngjohn, who was fourteen in 1935, recalls how the Parrys were supposed to be visiting them in El Cajon for a few days, that the prospective visit, coming in December, carried a whiff of Christmas fete, and that her mother had much prepared for it. On December 3, her father, Ramiel Youngjohn, drove to San Diego, a distance of about twenty miles, to pick them up—only to be paged once he'd arrived and informed that the Parrys weren't coming, that his brother-in-law was dead.

Word of Parry's death reached Harvard and Cambridge almost immediately, with condolence letters addressed to Marian dated as early as the next day:

> This is too dreadful for words.
>
> . . .
>
> I have no words with which to express my feeling. I can only send to you my love and most understanding sympathy.
>
> . . .
>
> It seems so completely incomprehensible. How can it be. . . . It is simply unbelievable!

Harvard's Classics department voted to convey to Mrs. Parry its "sympathy and deep sense of loss in the death of assistant professor Milman Parry, her husband, who shot himself accidentally on Tuesday, December 3, in . . ."—mistaken facts were already drifting into the world—". . . San Francisco, Calif." Practically every news account differed in large ways or small from all the others. A single *Boston Globe* article misspelled Mrs. Parry's maiden name; made Milman two years older than he was; said he was born in San Francisco, not Oakland; made him a graduate of UCLA; said he became assistant professor only in 1933; and made him "an authority on Horace," which he was not.

A memorial service was held at Appleton Chapel, at the north end of Harvard Yard, on December 19, at which C. B. Gulick of Harvard Classics sang Parry's praises. Two months later, Parry's friend John Finley wrote of the event to Parry's father: "The ceremony held here in the college chapel was a very beautiful one and, as such, fitting . . . [suffused] with dignity and feeling. To his many friends the ceremony was a great comfort." Many of Parry's books were being placed in the library with commemorative bookmarks. Provision was being made "for the carrying on of his work."

Yet such steps, however fitting, give little comfort. It is impossible to replace his keen mind and noble, decisive spirit. To myself he had been for many years an inspiration as a scholar and a constant source of joy as a friend. The future here, which was brightened by the prospect of his companionship, seems darker now. Nevertheless, his life could hardly have been more perfect even if it had been much longer. He was known, respected, and admired in the way that few men are who die after a long life.

There was one more thing about which Finley advised Isaac Parry, if he didn't know of it already: Marian and the children had left Cambridge. "The climate is bad here, living expensive, and social life restless and uncertain because all are busy. There is therefore much to be said for their living in California."

It was as if Marian couldn't wait to get away from Cambridge and the anti-Semitism and elitism that wounded her there. She gave away many of Milman's books and records and left for Berkeley, where she and the children would live in a modest cottage on Dwight Way, easy walking distance from the Cal campus. That summer she took a few classes and then, in the fall, enrolled for a full load of four French classes, earning A's in all of them. By the following May she had secured the bachelor's degree, with honors, from which married life had deflected her fourteen years before.

27

THE HOUSE OF ACADEME

After his death, whatever was to be made of Milman Parry's work rested on the shoulders of Albert Lord.

In later years, and in most settings, Lord never spoke much of Parry. One of his graduate students, Margaret Beissinger, would depict Parry's death as "almost a taboo topic" with him: "I never really dared to speak to him about Parry in personal terms." To quiz him for details would have been "just so out of bounds." In his courses on oral epic, Lord invariably returned to the theme of the "death of the companion," as in Achilles and Patroclus of the *Iliad;* Beissinger and her classmates instinctively grasped that it "figured prominently in Lord's life when he lost Parry."

Referring to their growing-up years in the 1960s and '70s, Lord's children allude to similar sensitivities. "My family is very reserved," said Nate Lord, the older son; his parents were "old-school, reserved, polite." Their father never spoke of Parry's death; "that would have been enormously painful" to him. But Parry had exerted a deep and lasting hold on him. So, professionally, his father was driven to complete and extend Parry's work, which bore "a sense of mission."

December 1936 marked a year since Parry's death. At a meeting of the American Philological Association in Chicago, Lord, then just twenty-four, gave a paper devoted to "The Singer's Rests in Homer and Southslavic Heroic Song." He'd worked it up, he explained, from an abstract Parry prepared before his death, and from Parry's unpublished notes.

The customary division of the *Odyssey* and the *Iliad* into twenty-four books each—the chapters, or "chants," to which almost all editions and translations of the epics still adhere—went back to third-century BCE Alexandria, hundreds of years after Homer is thought to have lived. These traditional chapter breaks never made much sense to him, Parry wrote in "Ćor Huso"; he entitled his notes "The Falsity of the Notion of the Chants of the Homeric Poems." To him, they seemed arbitrary, and meant nothing to the singers. Like Victor Bérard, he had wondered what might be other, presumably more natural divisions in the texts, but never found any: "It was only when the Southslavic poetry showed me the actual practice of a sung poetry that I saw how foolish my notions had been."

Yugoslavian singers of long poems felt no need to stop at "chapter" breaks, or other artificial divisions within the songs. Rather, they rested when their voices, minds, and bodies needed to rest, or when outward circumstances demanded. They could stop wherever they were and, an hour or a day later, gracefully pick up the song again. There was no unity or significance to any part or division of the song, only that of the song as a whole. So it was with Homer, said the dead Milman Parry. And so said now the living Albert Lord.

This was one example, Lord wrote in his first attempt to advance the work of his master, of how, through the Yugoslav analogy, "we can begin to reconstruct more exactly Homer's milieu, his tradition, his technique."

*

In 1960, twenty-four years after his Chicago paper, Lord's magnum opus, *The Singer of Tales,* finally came out, embodying Parry's ideas and insights as well as Lord's own from his youthful experience in Yugoslavia and later visits there. It was much more than anything he could have written with any grace or confidence in 1935. But the intervening years had transformed Professor Parry's young typist and jack-of-all-trades into a seasoned scholar.

As the first chapters of this book have recounted, Lord early suffered what he'd frankly call a "breakdown," leading him to withdraw into a job at the Charlestown Navy Yard for eight years of intellectually unde-manding work. Finally, he'd reeled himself in, begun to publish articles based on the Yugoslav work, completed his dissertation, earned his doc-torate, returned to Yugoslavia in 1950 and 1951, and written a substantial

introduction to one piece of the Parry project, that devoted to singers from Novi Pazar; the first volume of *Serbocroatian Heroic Songs* was
published jointly in 1954 by Harvard University Press and the Serbian
Academy of Sciences. And now, *The Singer of Tales*—it was Parry's own
title—at last appeared. It began:

> This book is about Homer. He is our Singer of Tales. Yet, in a
> larger sense, he represents all singers of tales from time imme-
> morial and unrecorded to the present. Our book is about these
> other singers as well. Each of them, even the most mediocre, is
> as much a part of the tradition of oral epic singing as is Homer,
> its most talented representative.

In *Singer,* Lord cited Parry's insistence "that a theory of composition
must be based not on another theory but on the facts of the practice of
the poetry." And by now, Lord had facts in abundance—in the hundreds
of songs he'd watched and heard sung, absorbed, translated, and allowed
to reach into him with their poetry and passion, songs by the guslars of
Yugoslavia.

In his 1945 novel, *The Bridge on the Drina,* Ivo Andrić conveys something of the hold guslars could exert on their listeners.

> Then suddenly, after he had more or less attuned his voice to
> the *gusle*, the Montenegrin threw back his head proudly and
> violently so that his Adam's apple stood out in his scrawny neck
> and his sharp profile was outlined in the firelight, and sang in
> a strangled and constrained voice. . . . The peasants pressed
> closer and closer around the singer but without making the
> slightest noise: their very breathing could be heard. They half-
> closed their eyes, carried away with wonder. Thrills ran up and
> down their spines, their backs straightened up, their breasts
> expanded, their eyes shone. . . . Carried away and insensible to
> all else, [they] followed the tale as if it were their own more
> beautiful and more glorious destiny.

It was the memory of moments like this that Lord brought back with
him from Yugoslavia while still almost a boy, that held him in thrall all

his life. "My father," Nate would report, "never forgot what it was like to actually be in the presence of one of these singers." It meant everything to him.

Appearing in a second edition in 2003, together with an audio compact disc, *The Singer of Tales* was a revelation, alive with observations and insights not apt to materialize from yet another dive into ancient texts. Its Part I reported, intimately, from Yugoslavia. Parry's "facts of the practice of poetry" bubbled up from every page:

> The singer has to contend with an audience that is coming and going, greeting newcomers, saying farewells to early leavers; a newcomer with special news or gossip may interrupt the singing for some time, perhaps even stopping it entirely.
>
> . . .
>
> There seem to be two things that all our singers have in common: illiteracy and the desire to attain proficiency in singing. If the second of these sets them apart from their fellows, it is the first, namely their illiteracy, which determines the particular form that their composition takes, and which thus distinguishes them from the literary poet.
>
> . . .
>
> In the Yugoslav tradition, [the rhythmic pattern to which the young singer must conform is] . . . a line of ten syllables with a break after the fourth. The line is repeated over and over again, with some melodic variation, and some variation in the spacing and timing of the ten syllables. Here is a rhythmic fixity which the singer cannot avoid, and which gives him his first real difficulty when he sings. His problem is now one of fitting his thoughts and their expression into this fairly rigid form.
>
> . . .
>
> Moslem singers, when asked how many songs they knew, frequently replied that they knew thirty, one for every night of Ramazan.
>
> . . .
>
> A performance [in the Yugoslavian oral tradition] is unique; it is a creation, not a reproduction, and it can therefore have only one author.

In *Singer,* Lord dissected much that Parry had only begun to think about or that death had foreclosed to him entirely. One theme, in particular, was how oral poets, in Homer and in the South Slavic lands, repeatedly returned to certain typical scenes—feasts, councils, journeys by sea or land, arrivals, armies gathering, warriors preparing for battle—that differed in detail, yet conformed to pattern:

> *First he wrapped his legs with well-made greaves,*
> *fastened behind the heels with silver ankle-clasps,*
> *next he strapped a breastplate round his chest,*
> *his brother Lycaon's that fitted him so well,*
> *Then over his shoulder Paris slung his sword,*
> *the fine bronze blade with its silver-studded hilt*

[FAGLES *Iliad,* 139]

Parry had begun to address the subject in "Ćor Huso" and in a review, published after his death, of a German scholar's article, "Typical Scenes in Homer." In it, Parry dismissed the author's "philosophic and almost mystic theory," inspired by Nietzsche, to explain their pervasiveness; no, it was much simpler, he held, a natural outgrowth of oral composition: "The singer of tales, unlike the writer of poetry . . . , has no pen and ink to let him slowly work out a novel way of recounting novel actions, but must make up his tale without pausing, in the speed of his singing." The epithets Parry had closely studied helped him do that—and so did these familiar, patterned scenes.

Now, in *Singer,* Lord devoted most of a long chapter, "The Theme," to fleshing out Parry's ideas. The young bard listens to his elders, "taking up the patterns and themes of their songs." He absorbs, for instance, "what preparations are made to receive the assembling host, and how each contingent arrives, what its heroes are wearing and what horses they are riding and in what order they appear." When it's time to sing his own song, the narrative structure fairly tumbles out.

Part II of Lord's book first turned back to the *Odyssey* and the *Iliad* but then, as we saw earlier, veered off in its surprising new direction, toward medieval epic, *Beowulf,* and the *Chanson de Roland* of the eleventh and twelfth centuries. And with it, Parry's ideas began to spread to realms far distant from Homer, splitting off to "all singers," in all ages;

oral tradition became a new *subject*. "The world never looked the same again to me after I'd read *The Singer of Tales*," the British anthropologist Ruth Finnegan wrote to Mary Louise Lord after Lord's husband's death in 1991. "There can't be many scholars who've had a greater influence on the intellectual life among the humanities in the 2nd half of the 20th century."

Back at Harvard in late 1935, Lord wrote later, "it was decided that I should work for a doctorate in comparative literature, with a major in English and minors in ancient Greek and Serbo-Croatian." His graduate adviser that first year was the vastly erudite folklorist Lyman Kittredge: "Sitting with me on the steps of [Harvard's] Warren House, Kittredge assigned me to take Anglo-Saxon and Middle English." The following

Albert Bates Lord, professor of Slavic and comparative literature at Harvard. He lived until 1991, fifty-six years after the death of his mentor.

year Lord took Old Norse and later, Middle High German. "I cite all this to explain how someone who was essentially a classicist found himself studying Germanic, particularly medieval English, epic poetry and Old Norse sagas in addition to South Slavic."

Later, with the extension of "oral theory" to new cultures and traditions, there would be scholars who drew on the insights of Parry and Lord yet could never have worked through a single line of dactylic hexameter in the original, nor have had an intelligible word to say about Serbian folk heroes. As John Miles Foley wrote of Lord: "What he accomplished after 1935 went far beyond any blueprint Parry provided, either formally or informally. For Lord . . . made Oral-Formulaic Theory a discipline of its own, a field that was eventually to touch on more than one hundred ancient, medieval, and modern traditions."

*

In August 1958, soon after his promotion to full professor at Harvard but before publication of *The Singer of Tales,* Lord received a letter from Milman Parry's son, Adam. Now thirty, Adam had followed in his father's footsteps; by one survey of his early career, he had "gyrated in the American fashion from junior post to junior post, from Amherst to Yale to Harvard to Amherst to Yale," where he would later become full professor. Adam married early and had three young children. Just now, he was writing Lord about the prospect of having his father's collected works published in a single volume, in English.

Decades after Paris, Milman Parry's longest and most important works, the two doctoral theses, were still to be had only in French. Cedric Whitman, a Homer and Sophocles scholar at Harvard, was suggesting that Adam translate them. Such a book "seems to me a terribly good idea," Adam wrote Lord. "The general interest in my father's work is as great now as ever." But, he added, "his writings are scattered and hard to get at, the theses especially being rare." The name of James Notopoulos, a classicist at Trinity College in Hartford, Connecticut, who was much taken with Milman Parry's ideas, had been suggested for the crucial introduction such a book needed. But no, maybe not, said Adam. Maybe, he ventured to Lord, it should be Whitman; or maybe John Finley, Milman's Harvard friend.

Or maybe himself.

By December 1959, Adam could report the project was under way. Oxford University's Clarendon Press would be the publisher. Adam was to supply the introduction, which would survey the Homeric Question and make for the nearest his father had had to a proper biography.

But translating Parry's "L'Épithète traditionnelle dans Homère" along with the shorter, supplementary thesis, Adam wrote Lord early the following year, was "much slower work than I had imagined it would be." He'd put countless hours into it, he wrote his sister around this time, and still it was taking him an hour to get through one page; Oxford was paying him £150 for the job, "which means I am working for about $1.50 an hour." Along the way he'd found occasional discrepancies in his father's work, including numbers his father cited that were "unobtainable from the statistics he himself gives: rather curious. His argument is still good"—but "less spectacularly" so. Altogether, the translation bogged him down, much interfering with his other scholarly work. The final 483-page volume, *The Making of Homeric Verse: The Collected Papers of Milman Parry*—with Adam's fifty-two-page introduction, some of the "Ćor Huso" notes, the master's thesis, and a 1948 paper by Albert Lord, "Homer, Parry, and Huso"—wouldn't come out until 1971.

Across the dozen years it took him, Adam Parry divorced and married a classicist recently come to Yale, Anne Amory. Together, they wound up on the opposite side of a bitter scholarly divide from Lord over a 1966 essay by Amory. Years later, Mrs. Parry and Pamela Newhouse, then a graduate student, would reminisce about it. Amory's article was about a famous passage in the *Odyssey* about "the gates of horn and ivory"; in it Penelope tells Odysseus, finally back in Ithaca but still disguised as a beggar, of her dream—true or false depending on whether it had reached her through gates of "honest horn" or those of duplicitous polished ivory. "There was nothing in it about Albert, nothing," said Newhouse. "Albert then simply took it upon himself to attack that first article." Lord's was "Homer as Oral Poet," a forty-eight-page piece in which he challenged both Adam and his new wife. Amory's article, "Homer as Artist," in *Classical Quarterly*, retaliated. "Lord's view of the nature of the Homeric poems has not attained the status of Revealed Truth," wrote Amory, who then added: "We would all benefit if Lord were to proceed more rapidly than he has with the publication of the

Yugoslav material which has been sequestered for thirty years and more in the Milman Parry collection at Harvard."

Albert was twenty-two when he'd first known Adam as a boy, then just six, in Dubrovnik. And now, their oddly asymmetric relationship had degenerated into feud. Adam's writings are clotted with barbs at the expense of his father's disciple. In one, he refers to "the fuzzy repetitions and condescending wafflings of the warmed-over dissertation of Albert Bates Lord." In another he describes Lord as "a very nice man, if a little dumb." Of course, Lord was anything but dumb, if perhaps not so bold and quick in the Parry way.

When Adam's own book at last made its way into print, it was welcomed into the classical community by, among others, C. A. Trypanis of the University of Chicago. "There is, of course, no longer need to stress the significance of Milman Parry's work for the students of Greek literature. His contribution can be safely said to be the greatest made by any American scholar to the field of classical studies." What struck Trypanis after encountering Parry's master's thesis for the first time was "how early in his life Parry conceived an 'oral Homer' and realized the power of the epic tradition." He praised Adam for his "long and balanced introduction."

Trypanis's review appeared in the *American Journal of Philology,* a natural home for any assessment of Parry's life's work. More surprising for a scholarly work, whole pages of it gray with Greek, was the review in the *New York Times Book Review,* its middlebrow readers rarely grounded in the classics. "It is almost incontestable," the reviewer began, "that anything could radically alter our concept of classical literature, especially if it did not involve a new manuscript or an archeological find. Yet in 1928, a young man woke literati out of centuries of complacency." Milman Parry's unearthing of Homer's oral roots meant that those of literary bent "must surrender certain cherished assumptions: that literature is inextricably associated with reading and writing, that lack of literacy means lack of culture." The review's author, Erich Segal, was an associate professor of classics at Yale. But he had other credentials attesting to a more common touch. The previous year, his novel *Love Story* had become a publishing sensation, propelling the catchphrase "Love is never having to say you're sorry" into the annals of American pop culture.

Adam, though, could not appreciate the sweet, surprising pleasure of seeing his book, and his father's career, saluted in the pages of the *New York Times*. The review came out on August 15. Two months earlier, in France, Adam had taken possession of a new BMW motorcycle. He was an experienced motorcyclist—if "experienced" means lots of mileage under one's belt. But by every account, he was an atrocious, preternaturally dangerous one. On this day, near Colmar, in the Alsace countryside, at about six in the afternoon, he came to an intersection, Anne tucked in behind him, a bus approaching from the other direction. Adam turned left directly into the path of the oncoming vehicle with its fifty-two passengers. As judged by French officials who examined evidence of the crash, he was killed instantly, along with his wife, both vehicles consumed in the flames of the collision. Adam was forty-three years old.

*

Lord's *Singer of Tales* was a scholarly work, in all the best ways. But it was a paean to Milman Parry, too. The debt he owed Parry showed on every page. Lord's work across the years, carrying the work of his mentor into new places, eras, and disciplines, helped ground "Parry-Lord theory" and "Parryism" in the larger scholarly world.

In 1973, two substantial bibliographies were published. One of them, *A Bibliography of Studies Relating to Parry's and Lord's Oral Theory*, listed more than five hundred books, articles, and dissertations, and amounted to what Edward R. Haymes, its compiler, called a "directory of the humanistic research stemming from Milman Parry's discovery forty years ago of oral style in Homer." A bibliography, of course, merely lists works on a particular subject; but the very impetus to create it testifies to that subject's significance. Haymes's included Parry's own work, and much of Lord's by now voluminous oeuvre; in 1973, "young Albert" was fifty-one. Predictably, it included Homer-related articles like "The Arming Motif in the *Iliad*." But it ranged far from Homer, too, with articles on medieval Spanish epic, the thirteenth-century German *Nibelungenlied* epic, the oral poets of South India, Gaelic oral literature, and the oral literature of Africa. Bruce A. Rosenberg was represented by "The Formulaic Quality of Spontaneous Sermons" as well as by a book, published in 1971, *The Art of the American Folk Preacher*.

Rosenberg, a young folklorist captivated by *Singer,* heard echoes of the guslars among preachers in Bakersfield, California, and in Kentucky, North Carolina, and Virginia. These mostly black preachers sang not epics but "chanted sermons": they "almost never rhyme, they seldom alliterate, the imagery is meager, yet they are poetic," wrote Rosenberg. "The lines are metrical, the language is ordered, and the effect is often pleasing." And they exhibited just the sorts of formulae, repetitions, and patterns of enjambment Parry and Lord had found in Homer and in the Balkans.

> *Keep your hand in God's hand*
> *And your eyes on the starposts in glory*
> *Lord said he would fight your battles*
> *If you'd only be still*
> *You may not be a florist*
> *Am I right about it?*
> *But you must tell them, that He's the Rose of Sharon.*
> *I know that's right*
> *You may not be a geologist*
> *But you must tell them, that He's the Rock of Ages*
> *I know that's right.*
> *You may not be a physician*
> *But you must tell them, that He's the great Physician*
> *You may not be a baker*
> *But you must tell them, that He's the Bread of Life.*

Here, again, was the relentlessly "adding" style that served the unforgiving pressures of oral composition.

After Parry and Lord, it seems, you couldn't help but wonder how words uttered alive in church, by rural preachers, across many generations, got there; you couldn't help but see and hear a little differently. It was as if the Yugoslav work had forged a new master key, one opening not one door to a little room cluttered with Homeric artifacts only, but to a tangle of branching rooms rich with oral traditions from every place, culture, and time.

The swelling of the oral theory into something so various, suggested Joseph Russo, a former colleague of Adam Parry's at Yale, in 1992, owed something to the "ethnographic impulse, as old as Herodotus, that finds different cultures irresistibly fascinating." This "burgeoning comparativism has produced a giant bibliography and has made Milman Parry a familiar name in the house of academe." Indeed, he would write later, Parry and Lord had become the new orthodoxy, "the position against which dissenters must argue."

In 1974, Lord's translation and close study of Avdo Međedović's "Meho" epic finally appeared in print. Once she'd gotten a chance to digest it, Dorothea Wender, a classicist at Wheaton College in Massachusetts, reviewed it in the pages of the *American Journal of Philology*. "Meho," she observed, was "Parry's prize, the work that almost rivalled Homer." That "almost," of course, went to the heart of the matter, and to the worth of the Yugoslav analogy. "The work is at last in our hands," she wrote—that is, in English; she herself did not read Serbo-Croatian. "Some scholars, no doubt, are disappointed that it isn't a better poem than it is; others, just as surely, are disappointed that it isn't worse." That is, were it better, the whole edifice of Parry's thinking would stand taller; were it worse, comparison inconceivable between it and Homer, correspondingly lower.

"The chief difference between the Homeric poems and *The Wedding of Meho*," Wender led off her critique, "is that they are masterpieces and it is not." But there was more to her verdict than that. "Meho," she wrote, was "not a contemptible poem; I would put it in a class with, say, the *Nibelungenlied*," which it surpassed "in unity, coherence, and polish." Overall, she concluded, "I do not now find it hard to conceive of an oral poet with Homer's abilities creating an *Iliad* or an *Odyssey* without a written outline or a text to refer to." Not that we know it happened that way, only that "Meho" showed it could have.

*

At a 1979 conference in Ankara, Lord met the Albanian novelist Ismail Kadare, not yet famous in the West. They spoke only briefly, but it wasn't long before Kadare had made a novel out of Parry's and Lord's travels in Yugoslavia; it came out in 1981 as *Le Dossier H.*—the "H" is for Homer—and, in its 1998 English translation, *The File on H*. In it, our two heroes metamorphose into Irish-American scholars Max Ross and Bill Norton, both from Harvard, who descend on Albania (which Lord visited in 1937), with their tape recorders, to record epic song. A kind of comic spy novel, it's full of cultural misunderstanding, bits of Homer, and a sprinkling of sex. Altogether, a light and frothy romp—yet testimony for just how far the rudiments of Parry's story, almost half a century since his death, had penetrated world culture.

Or else, turned the other way around, how it had become *old*.

Like any idea that's been around for a while, a reaction to the "oral theory" set in, with "Parryites," "Parryans," or "Parryists" variously named as intellectual targets. Scholars poked at its blind spots, probed its assumptions, dug more deeply into its founding books and essays. What *exactly* did Parry mean by a Homeric "formula"; why, if you parsed it sharply enough, one scholar argued, he could seem to mean seven *different* things. Some became irritated by Lord's "litmus test" for oral, as opposed to literary, composition, which seemed to demand a certain proportion of formulaic expression. In Germany, especially, a breed of "neoanalysts" challenged it, seeing oral tradition less the motive force behind the Homeric epics than other, earlier poetic sources. "The Parry-Lord theory," wrote one scholar, risked slipping into "an unreflexive orthodoxy."

In a long 1996 essay, "In Defense of Milman Parry: Renewing the Oral Theory," Merritt Sale set out the case against Parry as he imagined Parry's scholarly opponents might have done, beginning with this qualification:

> Let me say, I hope without impudence, that while Parry was a consummate linguist, an excellent scientist, and a man of wide literary culture, he was an imperfect theorist who made a number of broad claims that conceal some deep and important confusions. He was young, and justly excited by the power of his position and the force of his individual genius; he therefore took extreme positions.

Even back in Paris, Aimé Puech had taken note of Parry's penchant for the categorical and the extreme: Parry brought to his work "great ingenuity and clarity" but, Puech pointed out, he was given to a "certain excess." So often he turned to "all" or "always" where more measured assertions might have served him better. Worst of all, by emphasizing the ready-at-hand formulae that made oral composition work, he could seem to make no room for Homer's "natural genius," if that is what it was.

Here was the most disquieting element of Parry's big idea, troubling right from the start: The brilliance of the Homeric epics hadn't billowed up from that of an individual human being? Their most remarkable qualities had emerged from formulaic expressions wielded by a procession of illiterate peasant singers? Their seeming originality, freshness, and force, their larger-than-life characters, their high-minded speeches, were the product of singers who weren't even *trying* to be original, fresh, and forceful? Rather, they clung to time-tested formulae they rudely fashioned into song, which others borrowed from, refashioned, and corrupted? This—*really?*—was how, after Parry, we were supposed to think of the Homeric epics? It could seem too much to bear, a species of betrayal. "Parry's theory," wrote one classicist, D. C. Young, in 1965, was "an unconscionable libel against one of the supreme men of letters."

Back in 1952, a few years after earning his doctorate but long before finishing *The Singer of Tales,* Albert Lord had addressed the issue himself. In a paper for the American Philological Association, he acknowledged the belief among some "that the work of Milman Parry in the 1930s was an attack on the citadel of Homer's creative greatness." He cited the British classicist H. T. Wade-Gery's now familiar depiction of Parry as "the Darwin of Homeric Studies," as well as his implicit reproach: As Darwin seemed to remove "the finger of God from the creation of the world and of man," Wade-Gery wrote, so Milman Parry seemed to "remove the creative poet from the *Iliad* and *Odyssey.*" But Parry's earliest ideas, Lord reminded his readers, were born of the Homeric texts alone, from a time when he had never seen or heard an oral poet; confronted with the limits of his understanding, he hastened to Yugoslavia. And from its singers, Parry learned that "originality" in oral performance was more nuanced than he'd supposed; a poem passing through many minds and voices was no simple thing.

Lord's attempt to resolve the problem didn't put an end to it; the gap between two discordant ideas—the force of Parry's arguments set against the reverence accorded Homer—could seem too wide, attempts to transcend it bound for frustration, contradiction, and divide. Here, then, was the hard kernel of resistance to Parry's ideas—and the subject of another bibliography, appearing in *The Classical World* within a few months of Haymes's in 1973. Annotated with capsule summaries of 214 articles, it dealt specifically with "Homeric Originality."

It was by then a commonplace, began its editor, James P. Holoka, "to say that the Parry-Lord theory of oral composition has radically altered the direction of modern Homeric scholarship. The purpose of this survey will be to reveal an aesthetic crisis which has arisen from this change of direction."

Oral theory "has become our critical conscience. The most basic instinct of the literary critic is to approach a text as the original product of a single inventive genius." But Parry said there *was* no single inventive genius behind the *Iliad* and the *Odyssey;* Holoka's bibliography was there to assess the intellectual damage, collectively making for a disquisition on the nature of creativity.

In the years since, Parry's ideas have been carved up in new ways, seen from new directions—and supplied with new defenses: Was the oral poet, so sadly circumscribed by his stock of formulae and type scenes, any more constrained than the rest of us with our own limited vocabulary, in our own sadly limited language? Didn't any artist—even, say, an unassailably brilliant jazz musician, a John Coltrane or Charlie Parker—work within a set tradition?

Writing seventy-two years after Parry's death, Johannes Haubhold summed up the conundrum in a charmingly provocative way reminiscent of a Zen *koan:*

> For Parry, Homer's poetry was supremely beautiful, but Homer could no longer be regarded as its author in the usual sense. He was still the best stylist, though he had no style of his own. His language was still superior, though many of its words had little or no meaning.

*

The challenge of new ideas and their emergence into new orthodoxies, one worldview supplanting an older, long-established one, raising new questions, and new *types* of question, is common in fields far from

Homeric studies. In his landmark 1962 book, *The Structure of Scientific Revolutions,* Thomas Kuhn showed how it worked in science and technology. Kuhn memorably argued that science doesn't progress in fine, agreeable little shifts but in unsettling, relatively abrupt revolutions that don't merely adjust, modify, or fine-tune existing ideas but overthrow them entirely. Perhaps for years, an established field's explanation for how, say, the planets move, overlooks anomalies that don't fit the orthodoxy of the age. But finally—as in Copernicus's sun-centered cosmology, or Darwin's evolution, or Einstein's relativity—a new theory comes along, bringing with it a "paradigm shift," that resolves the objections in a new way and asks new questions no one before had even thought to ask.

Something much like this happened with Parry. Many of the Homeric Question's contradictions and conundrums vanished when it became clear that the *Odyssey* and the *Iliad* were works not of a writer, or writers, but of oral poets. Parry's work over the scant few years of his adult life, coupled with the infiltration of his ideas into new cultures and traditions, together made for a revolution. Harry Levin's fetching 1937 "Portrait of a Homeric Scholar" suggested that, with Parry, all the old controversies had been turned on their heads or rendered irrelevant. But of course in a world of scholarship that rewards close argument and fine distinctions, it wasn't so simple. The originality problem lies open. There is no "final" proof, and won't be, Yugoslav analogy or not, for just how Western civilization got the *Iliad.* And there is no answer in Parry to who, when, and how the oral poems of the bards were reduced to written text. Despite the "scientific" aura surrounding Parry's Paris theses, absolute and final answers are hardly to be expected from humanistic scholars, who ask questions that encourage us to imagine and explore across eons of time and space.

What does it mean to be a great scholar in the house of academe? To gather facts? Draw insights? Reveal new patterns? Comment incisively on the work of others? Parry did all that. But in the end, as in all the arts and sciences, a great thinker makes something new, something that didn't exist before; a painting, poem, book, or theory doesn't exist before someone makes it. We willingly appreciate the creation of clever devices and beautiful objects. Wet clay thrown on the potter's wheel, shaped, and fired to create fanciful teacups or luminously colored bowls: This we *get.* But the further we draw away from the physical and tangible, the more difficult it can be to see a new creation for what it is. And yet the great distinction remains: A new theory—scientific, humanistic, or otherwise—offers a new way to understand the world; it is nothing before it exists, everything once it has come into being.

In *A Mathematician's Apology*, the great early-twentieth-century English pure mathematician G. H. Hardy—whom we welcome here as ambassador from a field that, like classical studies, some disdain as unworldly or irrelevant—once wrote:

> I have never done anything "useful." No discovery of mine has made, or is likely to make, directly or indirectly, for good or ill, the least difference to the amenity of the world. . . . The case for my life, then, or for that of any one else who has been a mathematician in the same sense in which I have been one, is this: that I have added something to knowledge and helped others to add more; and that these somethings have a value which differs in degree only, and not in kind, from that of the creations of the great mathematicians or of any of the other artists, great or small, who have left some kind of memorial behind them.

Likewise with Parry. He created a new idea of poetic artistry; this is his memorial. He made one of Hardy's beautiful "somethings"—a new way of looking at old words and how they'd come into the world that profoundly influenced all of classical studies and, in time, the humanities generally. Turning to the same facts and the same ancient texts, he saw in new ways what they implied, asked new questions, and fashioned new tools with which to study this variant species of poetic expression, one formed on the breath of word and song long before anyone was there to take it down.

Acknowledgments

For its generous grant in support of this book, I wish to thank the National Endowment for the Humanities and its Public Scholar program, which encourages the writing of humanities-themed books for general readers. I am honored to receive this award, and grateful for it. It has enabled me to take on a complex project, in all its dimensions, with less financial strain and worry. It has encouraged me to follow up leads and lines of thought I might otherwise have forsaken, and so, I hope, made for a better book. The views expressed in this book, however, do not necessarily represent those of the NEH.

*

The aluminum discs with which Parry and Lord returned to America in 1935 are today housed in the Milman Parry Collection at Harvard University, together with its rich stock of correspondence, photos, and background material on their adventures in Yugoslavia. The Collection is presided over by David Elmer, Eliot Professor of Greek Literature, who has made its resources available to me and otherwise aided me in the pursuit of this project. He alerted me as correspondence and other materials came his way; arranged for graduate student helpers during my stints at the Collection; and answered questions, however slight or outlandish, always with good cheer. I deeply appreciate his cooperation and kindliness.

In addition to David Elmer, I wish to publicly thank Richard Martin of Stanford University, Philip Khoury of MIT, and Judith Hallett of the University of Maryland at College Park for their care and trouble on my behalf early in this project.

At Harvard University, I would like to thank the staffs of the Houghton, Pusey, and Widener libraries. I am especially grateful to Tim Driscoll, senior reference archivist, who, while I was still back in Baltimore, went the proverbial extra mile to dip into key archival material for me—an act of care and kindness that, at a stroke, clarified my next research steps. Thanks also to Scott Hayward for his tour of Kirkland House; to Peter McMurray, Greg Nagy, Stephen

Mitchell, and Leonard C. Muellner, all expert in Greek, Homer, and the oral tradition, for warmly welcoming me to the Harvard classics community; and to Blaž Zabel, for sharing with me materials he gathered in the course of his own studies at Harvard. For making my trips to Harvard a warmer and more comfortable experience, I thank Anne and Dick Tonachel, who shared their house, their friendship . . . and their luggage—in particular, a piece sturdy enough to bear the weight of the unexpectedly large cache of Parry family letters I was taking on the plane back to Baltimore.

In Berkeley and Oakland, my thanks go to Dorothy Lazard and her able staff at the Oakland Public Library; Kristen R. Southworth and Cathy Rosenfeld, Oakland Technical High School; the staff at the Bancroft Library, University of California at Berkeley; Emily Thornbury, for her useful tour of Wheeler Hall; and Dea Lee, Rachele, and Laird for their support and interest.

In Los Angeles, thanks to Andrea Vargas, Richard Kennemer, and the residents of Parkville on the Park; and to Andy and Caren, Bruce and Sumona, for their friendship and understanding at a problematic moment.

For the Paris side of my research, thanks to all who endured my fractured French, including Vincent Mohnen, of the Rectorat de l'academie de Paris; the highly competent staffs of the Archives nationales, Pierrefitte-sur-Seine, and of the École Pratique des Hautes Études, Paris; Jacques and Claude Blanchard, for their welcome to Paris; Aldine Martini and Alain Carron in Sceaux; Gisèle Jullemier and Yahyaoui Mehdi in Clamart; Arthur Goldhammer, for his suggestions and leads; Jack Kessler, for his spirited epistles on the academic worlds of Paris and Berkeley; and Étienne Bérard, for his rewarding correspondence about his grandfather. Special thanks to Katia Sainson for so ably persevering through the handwritten jury report of Parry's *soutenance* and, with her husband, John Hessler, alchemizing it into an animated afternoon of scholarly detective work.

For their help in supplying leads and practical advice as I weighed the prospect of a trip to the former Yugoslavia, I wish to thank Carol Hyman and the friends she martialed on my behalf, including Carol Silverman and Larry Weiner; also Danka Lajić-Mihajlović, Carol Bier, Selena Rakocević, and Ana Hart. In Sarajevo, my thanks go to Jasmina Talam and her husband for graciously showing my wife and me around the city; in Stolac, to our innkeeper, for the heaping trays of fresh strawberries laid at our door the morning we left; in Dubrovnik, to Frane Čizmić and Zoran Perović of the city's archives; and in Kolašin, to Davor Sedlarević, art director of the town's cultural center, for giving me the chance to play a gusle, and for giving Sarah and me an impromptu concert of his singers. And finally, to David Bynum, who, though faced by health problems, engaged with me in a spirited email dialogue over several years that left me with rich insights into the Parry-Lord adventure in the Balkans.

A special appreciation to Pamela Newhouse Mensch. In December 1981 Ms. Mensch—then a graduate student, today a distinguished translator of ancient texts—conducted a patient, persistent, deeply engaged three-day interview of Marian Thanhouser Parry. Now, forty years later, it has proven invaluable in giving me a deeper understanding of the Parry marriage, of the life they shared, as well as of the life they didn't share.

The various corners of the far-flung Parry family have been invariably cooperative and welcoming to me. I owe much gratitude to Laura and Andrew Feld, who wrote or spoke with me on many occasions, filled me in on family lore, forwarded me batches of correspondence, shared family photographs, and so, it could sometimes feel, welcomed me to at least the outer reaches of their family. I thank Catherine Marcial for her patience, substantial help, and extraordinary kindness at a gridlocked moment in the research; Milman Youngjohn, for the eager intelligence with which he reflected back to times long past, and for furnishing me with key documents; Christine Henry and Lee Perry; and Stephen Parry, who, for an absorbing couple of hours at the Lawry Steak House in Los Angeles, shared with me his memories and insights into the Parry family.

Many thanks are owed Meg Alexiou, professor emerita of modern Greek at Harvard, who led me to Milman Parry in the first place. While researching one of my previous books, *On an Irish Island,* I had become intrigued with her father, George Thomson, a classics professor at the University of Birmingham in England. Meg told me much about her father. But more, in an essay about him, she wrote intriguingly of Milman Parry and Homer, and of her father as "the first classicist to acknowledge and acclaim the full significance of Parry's findings."

Hearing Homer's Song is, in some measure, a dual biography; certainly the role Albert Bates Lord played in the spread of Parry's ideas is incalculable. I want to thank members of the Lord family, including Mark and Kit Lord, for their help and kindnesses in Portsmouth, and for sharing with me various documents from their father's life; and Nate Lord, for fielding questions and rounding up key bits of family information.

In addition to those listed above, I acknowledge the following for sharing thoughts, documents, and insights in phone or in-person interviews and correspondence: Alessandro Barchiesi, Margaret Beissinger, Charles Beye, Sandy Blakeley, Claudia Frazer, Juan Garcia, Steve T. Reece, and Joseph Russo.

My thanks and appreciation also go to Michele Asuni, then a graduate student in classics at Johns Hopkins University in Baltimore, for his informal lessons in the rudiments of ancient Greek and for later reviewing the finished manuscript. In Baltimore, too, Joel Marcus constructively challenged me on an aspect of the writing I had taken for granted, and fellow author Arthur Magida and I enjoyed many a cheerful lunch comparing notes on our biographical subjects.

I write this in the middle of the pandemic, during which Knopf's band of editorial brothers and sisters have had to do their good work from home, or otherwise apart from their colleagues. One might be apt to credit digital technology for making it all possible; but I credit them, for their flexibility: Thanks to designers Tyler Comrie and Soonyoung Kwon; production editor Victoria Pearson and copyeditor Chris Jerome; and marketing and publicity virtuosos Morgan Fenton and Jessica Purcell. Ann Close is the editor of this book, Todd Portnowitz her capable assistant; I warmly thank them both for their energy, care, and clear thinking over the several years Milman Parry has been part of their lives; as well as Michael Carlisle, my agent, for his backing along the way.

I am grateful to my wife, Sarah, for her understanding, patience, and love. But it will not do to say just that. For what Sarah has *also* done on behalf of this book is translate letters from the German; fruitfully grill me on parataxis in the epics; drive us safely through the dizzying mountain roads of Montenegro; help work through my computer glitches; read the manuscript through, parts of it several times, always with smart suggestions; alert me when I ran off on rhetorical deep ends; challenge me on points seemingly "self-evident"; and enrich me and the book through her own knowledge of, and practice of, poetry. This and much more needs to be noted of the remarkable woman who is my wife.

Notes

Names appearing most frequently have been abbreviated as follows:

ABL—Albert Bates Lord, born 1912
AP—Adam Parry, born 1928
IP—Isaac Parry, born 1865
MP—Milman Parry, born 1902
MTP—Marian Thanhouser Parry, born 1899

*

The following most frequently cited books, articles, personal papers, and archival records have been abbreviated as follows:

"Across"—Albert Bates Lord, "Across Montenegro, Searching for Gusle Songs," unpublished typescript, March 1937, Milman Parry Collection.

Adam—A large body of correspondence linked to Adam Parry, including many letters to and from his sister, Marian, furnished the author by Milman Parry's grandchildren, Laura and Andrew Feld, later transferred in their entirety to their cousin Catherine Marcial, Adam Parry's daughter. From these papers, I culled a small subset of special interest, numbering them Adam 001 to Adam 066.

AdamIntro—Adam Parry's introduction, pp. ix–lvii, to his edited work *The Making of Homeric Verse: The Collected Papers of Milman Parry*. New York: Oxford University Press, 1987, originally published 1971.

Bynum—Email interviews and supplemental correspondence with the author beginning May 2017; for medical reasons, David Bynum could not comfortably speak, so that our ongoing conversations took place through extended email, in which he forwarded to me postings from his now defunct website, enargea.org. In the citations below, I sometimes use references to my own numbering system, as in "Bynum, Field 108."

Ćor Huso—Portions of "Ćor Huso," itself a fragmentary and incomplete work, reached me in three forms: through *The Making of Homeric Verse,* pp. 437–464; through a typewritten version, numbered, sometimes dated, sometimes with photographs pasted in, from the Milman Parry Collection; and through David Bynum, on his former website enargea.org. The Notes cite "Ćor Huso" either by page-number references to *Making,* or by part-and-page number.

Dow—Papers of Sterling Dow, Harvard University Archives, three notebooks devoted to Parry. Unless otherwise noted, all citations are to Book II. In the absence of other identifying description, I sometimes use references to my own numbering system for Dow's Part II, as in "Dow 52."

EpicSingers—Albert Bates Lord, *Epic Singers and Oral Tradition.* Ithaca and London: Cornell University Press, 1991.

Fagles *Iliad*—*The Iliad,* translated by Robert Fagles, with an introduction and notes by Bernard Knox. New York: Penguin Books, 1991.

Fagles *Odyssey*—*The Odyssey,* translated by Robert Fagles, introduction and notes by Bernard Knox. New York: Viking, 1996.

Feld—A body of letters, papers, and photographs furnished by Laura and Andrew Feld in 2017, all or many of them also deposited in the Milman Parry Collection, supplemented by email correspondence and additional papers later. The dates of letters from this collection sometimes do not include the year, though it can usually be inferred from the content of the letter and its relationship to known events and other elements of chronology. The Feld papers include "Newhouse" and "JugoDiary," below.

Fitzgerald *Odyssey*—*The Odyssey,* translated by Robert Fitzgerald. Garden City, NY: Doubleday, 1961.

Garcia—John F. Garcia, "Milman Parry and A. L. Kroeber: Americanist Anthropology and the Oral Homer," *Oral Tradition* 16, no. 1 (2000): 58–84.

Harvard—Pusey Library, Houghton Library, and Widener Library, Harvard University.

JugoDiary—"Jugoslavia: A Diary," kept by Milman Parry's daughter, Marian, during the second trip to Yugoslavia. Part of Feld papers.

JugoWork, I and II—Milman Parry's "Report on Work in Jugoslavia, I, June 18–October 19 [1934]; and II, October 20, 1934–March 24, 1935," typescripts, Milman Parry Collection.

Jury—Puech, A., "Rapport sur les thèses de M. Milman Parry." Archives nationales (Pierrefitte-sur-Seine), AJ/16/7098, handwritten four-page document prepared by Puech as Président du Jury, transcribed by Katia Sainson, professor of French, Towson University, translated by the author.

de Lamberterie—Charles de Lamberterie, "Milman Parry and Antoine Meillet," in *Antiquities,* edited by Nicole Loraux, Gregory Nagy, and Laura Slatkin. Translated by Arthur Goldhammer. New York: The New Press, 2001, pp. 409–438.

Lattimore *Iliad*—*The Iliad of Homer,* Richard Lattimore, translator. Chicago: University of Chicago Press, 2011.

Levin—Harry Levin, "Portrait of a Homeric Scholar," *The Classical Journal* 32, no. 5 (February 1937): 259–266.

Making—*The Making of Homeric Verse: The Collected Papers of Milman Parry,* ed. Adam Parry. New York: Oxford University Press, 1987, originally published 1971. This book includes his Paris theses, his master's thesis, parts of Ćor Huso, Parry's other published works, plus a 1948 essay by Albert Lord, "Homer, Parry, and Huso."

Marcial—Family papers furnished by Catherine Parry Marcial, daughter of Milman Parry's son, Adam.

Meho—Albert Bates Lord and David E. Bynum, eds. *Serbo-Croatian Heroic Songs, Vol. 3: The Wedding of Smailagić Meho,* by Avdo Međedović. Cambridge, MA: Harvard University Press, 1974.

MPColl—Milman Parry Collection, Harvard University.

Murko—Matija Murko, "The Singers and Their Epic Songs," *Oral Tradition* 5, no. 1 (1990): 107–130. Translation by John Miles Foley of Murko's *La Poésie populaire épique en Yougoslavie au Début du XXᵉ Siècle.* Paris: Librairie Ancienne Honoré Champion, 1929, which includes annotated photo section not included in the Foley translation.

Newhouse—Pamela Newhouse interview with Mrs. Marian Parry, conducted 3–5 December 1981, titled "A Verbatim Transcription of Three Conversations with Marian Parry," page-numbered, 1–80, by Ms. Newhouse. Part of Feld papers.

NoviPazar—Albert Bates Lord, *Serbo-Croatian Heroic Songs, Vol. 1: Novi Pazar: English Translations.* Cambridge and Belgrade: Harvard University Press and Serbian Academy of Sciences, 1954. When not otherwise noted, names of songs, singers, and collection sites in Yugoslavia come from *NoviPazar,* pp. 21–40, "A Digest of Serbocroatian Epic Songs in the Milman Parry Collection of Southslavic Texts."

PopOral—"Project for a Study of Jugoslavian Popular Oral Poetry, July 1933 to September 1924 [*sic*]," 9 pp., typewritten, MPColl. (Parry must mean the dates to be July 1934 to September 1935. Most likely time of writing, based on its contents, is fall 1933 or early January 1934.)

Reminiscences—Albert Bates Lord, "Reminiscences," 3 pp., typed, undated, MPColl.

Mitchell&Nagy—Stephen Mitchell and Gregory Nagy, eds. Introduction to *The Singer of Tales*, 2nd edition, by Albert Bates Lord.

Singer—Albert Bates Lord, *The Singer of Tales,* 2nd ed. Cambridge, MA: Harvard University Press, 2000. (Lord's 1949 doctoral thesis has almost the same title, "A Singer of Tales," but is significantly different, and is cited separately when it appears in the Notes.)

Wilson *Odyssey*—*The Odyssey,* translated by Emily Wilson. New York: W. W. Norton, 2018.

Youngjohn—Interviews and email correspondence with, and personal papers furnished by, Milman Youngjohn, son of Milman Parry's sister Lucile.

Zabel—Collection of Harvard University archival papers gathered independently by Blaž Zabel as part of his doctoral research and furnished to me in October 2018, subsequently culled for their relevance to this book, and numbered Zabel 1–38. Most of these papers are from Accession 2018.170. Zabel's research culminated in his thesis, "Homeric Epic and World Literature: A Comparative Study of Method," for Durham University's Department of Classics and Ancient History.

OTHER ARCHIVAL SOURCES

Archives nationales, Pierrefitte-sur-Seine, Paris
Bancroft Library, University of California, Berkeley
National Archives and Records Administration, St. Louis, Missouri
Oakland Public Library, courtesy Dorothy Lazard and staff
Oakland Technical High School, Oakland, California, courtesy Kristen R. Southworth and Cathy Rosenfeld

INTERVIEWS

In-person and telephone interviews, and/or correspondence with: Margaret Alexiou, Michele Asuni, Alessandro Barchiesi, Margaret Beissinger, Étienne Bérard, Charles Beye, Sandy Blakeley, David Bynum, Frane Čizmić, David Elmer, Andrew Feld, Laura Feld, Marian Parry Feld, Juan Garcia, Arthur Goldhammer, Judith Hallett, Ana Hart, Scott Haywood, Christine Henry, Gisèle Jullemier, Jack Kessler, Jessica Lamont, Kit Lord, Mark Lord, Nate Lord, Catherine Parry Marcial, Richard Martin, Aldine Martini, Peter McMurray, Yahyaoui Mehdi, Pamela Newhouse Mensch, Stephen Mitchell, Leonard C. Muellner, Greg Nagy, Stephen Parry, Zoran Perović, Lee Perry, Steve T. Reece,

Joseph Russo, Mark Usher, Davor Sedlarević, Jasmina Talam, Emily Thornbury, Milman Youngjohn, Blaž Zabel.

*

PART ONE
Edifice

1—YOUNG ALBERT AND MR. PARRY

3 "my father explained": handwritten notes, "Jugoslavia," MPColl.

5 "with copious material": "Service in Memory of Milman Parry" at Harvard, 19 December 1935, G. B. Gulick.

5 "had not the slightest idea": Bynum, Field 105.

6 "no opportunity whatever": Ibid., Field 106.

6 "In spite of moments": ABL, *25th Anniversary Report*, Harvard Class of 1934, p. 826.

6 "the Darwin of Homeric Studies": H. T. Wade-Gery, *The Poet of the Iliad*. Cambridge: Cambridge University Press, 1952, p. 38.

6 "the spirit of a whole race": MP master's thesis, *Making*, p. 425.

7 "The *Iliad* and the *Odyssey* have been commonly regarded": Walter Ong, *Orality and Literacy: The Technologizing of the Word*. London: Routledge, 1988, p. 18.

9 "never solved the Homeric Question": Levin, p. 261.

10 "to visit the local pashas": Ibid., p. 264.

2—SINGER OF TALES

12 boiler room of the university's: Interview, Stephen Mitchell.

12 "painful and unmanageable": ABL, "Further Recommendations to the Committee of the Parry Collection of Southslavic Texts," 7 March 1937, MPColl.

13 "the same charming place": ABL to parents, 29 June 1937, MPColl.

13 "to hear the gusle again": ABL to parents, 1 August 1937, MPColl.

13 "by the chief elder. They killed a sheep": ABL to parents, 11 September 1937, MPColl.

13 "it has proven something of a burden": ABL to George Herzog, 17 November 1938, MPColl.

14 "wretched and disappointing winter": ABL to George Herzog, 23 April 1940, MPColl.

14 "a nervous breakdown": ABL to MTP, 27 November 1949, Feld.

14 "for a combination of work": ABL to George Herzog, 4 July 1940, MPColl.

14 On January 22, 1941: Unless otherwise noted, my account of ABL's ship-yard years is drawn from his forty-two-page Official Personnel Folder, National Archives and Records Administration, St. Louis.

15 Rising at 6:30: ABL to George Herzog, 16 March 1941, MPColl.

16 "For eight years": ABL, *25th Anniversary Report,* Harvard Class of 1934, p. 827.

17 "in the real sense of": Mitchell&Nagy, p. xx.

17 "It is a strange phenomenon": *Singer,* p. 11.

18 an African tribe: *Making,* p. 445.

18 "What is called oral tradition": *Singer,* p. 141.

20 never any true final version: Richard F. Thomas, "The Streets of Rome: The Classical Dylan," *Oral Tradition* 22, no. 1 (2007): 30–56.

20 "poetry depends on oral performance": Gordon Ball, "Dylan and the Nobel," *Oral Tradition* 22, no. 1 (2007): 14–29.

20 "It was a decision that seemed": Horace Engdahl, Nobel Prize "Award Ceremony Speech," 10 December 2016.

20 Homer, Parry, and Lord: Nicholas Frankovich, "Bob Dylan and the Sound of Music," *National Review,* 17 October 2016; "The Swedish Academy's Surprise Definition of Literature," *Diasporian News,* 21 October 2016. (Retrieved from GhanaWeb.)

21 "From that pioneering effort": John Miles Foley, *Homer's Traditional Art.* University Park: Pennsylvania State University Press, 1999, p. 37.

21 "Working from the clues he left": *Singer,* p. 12.

PART TWO

California

3—DOWN IN THE FLATS

26 His boyhood played out: Details of Parry's childhood and youth in Oakland drawn from street directories 1901–1924 and Sanborn fire insurance maps, Oakland History Room, Oakland, California, public library; tours of what remains of the old neighborhood; correspondence with Dorothy Lazard, Oakland History Room; Sterling Dow's notes of talk with Addison Parry, 18 September 1964, Dow.

26 "ran away with a Miss Milman": Newhouse, p. 22.

27 "no one expected aid": IP to AP, 17 January [1956], Marcial.

27 Their fourth child: "Return of a Birth in the City of Oakland," which lists

his parents' residence as 478 22nd Street. MP's birthday has often been erroneously recorded as June 20.

28 Santa Cruz Mountains: "Boys Off for Pescadero Camp," *Oakland Tribune,* 8 June 1916.

28 regularly invited: For example, "Friends Assist Youth to Celebrate Birthday," *Oakland Tribune,* 13 April 1910.

28 French program: "French Classes Will be Held in the Schools," *Oakland Tribune,* 31 January 1914.

28 Rotary Club: "To Honor Boys for Achievement," *Oakland Tribune,* 22 February 1916.

28 a photo taken around this time: Dow, Book II, original in glassine envelope.

4—THE OLD DEAR

29 "I have no right to do this": IP to AP, 26 April 1950, Adam 08.

29 "Our father was the 'student' ": Addison Parry to Sterling Dow, 15 June 1964, Dow.

29 "He was a very scholastic man": Youngjohn.

30 "a sepia Galahad": Addison Parry to Sterling Dow, 15 June 1964, Dow.

30 introduction to the classic myths: Sterling Dow's notes from talk with Addison Parry, 18 September 1964, Dow.

30 "little parental sense of responsibility": Youngjohn.

30 "poor and hard-pressed": Telephone interview, Christine Henry.

31 "registered pharmacist": "State Board of Pharmacy," *Los Angeles Herald,* 19 October 1898. See also "History of Drug Stores" in Berkeley and Oakland, CA, typed manuscript, October 1958, courtesy Bill Roberts, archivist, Berkeley Historical Society.

32 "life there was too hard": Addison Parry to Sterling Dow, 15 June 1964, Dow.

32 "a drugstore of his own": Newhouse, p. 22. See also online "Oakland Wiki" entry, Isaac Parry.

32 "He was compelled to take flight": "Detective Hodgkins Is Shot," *Oakland Tribune,* 3 February 1909, begins the paper's two-month coverage of the incident, which culminated with Clifton's trial at the end of March and included many references to the heroic clerk. An illustration included with this first article shows the layout of the drugstore. " 'No you don't,' daringly shouted I. M. Parry, a clerk," when confronting Clifton, according to a *San Francisco Call* article on 3 February 1909, "and he lifted the cash register from the counter and hurled it at the holdup man," who later fired twice at him.

32 "gargles, inhalations": Thomas J. Schlereth, *Victorian America: Transformations in Everyday Life, 1876–1915*. New York: HarperCollins, 1991, p. 284.

32 "Your Hair Can Be Long": *Oakland Tribune* display ad, 2 October 1911.

33 "There is absolutely no use to keep the stores open": "Druggists Discuss Hours of Closing," *Oakland Tribune*, 1 February 1913.

34 "His candor is such": MP to Addison Parry, 11 January [1935], Feld.

34 "Hello Grandson": IP to Milman Youngjohn, Christmas 1953, Youngjohn. Isaac Parry's penchant for blithe assertion occasionally surfaced in awkward ways: During World War II, around 1942, he blamed Hitler's campaign against the Jews on the Jews: *Oh, they've just brought it on themselves.* His widowed daughter-in-law, Milman Parry's Jewish wife, Marian, never spoke to him again, reports her grandson Andrew Feld.

35 They were close: Sterling Dow summary of talk with Addison Parry, 18 September 1964, Dow.

35 "snuggled up to her": Newhouse, p. 69.

35 "Our mother was artistic": Addison Parry to Sterling Dow, 15 June 1964, Dow.

36 "They felt they were superior": See Newhouse, pp. 21–22; interview, Stephen Parry.

36 "Oh," she gushed: Youngjohn.

36 "overburdened adolescence": Levin, p. 259. In "Four Generations of Oral Literary Studies at Harvard University," MPColl, David Bynum variously pictures MP's father as a carpenter and as an "independent artisan," and MP himself as a poultry farmer, but these fail to square with other evidence.

36 Milman worked: Numerous references in Newhouse.

36 "they went to any church": Sterling Dow summary of talk with Addison Parry, 18 September 1964, Dow.

36 she learned for the first time: Youngjohn.

36 "Sometimes I think I loved him too much": IP to John H. Finley, 28 June 1954, Zabel 4.

37 "He liked the domesticity": Newhouse, p. 59.

37 "reared in a secure and loving home": Addison Parry to Sterling Dow, 31 October 1964, Dow.

37 "in a way in love": Newhouse, p. 62.

37 she wrote several stories: Addison Parry, "The Great Hate," "The Spirit of His Music," Oakland Tech literary magazine, *Scribe*, circa 1916.

37 "We are having a bit of fairly good weather": MP to Addison Parry, 24 June [1925], Feld.

37 "Fine description, is it not?": MP to Addison Parry, 8 June [1925], Feld.

38 "written on a thin paper": MP to IP, 18 August [1925], Feld.

39 new crown jewel: *The Architect* xiv, no. 1 (1917). See also "Oakland Wiki," online site; "Oakland Tech: One Hundred Years," video history narrated by Ted Lange, 2015; *Scribe,* during MP's tenure there; Oakland Technical High School Centennial Book.

40 shattered the normal routines: For Spanish flu, see "The American Influenza Epidemic of 1918–1919: Oakland, California," in *Influenza Encyclopedia,* digital publication of University of Michigan Center for the History of Medicine; Rex W. Adams, "The 1918 Spanish Influenza, Berkeley's 'Quinta Columna,'" *Chronicle of the University of California,* spring 1998; Georgia Graves Bordwell, "That One Touch of Nature," *Oakland Tribune,* 3 November 1918.

40 "After we've washed the dishes": Agnes Edwards to her parents, 19 October 1918, Bancroft Library, University of California, Berkeley, LD759.P37 2006.

40 Parry's mother died: Given her date of death, at the very height of the flu epidemic, and her relative youth, one might reasonably assume it was the flu that killed her. But Alameda County records are clear: "Cause of death: cancer of the stomach." In a telephone interview, Christine Henry, daughter of MP's sister Lucile, reports also having heard that her grandmother died of cancer, possibly ovarian cancer.

40 "The world is a different one": *Scribe,* 4 December 1918.

40 "a brainy lot": Ibid., 15 May 1919.

40 "glimpsed [Milman's] potentialities": Addison Parry to Sterling Dow, 15 June 1964, Dow. Elsie Henrietta Martens presented at a joint session of the Classical Association of the Pacific States and the California High School Teachers' Association on 18–19 July 1918: *The Classical Journal* 14, no. 1, p. 66.

41 "Latin Club's Lively Plans": *Scribe,* 3 November 1915.

41 "Twenty-seven members": Ibid., 1 and 15 May 1915.

41 "Give the principal parts": Ibid., 4 December 1918.

41 four years of Latin: MP's University of California (Cal) transcript, Summary of Entrance Credits.

42 Milman in uniform: Photo, Marcial.

42 "one of those rare and happy scholars": "Service in Memory of Milman Parry" at Harvard, 19 December 1935, G. B. Gulick.

42 hopped a freight train: Interview, Milman Youngjohn. Addison Parry seems to refer to the same incident in an interview with Sterling Dow, 18 September 1964, Dow.

43 "From his earliest youth": *Occident,* September 1921, pp. 223–225 and 238.

44 becoming a physician: Newhouse, p. 11; MP's Cal transcript shows him signed up for Anatomy 102 for the spring 1921 semester, later formally withdrawing "by petition."

6—MRS. PARRY

45 In a story: MTP, "At Twenty," *Occident* 76, no. 1 (September 1920): 9–12.
46 trip to Atlantic City: Photo, Feld.
46 weak, sick, and dependent: Newhouse, p. 4.
46 "our class poet": Riverside High School *Mercury,* 1917.
46 "Sometimes at night": MTP, "At Night," *Poetry,* September 1921, p. 313.
46 "life's one and valiant truth": MTP, "To Rupert Brooke," *Wisconsin Literary Magazine,* February 1919, p. 125.
46 "I had to be taken care of": Newhouse, p. 5.
47 loaded up on economics: University of California transcript, Mildred Thanhouser.
48 "being ill and trying to get strong": Newhouse, p. 6.
48 "it was our tastes and things": Ibid., p. 43.
49 "I was very ambitious": Ibid., p. 52.
49 "Stowitts, through whose brain now whirl": MTP, "A Track Star with a Russian Ballet," *Occident,* February 1921, p. 85.
49 *Why, he isn't even 20:* Newhouse, p. 9.
50 Milman was not a member: For student life at Cal during this period, see Clarkson Crane's novel, *The Western Shore.* Salt Lake City, UT: Peregrine Smith Books, 1985, originally published 1925.
50 Alfred Kroeber: See Garcia; Theodora Kroeber, *Alfred Kroeber: A Personal Configuration.* Berkeley: University of California Press, 1970; Julian H. Steward, "Alfred Louis Kroeber," *Biographical Memoirs,* National Academy of Sciences, 1962.
50 "All my friends turned into buildings": Newhouse, p. 7.
50 Raina Prohme: Ibid., pp. 6–7.
50 formed a dislike: Gregor Benton and Arthur J. Knodel, *Reporting the Chinese Revolution: The Letters of Rayna Prohme.* London: Pluto Press, 2007, p. 27.
50 "wasn't in the air": Newhouse, p. 7.
50 "I was more or less the leader": Ibid., p. 20.
51 "masculine reactions": Ibid., p. 44.
51 "That's the beginning of the baby": Ibid., p. 10.
51 hitchhiked down the Pacific coast to Carmel: Ibid., p. 9.
52 Their first home: Caption for original photo in glassine envelope, Book II, Dow.

52 took a few graduate courses: Cal transcript, MP.

52 poultry farm: Newhouse, pp. 11–12. ABL was "quite vexed to think of anyone's remembering such lowly, loathsome details of Parry's life," recalls David Bynum.

52 Molino Avenue: *Mill Valley Record,* 1 December 1923, Laurie Thompson to the author, 16 October 2017; Newhouse, p. 11.

52 at the door of Ivan Linforth: Sterling Dow conversation with I. M. Linforth, 6 March 1964, Dow.

52 Senior Extravaganza: *Oakland Tribune,* 13 February 1923.

53 hands behind his back: Cal yearbook, *Blue and Gold,* 1923, p. 116.

53 all he could talk about was Homer: Sterling Dow summary of conversation with I. M. Linforth, 6 March 1964, Dow.

7—MILMAN ON THE BEACH

54 "As soon as Dawn": Fagles *Odyssey,* Book 12, line 10.

55 "But *he* raged on": Fagles *Iliad,* Book 1, line 581.

55 as it appears he did not: Sterling Dow unpublished comments on MP not included in his 1964 Sather Lecture at Cal, Dow 10–13: "During his undergraduate years, Parry had put no special emphasis, had taken no famous course regularly given, on Homer"; see also MP's Cal transcript.

55 "Now, the lustrous queen": Fagles *Odyssey,* Book 21, line 50.

56 "Parry had some ideas": Sterling Dow summary of conversation with I. M. Linforth, 6 March 1964, Dow.

56 "became his deep and abiding love": Addison Parry to Sterling Dow, 15 June 1964, Dow.

57 Across his undergraduate years: MP's Cal transcript.

57 "as excellent a Greek faculty": Joseph Fontenrose, "Classics at Berkeley: The First Century," Department of Classics, 1978, p. 29. Fontenrose, pp. 13–29, supplies capsule biographies of James Turney Allen, Roger Jones, George Calhoun, and Ivan Mortimer Linforth.

57 Roger Jones: In a listing of potential research leads, Dow 38 puts Roger Jones under "Berkeley friends" rather than "Faculty."

59 Linear B: See Margalit Fox's excellent *The Riddle of the Labyrinth: The Quest to Crack an Ancient Code.* New York: Ecco, 2013.

60 "Now the great array of gods": Fagles *Iliad,* Book 2, line 1.

61 "not even the most hardened cynic": Richard Martin, "Introduction," Lattimore *Iliad,* p. 37.

61 "how this inspiration came": Newhouse, p. 51; see also Sterling Dow comments on MP not included in his 1964 Sather Lecture, Dow 10–13.

62 "the idea of this book": *Making,* p. 1.

8—*GLAUKOPIS ATHENE*

63 "A Comparative Study": *Making,* pp. 421–436.

63 "Just as the story": Ibid., p. 421.

64 "They flow unceasingly": Ibid., p. 426.

65 "Plenty of insults": Ibid., Fagles *Odyssey,* Book 20, line 285.

65 "Ships are swift": *Making,* p. 426.

65 "for the sake of introducing": Ibid., p. 427.

65 "dictated by convenience": Ibid.

66 coterie of devoted admirers: See, for example, Suzanne B. Riess, interview of Grace L. McCann Morley, "Art, Artists, Museums, and the San Francisco Museum of Art," University of California Regional Cultural History Project. Berkeley," 1960, pp. 12–13.

66 Ten times: Garcia, p. 69.

66 "overzealous": *Making,* p. 427.

67 "with uncovered head": Ibid., p. 424.

67 "By following this tradition": Ibid., p. 425.

67 two brief essays: *Occident,* November 1922, p. 165, and December 1922, p. 229, which both appear in the journal's "Concerning Books" column. MP's likely authorship deduced from content and context of the essays, and his position as *Occident's* book editor.

67 "the unrestricted range": *Making,* p. 421.

68 "An audience of the period": Ibid.

69 "I never asked him": Newhouse, p. 51.

69 "Milman tore from his apartment": Addison Parry to Sterling Dow, 31 October 1964, Dow.

69 Its forty pages: Dow, Book III.

70 "But the first few pages": Sterling Dow unpublished comments on MP not included in his 1964 Sather Lecture, Dow 10–13.

70 "An astonishing piece of work": Hugh Lloyd-Jones to AP 23 February 1971, Adam 066.

70 "Probably there are": *Making,* p. 422. Having written biographies of the Indian mathematical genius Srinivasa Ramanujan and of the Canadian-American writer and thinker Jane Jacobs, I cannot refrain from remarking on a certain kinship between them and Parry:

• The self-educated Ramanujan introduces himself: "I have not trodden through the conventional regular course which is followed in a University course, but I am striking out a new course for myself."

• Jane Jacobs writes to her patron of her progress on her seminal book,

The Death and Life of Great American Cities: "I am not rehashing old material on cities and city planning. I am working with new concepts."

• And here Parry declares that, in the light of his ideas, "modern critics must change their attitudes."

In each, we find a remarkable haughtiness—the conviction that a new understanding of the world rests on his or her shoulders.

PART THREE
Paris

9—THE PARIS DEAL

73 anatomy course: Newhouse, p. 11; MP's Cal transcript.

73 "Well, why not be a college professor": Newhouse, p. 11.

74 only job she'd ever held: Ibid., p. 10.

74 "Milman was by far the best": Ibid., p. 8.

74 "Mr. Linforth highly disapproved": Ibid., pp. 8, 55.

74 "distinguished in appearance": Joseph Fontenrose, "Classics at Berkeley: The First Century," Department of Classics, 1978, p. 20.

75 "it was as though he were carved out of a block": Newhouse, p. 53.

75 "I found domesticity": Ibid., p. 12.

75 "We came to feel": Malcolm Cowley, *Exile's Return: A Literary Odyssey of the 1920s.* New York: Penguin, 1994, p. 28.

75 "heart-broken": Newhouse, pp. 12–13.

75 "He didn't want": Ibid., p. 13.

76 "We'll go on our own": Ibid.

76 "After the war": Cowley, *Exile's Return,* p. 94.

77 went first to Milwaukee: Newhouse, p. 14.

77 "big enough for a room": Ibid., p. 17.

78 "I just threw them over the side": Ibid., p. 18.

79 "we were employing the whole neighborhood": Ibid., p. 48.

79 "a most imperfect knowledge": AdamIntro, p. ix; MP's Cal transcript credits Parry with a year of French at Oakland Tech.

79 "They consisted of little dictations": MTP to Addison and Allison Parry [circa Christmas 1924], Feld.

79 Clamart: Interviews with Yahyaoui Mehdi, Service Archives-Documentation, Mairie de Clamart; Gisèle Jullemier, Clamart historian, April 2018.

10—A WORLD TO HIM

81 "Here it is about three o'clock": MTP to Addison and Allison Parry, n.d.

82 "He gave me one day off": Newhouse, p. 49.

82 "This is something our mother told us": Andrew Feld to the author, 25 January 2018.

82 "You can't imagine": Newhouse, p. 39.

83 "was a great machine": Malcolm Cowley, *Exile's Return: A Literary Odyssey of the 1920s.* New York: Penguin, 1994, p. 135.

83 "Even more than the University": Levin, p. 260.

84 A Budapest woman, Liliane Olah: Information about their thesis subjects is drawn from "Registre des certificats d'aptitude au grade de docteur d'État ou d'Université, 1923–1959." Faculté des Lettres, Université de Paris. Archives nationales (Pierrefitte-sur-Seine), AJ16 7075, for the years 1923–1928.

85 "rosy and angelic": MTP to Addison and Allison Parry [circa Christmas 1924], Feld.

85 "well, unified and": Newhouse, p. 49.

85 "Milman gets his revenge": MTP to Addison and Allison Parry [circa Christmas 1924], Feld.

11—STUDENT WITHOUT A SCHOOL

86 "demands much more determination": Hugh A. Smith, "The American University Union at Paris," *The French Review,* January 1930, pp. 161–168.

87 Victor Bérard: Account of Bérard, his relationships with Parry and Meillet, drawn from correspondence with Étienne Bérard; extracts from unpublished book about his grandfather; *Portraits de Victor Bérard,* ed. Sophie Basch. Athènes: École française d'Athènes, 2015.

88 "a big handsome man": Edith Wharton, *A Backward Glance: An Autobiography.* Philadelphia: Curtis Publishing, 1934.

88 Sometime early in 1925: Sterling Dow's working time line of MP's life gives it as "*ca* June" 1925, Dow.

89 not merely disappointed: Newhouse, p. 14.

89 "Sorry you can't see this place": MP to Addison Parry, 8 June [1925], Feld. (In the typed transcript of this letter, the postmark on the accompanying envelope is recorded as 8 June 1926, but this, I believe, is an error; in every other way, it fits what we know of Parry's travels in the summer of 1925.)

90 "I had, I think, almost a motherly desire": Newhouse, p. 44.

90 "just as heavy and doughy as a doughnut": Ibid., p. 8.

90 often unprepared: Sterling Dow summary of his interview with Broneer, 24 April 1964, Dow.

90 "But this little place": MP to Addison Parry, 29 June [1925], Feld.

91 "A month at Athens": MP to IP, 18 August [1925], Feld.

91 "a sleepy girl, unbeautiful": MP's Greek journal, Zabel 38.

91 "From the sweating compartment": Ibid.

91 "Somewhere around here": MP to IP, 18 August [1925], Feld.

92 only Marian's last-minute switch: Sterling Dow's working time line of MP's life for fall 1925, Dow.

92 "Oh," Marian would lament: Newhouse, p. 14.

12—ALMOST EVERY SUNDAY

93 "such beginners as you": MP to Addison Parry, 9 November [1925], Feld.

93 "if you have nothing to tell us": MP to Addison and Allison Parry, 5 June 1926, Feld.

94 enrolled at the Sorbonne: Université de Paris, Faculté des Lettres, Immatriculation, 1925–26 on 26 November 1925; 1926–27 on 13 November 1926.

94 "days of many Greek books": MP to Addison Parry, 17 October [1925], Feld.

94 Maurice Croiset: See Edmond Faral, "Notice sur la vie et les travaux de M. Maurice Croiset," *Comptes rendus des séances de l'Académie des Inscriptions et Belles-Lettres*, 88ᵉ année, no. 1, 1944, pp. 78–101; Aimé Puech, "Maurice Croiset," *Bulletin de l'Association Guillaume Budé*, no. 47, avril 1935, pp. 3–9; Abel Lefranc, "Funérailles de M. Maurice Croiset, membre de l'Académie," *Comptes rendus des séances de l'Académie des Inscriptions et Belles-Lettres,* 79ᵉ année, no. 4, 1935, pp. 518–526.

95 Aimé Puech: See Charles Virolleaud, "Notice sur la vie et les travaux de M. Aimé Puech," *Comptes rendus des séances de l'Académie des Inscriptions et Belles-Lettres,* 1947, pp. 136–151; Mario Roques, "Éloge funèbre de M. Aimé Puech," *Comptes rendus des séances de l'Académie des Inscriptions et Belles-Lettres,* 1940, pp. 512–524.

95 "I was immediately charmed": Aimé Puech, "Milman Parry," *Revue des Études Grecques* 49, no. 229 (1936): 87–88.

96 "the religious life": Anna Radwan, *Memoire des Rues: Paris 5ᵉ Arrondissement.* Paris: Parigramme, 2016, p. 102.

97 "can only be truly interested": Aimé Puech, "Louis Méridier," *Revue des Études Grecques* (avril–juin 1933): 161–167.

97 master's thesis took up 15 pages: Both figures refer to their lengths as published in *Making.* Typewritten, the master's thesis was 40 pages.

13—THE HOMERIC QUESTION

98 "His theory of epic composition": Harry Levin, "Comparing the Literature," in *Grounds for Comparison*. Cambridge, MA: Harvard University Press, 1972, p. 78.

99 "the Homeric Question": AdamIntro offers a comprehensive review.

99 "The problem is as difficult as it is fascinating": Martin P. Nilsson, *Homer & Mycenae*. Philadelphia: University of Pennsylvania Press, 1933, p. 1.

100 "incoherent, immoral": Wilson *Odyssey*, p. 8.

100 "an original core narrative": Ibid., p. 9.

101 "he had so much as heard": AdamIntro, p. xxii.

101 How can we understand: *Making*, p. 2.

102 "Philological criticism": Ibid., p. 3.

14—ORNAMENTAL EPITHETS

105 "Yet though it is always": Bernard Knox, "Introduction," Fagles *Odyssey*, p. 13.

106 "Scholarship has always admitted": *Making*, p. 8.

106 "shocked the delicate sensibilities": de Lamberterie, p. 413.

106 "The epic poets fashioned": *Making*, p. 9.

106 "Then X replied": Parry begins to set out his argument at Ibid., p. 10.

108 "Noun-Epithet Formulae of Gods and Heroes": Ibid., p. 39.

109 "The fixed epithet": Ibid., p. 126.

109 "An epithet is not ornamental in itself": Ibid., p. 127.

109 "As we come to the end": Ibid., p. 171.

110 "The mind gives up": Ibid., p. 172.

111 "a remarkable fullness": Jury, p. 2. Storey's review appears in *Classical Philology* 23, no. 3 (July 1928): 305–306; Saussy's comment in *The Ethnography of Rhythm: Orality and Its Technologies*. New York: Fordham University Press, 2016, p. 43.

111 "One is tempted to reproach": P. Chantraine, review of MP's "L'èpithète traditionnelle dans Homère," *Revue de Philologie*, 1 January 1929, p. 299.

111 "My head is too full": MP to Addison Parry, 16 October 1926, Feld.

111 "It could fairly be said": AdamIntro, p. xxii.

111 "undoubtedly the most important": *Making*, p. 124.

112 "the melancholy conclusion": Ibid., p. 125.

112 "to bring us back to the days": Ibid.

112 "We shall find among the causes": Gilbert Murray, *The Rise of the Greek Epic*, Oxford, 1907, cited in James P. Holoka, "Homer, Oral Poetry The-

ory, and Comparative Literature: Major Trends and Controversies in Twentieth-Century Criticism." In *Zweihundert Jahre Homer-Forschung: Rückblick und Ausblick,* ed. Joachim Latacz. Stuttgart/Leipzig: B. G. Teubner, 1991, p. 459.

113 "the thoroughness of the argumentation": AdamIntro, p. xxviii.

113 "Must we give reasons": *Making,* p. 37.

114 "not twice, not thrice": Ibid., p. 130.

114 "Parry's statistical orientation": Holaka, "Homer, Oral Poetry Theory, and Comparative Literature, p. 463.

I 5 – TRAPPED

115 boardinghouse: The house, much altered, still exists. A photo, among the Feld papers, shows their bedroom.

115 "He did a good deal": Newhouse, p. 45.

115 "we are learning much bad French": MP to Addison Parry, 11 avril [1927].

115 Allards: 1926 census for 24 rue de Fontenay; correspondence and photos from Alain Carron, the house's current owner.

115 "still, clear autumn days": MTP to Addison Parry, October [1926], Feld.

116 Sceaux: Interview with Aldine Martini, chef du service Archives/Documentation, ville de Sceaux, who furnished photos, maps, articles, and books of local history.

116 "There in his garden": Simone Flahaut-Ollive, "Une Jeunesse à Sceaux de 1920 à 1940," *Bulletin des Amis de Sceaux,* nouvelle série no. 21, 2005, pp. 40–54.

116 "I was just there with Marian": Newhouse, p. 45.

117 "Remember how Mother": AP to sister Marian, 4 June 1950, Adam 017.

117 "Banlieue Parisienne": Zabel 36.

118 "I envy you": MTP to Addison Parry, October [1926], Feld.

118 "constantly at work": Sterling Dow's notes, under "Work Habits," Dow.

119 "I'm ashamed now": Newhouse, p. 39.

119 her questions more intrusive: Ibid., p. 45.

120 "I even refused to do that": Ibid., p. 47.

120 "I think Milman could have taken me": Ibid.

I 6 – SOUTENANCE

121 Antoine Meillet's: See Karl Krippes, "Meillet, the Researcher and the Teacher," *Histoire Épistémologie Langage* 10, no. 2 (1988): 277–283; Joseph Vendryes, "Antoine Meillet," *Annuaire 1937–38, École pratique des hautes*

études, Section des sciences historiques et philologiques 70, no. 1, 1937, pp. 5–37 ; Paul Boyer, "Antoine Meillet: L'Homme et le Savant," *Revue des Études Slaves,* 1936, pp. 191–198; see also Thérèse de Vet, "Parry in Paris: Structuralism, Historical Linguistics, and the Oral Theory," *Classical Antiquity* 24, no. 2 (2005): 257–284; and de Lamberterie.

122 "whose ideas were most in harmony": AdamIntro, p. xxiii.

122 "We have discussed many times": Antoine Meillet to MP, 7 April 1928, Harvard.

122 not *entirely* certain: de Lamberterie, p. 411.

123 compliment he'd recently received for his French: MP to Addison Parry, 13 December [1926], Feld.

123 "cost him much slow and careful labor": Sterling Dow's notes, under "Language Ability," Dow.

123 "While he spoke French": Aimé Puech, "Milman Parry," *Revue des Études Grecques* 49, no. 229 (1936): 88.

123 "I estimate that you have studied": Maurice Croiset to MP, 24 January 1927, Harvard.

124 "My thesis," Milman wrote: MP to Addison Parry, 11 April [1927], Feld.

124 *Docteur ès lettres:* See Édouard Des Places, "Cent Cinquante Ans du Doctorat ès Lettres (1810–1960)," *Bulletin de l'Association Guillaume Budé* 1, no. 2 (1969): 209–228.

124 "At that moment": MP to Addison Parry, 11 April [1927], Feld.

124 "Well, that was a little bit of a surprise": Newhouse, p. 40.

124 their son was born: Report of Birth of Children Born to American Parents, American Consular Service, Paris, 23 February 1928.

125 "Look, if you'll cook supper": Newhouse, p. 31.

125 "the bassinette": Fragment, beginning "Dearest Pussicat," young Marian to her mother, n.d., Adam 037.

125 Parry's was announced: *La Semaine à Paris,* 25 May to 1 June 1928.

126 ample room to point up: Reports on the theses of M. Jacques Paliard, Gabriel Perreux, and Mélitta Pivec-Stelè, respectively, can be found in the Archives nationales (Pierrefitte-sur-Seine), AJ/16/7098.

126 Salle Louis Liard: The *salle* looks today much as it did in 1928.

126 "like a bibliography of modern classical scholarship": Levin, p. 260.

127 "probably couldn't have understood": Newhouse, p. 14.

127 "with ease and precision": Jury, p. 4.

127 Vendryes faulted even its title: Ibid.

127 "less complete and less finished": Ibid.

127 "one of the most original": Ibid., p. 1.

128 "both flexible and broad": Ibid., p. 2.

128 "that Homeric style must": Ibid.

128 "a great number of seeming liberties": Ibid., p. 4.
128 "With the completion": Richard Martin, "Introduction," *The Iliad of Homer*, trans. Richard Lattimore. Chicago: University of Chicago Press, 2011, p. 40.
128 "reservations": Jury, p. 3.
128 "anonymous bards constrained": Review of Parry's Paris thesis, *Bulletin de la Société de Linguistiqe de Paris* 29: 100–102, cited in de Lamberterie, p. 412.
129 Matija Murko [who often appears in French-language texts as Mathias Murko]: See Aaron Phillip Tate, "Matija Murko, Wilhelm Radloff, and Oral Epic Studies," *Oral Tradition* 26, no. 2 (2011): 329–352; Sylva Fischerová, "The Role of Czechoslovakian Slavistics in the Forming of the Parry-Lord Oral-Formulaic Theory," in *Roman O. Jakobson: A Work in Progress,* eds. T. Kubíček and A. Lass. Olomouc, Czech.: Palacký University, 2014; Jasmina Talam, "Matija Murko and His Growing Interest in South Slavic Epics," The Complete Historical Collections, 1899–1950. Series 16: The collection of Matija Murko (1912, 1913), Phonogrammarciv of the Austrian Academy of Sciences, 2017, pp. 15–22.
129 "with his usual ease and clarity": *Making,* p. 439.
130 "the effort expended": Jury, p. 4.
130 "I knew cum laude": Newhouse, p. 15.

PART FOUR
Harvard

17—THE CALL

133 "We didn't know": Newhouse, p. 16.
133 "almost helpless invalidism": Charles Blanchard, *Building for the Centuries: A History of Drake University,* Des Moines: Drake University, 1931, p. 70.
134 "until," the university said: "Professor Denny Retires as Head of Department," Drake student newspaper, n.d.
134 long white envelope: Newhouse, p. 16.
135 "I am sending you": MP to Alfred Kroeber, 28 June 1928. Guide to Records of the [Cal] Department of Anthropology, Collection CU-23. (Parry also sent a copy of his thesis to Victor Bérard, 17 May 1928, courtesy Étienne Bérard.)
135 boarded the SS *Rochambeau:* Parry "time line" by Steve T. Reece.
136 "the dream of my heart": Newhouse, p. 18.
136 local paper interviewed him: "Parry Blames Teachers for Pupil's Failure,"

Des Moines Register, 9 September 1928. See also "Drake U. Names Milman Parry as Latin Head," *Des Moines Register,* 2 August 1928.

136 "little bit of a house": Newhouse, p. 19.

136 handwritten note: Herbert Weir Smyth to MP, 2 December 1928. Papers of Herbert Weir Smyth, Harvard. See also ibid., p. 7.

137 "revealed a scholarly mind": Eleanor A. Smyth to MTP, 9 December 1935.

137 "Is there not a good chance": Herbert Weir Smyth to MP, 2 December 1928. Papers of Herbert Weir Smyth, Harvard.

137 "The Homeric Gloss": *Making,* pp. 240–250. Parry's original title, as it appears in *Transactions and Proceedings of the American Philological Association* 59 (1928): 233, was "Did Homer Understand the Epic *Glottai?*"

137 "One's style": *Making,* p. 250.

138 "the impression he made": "Service in Memory of Milman Parry" at Harvard, 19 December 1935, G. B. Gulick.

138 A second letter: C. N. Jackson to MP, 15 December 1928, Harvard.

138 "I was left then in the snow": Newhouse, p. 19.

138 "his return to America": Levin, p. 260.

138 Harvard's "call": *Language* 5, no. 3 (September 1929): 199.

139 Morehouse's home: "Dr. Morehouse Entertains New Faculty Members," *Drake Delphic,* 14 March 1929.

139 Marian actually liked Des Moines: Newhouse, p. 19.

139 artless snapshot: Photo, Feld.

140 "Iowa's very much like Wisconsin": Newhouse, p. 20.

140 "I didn't want it in the house": Ibid.

18—HIS CAT-LIKE SMILE

141 "He could just do things": Newhouse, p. 13.

141 At noon on Mondays: "Announcement of the Course of Instruction," Faculty of Arts and Sciences, 1929–30, Harvard.

141 "Parry looking out the window": General Records of the Chairman of Classics, 1929–30, Harvard.

142 "over which presided": Robert Fizgerald, in Joseph L. Lant, *Our Harvard: Reflections on College Life by Twenty-Two Distinguished Graduates.* New York: Taplinger, 1982.

142 "if there was any suspicion": John B. Titchener to Sterling Dow, 14 July 1964, Dow.

142 "The incisive impression": Harry Levin, "Comparing the Literature," in *Grounds for Comparison.* Cambridge, MA: Harvard University Press, 1972, p. 78.

142 "after an anticipated routine": Levin, p. 260.

143 "The study of Greek": Ibid., p. 259.

143 "a charming and sympathetic": M. V. Anastos to Sterling Dow, 14 June 1964, Dow.

143 "cat-like smile": Marian Feld, MP's daughter, to her own daughter, Laura, 17 October 1976, recounting a recent talk by Fitzgerald, Feld.

144 "reflected a way of life": Ibid.

144 Homer and Virgil: *Harvard Crimson,* 16 April 1930.

144 "able and sagacious work": Martin P. Nilsson, *Homer and Mycenae.* Philadelphia: University of Pennsylvania Press, 1933, p. 179.

144 left him feeling appreciated: ABL doctoral thesis, "A Singer of Tales," p. 16, Harvard.

144 "The implications of his theory": John B. Titchener to Sterling Dow, 14 July 1964, Dow.

145 "was *not* a liberal": Newhouse, p. 77.

145 "he found nothing mystical": Sterling Dow's notes on Parry as a teacher, Dow 52.

145 "He respected the hierarchical nicety": Levin, p. 264.

145 selected her wardrobe: Newhouse, p. 79.

145 "to cut in": Ibid.

145 "I wonder exactly": AP to MTP, 14 December 1951, Marcial.

146 Sceaux's war dead: See Aldine Martini, chief researcher, *Les Scéens et la Première Guerre mondiale.* Ville de Sceaux, 2011.

19—THE ORAL TURN

148 "an awareness": AdamIntro, p. xi.

149 "was essentially a part of an oral poetry": *Making,* p. 429.

150 "Complicated groupings of ideas": Ibid., p. 251.

150 "upon a well-bound wooden raft": Wilson *Odyssey,* Book 7, line 264, p. 216.

152 70 percent of Homeric verses: *Making,* p. 254. These neat numbers do not appear in Parry's text, but can be derived from the comparison at the bottom of this page, where his I and II categories come to 48.5 and 24.8, or a total of 73.3 percent for the *Iliad,* and 44.8 and 26.6, or a total of 71.4 percent for his *Odyssey* text samples. The *Argonautica* and *Aeneid* samples add up to 50.8 and 50.5 percent, respectively.

152 "Homer was ever pushed on": *Making,* p. 262.

152 "new idea of poetic artistry": Ibid., p. 269.

152 "the scholarly caution": Joseph Russo, "The Meaning of Oral Poetry. The Collected Papers of Milman Parry: A Critical Re-assessment," *Quaderni Urbinati di Cultura Classica,* no. 12 (1971): 32.

152 "It must have been": *Making,* p. 317.

153 "we shall cease to be puzzled by much": Ibid., p. 269.

155 Jousse's 1925 book: *Le Style oral rhythmique et mnémotechnique chez les Verbo-moteurs.* Paris: Gabriel Beauchesne, 1925. See also Edgard Richard Sienaert, "Marcel Jousse: The Oral Style and the Anthropology of Gesture," *Oral Tradition* 5, no. 1 (1990): 91–106; Haun Saussy, *The Ethnography of Rhythm.* New York: Fordham University Press, 2016, p. 43.

155 "an idiosyncratic synthesis": Foley, p. 14.

155 assign it to his young student: *EpicSingers,* p. 15.

155 "marks the change of emphasis": AdamIntro, p. xxiii.

155 fashioned a one-hour documentary: *Sur les Pas de Marcel Jousse: La Mémoire, le Geste et le Vivant.* Pessac, France: L'Université Bordeaux Montaigne et l'Association Marcel Jousse, 2014.

156 "We may very well find": *Making,* p. 265.

20—NOTHING ELSE TO DO

157 "Life here": MP to Addison Parry, 14 April 1931, Feld.

158 "I did not at once give myself": *Making,* p. 439.

158 "had reached a crisis": ABL in Ibid., p. 468.

159 "rawboned, poor": John Gunther, *Inside Europe.* New York: Harper & Brothers, 1937, p. 356. The classic book on Yugoslavia from this period is Rebecca West, *Black Lamb and Grey Falcon: A Journey Through Yugoslavia.* New York: Penguin Books, 1982, originally published 1940. For an almost unrecognizably milder take on the country, see Grace Ellison, *Yugoslavia: A New Country and Its People.* London: John Lane, 1933.

160 "We live in harmony": Murko, p. 111.

160 "There is no condition or profession": Ibid., p. 114.

161 Murko's photos: These appear only in the original French-language booklet, not the Foley translation.

161 "scholar-gypsy": Levin, p. 264.

162 "obeys very different rules": Thérèse A. de Vet, "Marcel Mauss, the Gift, and the Oral Theory," in Emily Varto, ed., *Brill's Companion to Classics and Early Anthropology.* Leiden, Netherlands: Brill, 2018, p. 319.

162 "remarkable consequences": David Bynum, "Four Generations of Oral Literary Studies at Harvard University," MPColl, p. 11.

21—A DARKNESS THERE

163 "I wasn't interested": Newhouse, p. 21.

163 "Well, you know I'm Jewish": Ibid., p. 27.

164 "I wasn't there five minutes": Ibid.

164 seem surprised: Ibid., p. 29.

164 "terribly anti-Semitic": Ibid., p. 27.

164 "impossible to have a real conversation": AP to sister Marian, 13 November 1949, Feld.

164 "had always liked Mother immensely": AP to sister Marian, 25 January 1953, Adam 010. See also AP to sister Marian, 11 July 1955, Feld: "Mother's characterization of Finley, as a man of passions but no feelings, is rather good."

164 "If a Jew entered": Sterling Dow's notes of 28 March 1969 interview with H. T. Levin, Dow 14.

165 "Suggested Procedure": Susanne Klingenstein, *Enlarging America: The Cultural Work of Jewish Literary Scholars, 1930–1990.* Syracuse, NY: Syracuse University Press, 1998, p. 41.

165 "He felt that he had to make his way": Newhouse, p. 29.

165 "Out of all this sea": Ibid., p. 24.

165 "Milman was a terrific worker": Ibid., p. 25.

165 "the fabulous students": Ibid., p. 23.

165 $4,000 a year: General Records of the Chairman of Classics, UAV 288.6, Harvard, 1932–33.

165 "On Sunday": Newhouse, pp. 26, 41.

166 "it was a sort of life": Ibid., p. 42.

166 "It had so many flights of stairs": Ibid., p. 55. The Belmont House was at 90 Alexander Avenue. *Congressional Record,* May 25, 1932.

166 "I kept the house": Newhouse, p. 42.

166 "easier for him to work": Ibid., p. 37.

166 "It made him miserable": Ibid., p. 21.

167 Milman's "opacity remains intact": Pamela Newhouse to Marian Feld, 14 March 1982, Feld.

167 "didn't confide in you"; Pamela Newhouse to MTP, 14 March 1982, Feld.

167 " 'You slept well?' ": Zabel 38.

168 a useful record: That is, "Cor Huso."

168 "He was not the kind of person": John B. Titchener to Sterling Dow, 23 November 1964, Dow.

168 not inclined to chatty letters: Sterling Dow's notes from lunch with ABL, 25 November 1981, Dow.

168 "an impermeable steadfastness": Bynum, Field 102.

168 "I went over to see this French friend": Newhouse, p. 40.

169 "Milman was devoted to Marian": Ibid., p. 58.

169 "In the first two great periods": AP to sister Marian, 29 August 1949, Adam 01.

169 "I have always felt a darkness there": M. V. Anastos to Sterling Dow, 14 June 1965, Dow.

170 *Philoctetes:* Account drawn from "Classical Club to Put On 'Philoctetes' by Sophocles This Week," *Harvard Crimson,* 13 March 1933; "Harvard Classical Club, Philoctetes," statement of receipts and expenses, Department of Classics, Harvard; Edwin Honig interview with Robert Fitzgerald, Academy of American Poets, originally appearing in *The Poet's Other Voice.* Amherst: University of Massachusetts Press, 1985; Klingenstein, *Enlarging America,* p. 441.

170 "laughing at the abominable acting": Marian Feld, MP's daughter, to her own daughter, Laura, 17 October 1976, Feld.

PART FIVE
Yugoslavia

22—RECONNAISSANCE

175 "What Musa said he would do": Parry Text 1 (autograph), David Bynum's enargea.org website. See also Ćor Huso 1.11–1.12.

176 "women's songs": See Mary P. Coote, "On the Composition of Women's Songs," *Oral Tradition* 7, no. 2 (1992): 332–348.

177 "someone went out": Reminiscences, p. 2.

177 "nothing more than a mere musician's trinket": Beatrice L. Stevenson, "The Gusle Singer and His Songs," *American Anthropologist,* New Series 17, no. 1 (1915): 58–68; see also Jasmina Talam, "Creation, Transmission and Performance: Guslars in Bosnia and Herzegovina," *Musicological Annual* 51, no. 2 (2015): 203–221.

178 "I suppose I expected": Charles Simic, preface to *The Battle of Kosovo,* trans. John Matthias and Vladeta Vucković. Athens: Ohio University Press, 1987.

178 little left of the guslars: Murko, p. 113.

179 "I did not seek new songs": Ibid., p. 112.

180 "Dubrovnik is perhaps the most exquisite town": Rebecca West, *Black Lamb and Grey Falcon: A Journey Through Yugoslavia.* New York: Penguin Books, 1982, originally published 1940, p. 231.

180 "there simply wasn't any realistic alternative": Bynum.

180 "This is a lovely vacation-place": MTP to Addison Parry, 2 August 1933, Feld.

181 nearby *kafana:* Ćor Huso 1.1. Parry reports that the Arbulić *kafana* was located in the "Italian Market," which is not on current maps of

Dubrovnik. I owe its location to Zoran Perović and Frane Čizmić, Drzavni arhiv u Dubrovniku, the city archives.

182 interrogated him: Ćor Huso 1.7.

182 "altogether indifferent": Ćor Huso 1.8.

182 "Marko and Musa": *NoviPazar,* p. 359.

183 "Kutuzov would not believe": Ćor Huso 1.10.

183 "had steeped himself": ABL doctoral thesis, 1949, p. 18, Harvard.

184 One day in mid-August: Ćor Huso, 21 December 1934.

184 "with great difficulty and patience": Ibid.

185 "in a voice whose lack of beauty": Ćor Huso 6.2.

185 "Marko and Nina": *Singer,* Appendix II, pp. 235–241.

186 "the care and the scholarly control": AdamIntro, p xxxvii.

187 "to an admiring account": Ćor Huso 5.5.

187 "he didn't have very much time": Newhouse, p. 32.

187 Kutuzov's son: Young Marian to her mother, 4 August, unknown year, from Les Grouets, France, Adam 035.

187 "There were no rules laid down": AdamIntro, p. xxxvi.

187 "as a complete outsider": Bynum.

188 "the first person of any sort": PopOral, p. 4.

189 "The Song of Milman Parry": *Singer,* pp. 272–275.

189 fond farewell: Harry Levin, "From *Gusle* to Tape Recorder," in *Grounds for Comparison,* Cambridge, MA: Harvard University Press, 1972, p. 213.

23–KIRKLAND HOUSE

190 taught the *Iliad:* "Announcement of the Course of Instruction," Faculty of Arts and Sciences, 1933–34, Harvard.

190 "The Oral Poetry of the Serbian Peasants": *Harvard Crimson,* 6 March 1934.

190 "Whole Formulaic Verses": *Making,* pp. 376–390.

190 all but removed: AdamIntro, p. xxxv.

190 "When one hears": *Making,* p. 378.

191 "And addressing him": Ibid., p. 380.

191 "the sun set": Ibid., p. 383.

191 Mićo Savić: In ibid., p. 389, he is called Mitcho Savitch. Murko had met him years earlier and photographed him for his book.

191 "Two pashas we fought and overcame": *Making,* p. 390.

193 "It is necessary to keep them in spirits": PopOral, p. 8.

193 snapped a picture: Ćor Huso 6.1.

193 not wholly at home: *NoviPazar,* p. 7.

193 "The greater part": PopOral, p. 8.

193 "singing to himself": Ćor Huso 1.17.

194 "direct for the first time": Kirkland House scrapbook, undated but approximately February 1934—apparently taken from "Parry Broadcasts Talk from Emerson Hall over WNAC," *Harvard Crimson,* 8 February 1934.

194 the new one: Peter McMurray, "Fathers and Sons; or, Recalling the Sound of Time," in "Festschrift in Honor of Gregory Nagy," edited by Victor Bers, David Elmer, Douglas Frame, and Leonard Muellner. Washington, D.C.: Center for Hellenic Studies, 2012; details of the recording apparatus owe to JugoWork I and II; Mitchell&Nagy, p. x; and Bynum.

195 "Every part": "SoundScriber," informational brochure, The Sound Specialties Co., MPColl.

195 "I made a couple of trips with Parry": Reminiscences, p. 1.

195 thronged with alums: ABL's handwritten account of his youthful impressions of Harvard, written sometime after 1966. Zabel 17.

196 advanced Latin course: ABL was also taking a survey course in French literature. "This early attempt of mine at Comparative Literature first brought me to Parry's attention." Zabel 17. See also ABL transcript, Office of the Registrar, Harvard.

196 Kirkland House: See *Kirkland House Alumni News,* beginning with its first issue, 23 January 1933; Kirkland House Scrap Book, 1931–37, which includes article about Kirkland House by Herbert N. Stevens, '35, in unknown Harvard publication; interview with Scott Hayward, superintendent of Kirkland House in 2017.

196 "whimsies, scholarly essays": November 1931 announcement in Harvard publication, unknown title, author, and date, about Kirkland House, in Hicks House library.

196 office, off stairway H: It is now the superintendent's office.

197 "he lost himself": M. V. Anastos to Sterling Dow, 14 June 1964, Dow.

197 Kirkland poker sessions: Newhouse, p. 30.

197 "the slurring things": Ibid., p. 38.

197 "unbounded admiration": Zabel 27.

197 "a very good-looking woman": Newhouse, p. 38.

197 "Nineteen Thirty-Four was the first Harvard class": ABL, *Sexennial Report,* 1940, Class of 1934.

197 "with an interest in his Homeric research": ABL, Harvard Class of 1934, *25th Anniversary Report,* p. 826. According to David Bynum, Parry's "outstandingly able tutee had no pronounced interest in the Homeric poetry or any other of the classics, and Parry's research activities remained quite beyond his ken all that year," referring to his senior year, 1933–34.

197 "If I am not mistaken": MP to Edward A. Whitney, draft letter, probably 8 March 1935, in folder marked "Misc," MPColl.

198 "I can't remember ever": Newhouse, p. 33.

198 "with preparations during the last days": JugoWork I, item 28.

198 group photographic portrait: Kirkland House library, dated March 8, probably 1934.

198 His passport was issued: ABL's passport, courtesy Kit and Nate Lord.

24—THE ACTUAL PROCEDURE OF WORK

199 "You must go with your husband": Newhouse, p. 56.

199 "living as we did": Ibid.

199 Parrys lived in one of them: Location deduced from MPColl photos, examined by Zoran Perović and Frane Čizmić, staff at Drzavni arhiv u Dubrovniku, the city archives; walking tour of candidate neighborhoods on the hill behind the Old City; and Evito Fisković et al., *Dubrovnik on the Old Post Cards.* Dubrovnik, HR: Dubrovački Muzei, 1996.

200 "A little town": JugoDiary, p. 12.

201 He is there for Ibro Bašić: See *NoviPazar,* pp. 21–25.

201 "The actual procedure of work": JugoWork I, p. 5.

202 Kijevo: Account is generally drawn from Aaron Phillip Tate, " 'There Were Two Foreigners and One of Ours': Parry and Lord in Kijevo, Croatia, 24 September 1934," *Folklore* 212 (December 2010): 311–320. However, based on the following evidence, I believe that Mr. Tate errs in placing Lord in Kijevo: 1. The Dow papers include Sterling Dow's notes on his interview with Lord, in which Lord, just joining Parry after a postgraduation vacation elsewhere in Europe, says he only reached Dubrovnik on September twenty-seventh; by that time the Kijevo visit was over and Parry was in Glamoc. 2. The visa stamps in Lord's passport have him leaving Italy on 21 September 1934 and arriving in Split on 22 September, the first day of the Kijevo visit (*NoviPazar,* p. 35). 3. In Lord's "Reminiscences," in the Milman Parry Collection, he reports that "my first trip to the interior began on the 7th of October, 1934 . . . , my first collecting experience." This was two weeks after the Kijevo visit by Parry. 4. The body of Tate's article, as opposed to its subtitle, never actually attests to the contrary, never makes a specific claim to a Lord "sighting" in Kijevo. Who, then, was the second foreigner? Possibly Ilija Kutuzov, but this is only a guess. So closely linked did Parry and Lord later become that to assume the "two foreigners" referred to by Tate's respondent meant Parry and Lord is understandable. Parry was one of the two, certainly, but Lord was not.

202 "heard what others could only see": Peter McMurray, "Fathers and Sons; or, Recalling the Sound of Time," p. 3.

203 "the mere organization of the work": JugoWork I, p. 1.

203 "I should wish to add": Ibid., p. 12.

203 "to study Southslavic popular poetry": Ibid.

204 "Parry's headquarters": Reminiscences, p. 1.

204 He had no previous work experience: ABL's nonacademic experience at the time he started at the navy yard in 1941, according to his Official Personnel Folder, National Archives and Records Administration, St. Louis, consisted of a month's work at a photo store and a month as a salesclerk at Jordan Marsh department store, both in Boston, during the fall of 1940.

204 "a jack of all trades": Newhouse, p. 32.

204 "I trust," wrote Perry: JugoWork I, p. 13.

204 "a memorable one": Reminiscences, p. 1.

205 "whom we found, as usual, in the bar": Ibid., p. 2.

205 Sheep's cheese and bread: Lord's handwritten notes, MPColl.

205 Kalinovik: Reminiscences, p. 2.

205 "more interest in the foreigner": ABL doctoral thesis, p. 21, Harvard.

205 "a decent interval": Ibid., p. 22.

205 "while Parry was attempting": Reminiscences, p. 2.

206 back to Dubrovnik: Account drawn from ibid.; Bynum.

206 "All morning long": JugoDiary, p. 12.

206 took one of Milman's academic robes: Newhouse, p. 33.

206 "resembled a small-town dentist": John Gunther, *Inside Europe*. New York: Harper & Brothers, 1937, p. 356.

207 "huge chimney": Lord, notes on trip to Konevala, 19 October 1934, MPColl.

207 "Unflappable": Marian Feld to Mary Louise Lord, condolence letter, 16 August 1991, Harvard: "How Albert will be missed! Quietly extraordinary, brilliant, unvainglorious."

207 "I have found once more": MP to C. N. Jackson, 24 October 1934, MPColl.

207 "Every few weeks": Marian the younger, handwritten notes, "Jugoslavia," MPColl.

208 "which we shall decorate," AP to MTP, n.d., Adam 013.

208 "My brother and I": Marian Feld's talk at Harvard symposium, "Singers and Tales in the 21st Century: The Legacies of Milman Parry and Albert Lord," 3–5 December 2010, online audio transcribed by the author.

208 In one story, Mickey captures: AdamIntro, p. xxxvii.

208 "'a real hero'": Ibid., p. xxxvi.

209 "the sojourn in Jugoslavia": Ibid.

209 "Papa's feeling": AP to sister Marian, 13 November 1949, Feld.

209 "Mother was quite lonesome": Marian Feld's talk at Harvard symposium, "Singers and Tales in the 21st Century: The Legacies of Milman Parry and Albert Lord," 3–5 December 2010, online audio transcribed by the author.

209 "I could have had": Newhouse, p. 49.

210 "Well," replied Marian: Ibid., p. 50.

210 "Papa is going to Novi Pazzaar": JugoDiary, p. 22.

211 "was born and brought up": *NoviPazar,* p. 53.

211 "a patriarchal way of life": Murko, p. 112.

211 "first came to realize": *NoviPazar,* p. 16.

211 "Where we sit": Ibid., p. 90.

212 field experiments: Ibid., p. 14.

212 seventeen notable variations: Ibid., p. 350.

213 "By this almost revolutionary idea": *Singer,* p. 30.

213 "patriarchal terms of deference": Slavica Ranković, "Managing the 'Boss': Epistemic Violence, Resistance, and Negotiations in Milman Parry's and Nikola Vujnović's *Pričanja* with Salih Ugljanin," *Oral Tradition* 27, no. 1 (2012): 17.

213 "While Parry may be the boss": Ranković, p. 20.

214 "They both live with me": *NoviPazar,* p. 235.

214 "His rags do not become the hero poet": ABL, caption to Figure 10, in Lord's photo album, MPColl.

214 "We quarreled among ourselves": *NoviPazar,* p. 59.

215 "Nothing, he had no trade": Ibid., p. 61.

215 "symbolized the Yugoslav traditional singer": *Making,* 473.

215 never existed at all: See, for example, John Miles Foley, " 'Reading Homer' Through Oral Tradition" in *Approaches to Homer's Iliad and Odyssey,* ed. Kostas Myrsiades. New York: Peter Lang, 2010, pp. 15–42.

215 "I must stay a few weeks": MP to Addison Parry, 11 January [1935], Feld.

215 occupying "volumes": Ćor Huso, *Making,* p. 439.

215 "Being notes only": AdamIntro, p. xxxix.

25—AVDO

217 "No statement made by any singer": Ćor Huso 1.12.

218 "one of the final stages": Ćor Huso, *Making,* p. 448.

218 "The material which we have obtained": YugoWork II, p. 1.

218 "in a palpable near-panic": Bynum.

218 "It is generally felt at home": YugoWork II, p. 3.

219 electrical static: Ibid., pp. 10–11.

219 "In his characteristic headlong way": Bynum.

219 "in their native costumes": ABL to his family, 3 March 1935, MPColl; see also Mary P. Coote, "On the Composition of Women's Songs," *Oral Tradition* 7, no. 2 (1992): 332–348.

219 "So we landed in a flop house": ABL to his family, 3 March 1935, MPColl.

220 "I am terribly afraid": ABL to parents, 7 March 1935, MPColl.

220 "I like to think": *EpicSingers,* p. 56.

220 "we can go much further": *Making,* p. 441.

220 "a region of gray rocks": "Across," p. 2.

221 "we sought eagerly": Ibid., p. 6.

221 Kolašin: Ibid., pp. 6–8; maps, photos, and working gusles made available by Davor Sedlarević, art director, Kolašin cultural center.

221 "stretch forth their arms": Ibid., p. 8.

221 "These Montenegrins": Rebecca West, *Black Lamb and Grey Falcon: A Journey Through Yugoslavia.* New York: Penguin Books, 1982, originally published 1940, p. 1019.

222 It was market day: Account drawn from ABL, "Avdo Međedović, Guslar," in *EpicSingers,* chapter 3; "Across," pp. 10–11; *Meho,* pp. 3–34.

222 "from a pipe": ABL, caption for Figure 21, Market Day in Bijelo Polje, Lord's photo album, MPColl.

222 They arranged to record him: Zabel 18 (fragment beginning, "When we arrive in the square at Bijelo Polje . . .")

222 "We listened with increasing interest": "Across," p. 10.

222 Lord had begun a letter: ABL to parents, 3–7 March 1935, MPColl.

223 In recent years: "Conversations" with Avdo Međedović, trans. David E. Bynum, *Meho,* pp. 37–75.

225 "a doctor who didn't dare": Ibid., p. 41.

225 "When," as he told Nikola: Ibid., p. 75.

225 For two hours each morning: *Making,* p. 476.

226 Avdo's "singing ran ahead": *EpicSingers,* p. 68.

226 "amazing sensitivity to the feelings": *Meho,* p. 6.

226 "He was straining to prove himself": *EpicSingers,* p. 70.

226 A photo taken that summer of 1951: *Meho,* p. 299.

226 "Parry found what he had searched for": *NoviPazar,* p. 16.

226 more intriguing experiments: *Singer,* p. 78; *EpicSingers,* p. 68.

227 "his heart was wilted": *Singer,* Appendix I, p. 223.

227 "To those who have ears to hear": *EpicSingers,* p. 71.

227 "Now to you, sirs": *Meho,* p. 79.

228 "Meho, the hadji's son": Ibid., p. 83.

228 likens himself to a woman: Ibid., p. 87.

228 Meho becomes a worthy hero: *EpicSingers,* p. 67.

PART SIX
Memorial

26—AT THE PALMS HOTEL

233 Whitley Terrace: MP to Addison Parry, 16 November 1935, Feld; National Register of Historic Places Inventory—Nomination Form, U.S. Department of the Interior, November 1978, with description of Whitley Heights Historic District; visit to surviving house.

233 "I wouldn't go": Newhouse, p. 57.

233 suffragist pamphlets: Ibid., p. 61.

233 "My mother, you see": Ibid., p. 16.

233 "Marian is now in Lost [*sic*] Angeles": MP to Addison Parry, 16 November 1935, Feld.

234 "No one could go very far": Sterling Dow to Albert Travis, 21 September 1964, Dow.

234 Parry was to give a talk: *Harvard Crimson,* 16 November 1935.

234 "I believe we can let him go": MP to Arthur Stanley Pease, 18 November 1935, Houghton Library, Harvard.

234 "Suddenly and unexpectedly": "Parry Brilliant Scholar, Say Harvard Associates," *Boston Globe,* 4 December 1935.

234 "did not know the reason": "Mystery Death of Harvard Man: Prof. Milman Parry Dies, Victim of Bullet, in Los Angeles Hotel Room—Believed Accident," unknown publication, n.d., but about 4 December 1935, Marcial.

234 "I had sent a message": Newhouse, p. 55.

234 "a good-natured, pig-headed": Young Marian to Laura Feld, 9 July 1976, Feld.

235 " 'Well,' she'd say": Newhouse, p. 57.

235 "it was to end this menace": "Death of M. Parry," Sterling Dow's notes of interview with H. T. Levin, 28 March 1969, Dow 16.

235 "We had said good-bye": Newhouse, p. 68.

236 brief leave of absence: "Mystery Death of Harvard Man," Marcial.

236 "bubbling over with joy": Sterling Dow's notes on conversation with Addison Parry, 18 September 1964, Dow 36.

236 presidential address: Bay Area possibilities drawn in part from Steve T. Reece, "The Myth of Milman Parry: Ajax or Elpenor," draft of essay that would later appear in *Oral Tradition* 33, no. 1 (2019): 115–142.

236 "seemed happy, quiet, composed": Sterling Dow's notes of talk with Ivan Linforth, 22 March 1964, Dow.

236 "We came up to Berkeley": Newhouse, p. 68.

236 telegraphed word home: "Parry Brilliant Scholar, Say Harvard Associates," *Boston Globe,* 4 December 1935.

237 the Palms: Hotel identified in "Harvard Professor Dies in Pistol Mishap Here," *Los Angeles Times,* 4 December 1935; see Larry R. Paul hotel database, online; picture postcards; "Parkview on the Park" website, Los Angeles Housing Partnership; 1930s-era photo furnished by Richard Kennemer, Los Angeles Housing Partnership and accompanying correspondence; tour of the much transformed structure and surrounding neighborhood.

239 "a bit of the country": Captioned photo of original Hotel Park Vista, n.d., but before 1942, on website Noirish Los Angeles, p. 2021—SkyscraperPage Forum.

239 both physically inked out: Standard Certificate of Death, State of California, Milman Parry, 5 December 1935, Dow.

239 One was B. L. Jones, LAPD badge 374: Badge numbers appear in Albert Travis to Sterling Dow, 19 January 1965, Dow. Photos of Romero appear on several online sites in connection with Los Angeles murders.

240 Parry's body was at the morgue: Ibid.

240 inconsistencies and contradictions: Reports of Parry's death were carried by the *Chicago Tribune, Los Angeles Times,* Santa Rosa *Press-Democrat, New York Times, Boston Globe,* Associated Press, United Press International, *Boston Herald,* and *Oakland Tribune,* among others.

240 "Most people who know anything about him": Sterling Dow to Albert Travis, 21 September 1964, Dow.

240 sometimes bruited about: As, for example, in the original version of Alessandro Barchiesi's 2014 Sather Lecture, since revised. Alessandro Barchiesi to the author, 19 April and 28 May 2017.

240 "richly deserves this promotion": Chair, Department of Classics to Dean Murdock, 9 December 1931, Harvard.

241 "one of the most brilliant scholars": "Parry, Greek and Latin Professor, Killed Yesterday," *Harvard Crimson,* 4 December 1935.

241 "likely to have acted favorably": "Death of M. Parry," Sterling Dow's notes of interview with H. T. Levin, Dow 14–16.

241 rumor of homosexuality: Ibid.

241 "The very circumstances of the death": Sterling Dow's notes, "Suicide Theory," 29 November 1981, Dow.

241 "somewhat mysterious early death": *New Statesman,* 19 March 1971.

241 "no one has, to our knowledge": AP and Marian Parry Feld, letter to the editor, *New Statesman,* 16 April 1971.

242 "He was too fond of living": Sterling Dow's notes of talk with Addison Parry, 18 September 1964, Dow 34.

242 "I know of no man": J. B. Titchener to Sterling Dow's, 14 July 1964, Dow.

242 "It would be a service": Sterling Dow to Albert Travis, 21 September 1964, Dow.

242 police department's records: Albert Travis to Sterling Dow, 19 January 1965, Dow.

242 "There may be an insurmountable obstacle of tact": Ibid.

243 "Widowed by Chance Shot": ACME photo with its caption, purchased by the author on eBay. Reference numbers on back: LA328356; Ref. Dept. 12-21-35, A35149.

243 "questioned at length": Sterling Dow to Albert Travis, 21 September 1964, Dow.

245 "police came storming": Youngjohn.

245 "It would be hard": Sterling Dow's notes, "Suicide Theory," 29 November 1981, Dow 2.

245 "Before this happened": Newhouse, p. 43.

246 And his promise to help her return to school: "The other injustice that Milman inflicted on Marian Sr., according to our mother," Andrew Feld wrote the author, was that they'd agreed that, once back in America, she "could continue with her higher education and get a degree, but when they got to Harvard Milman reneged, because he thought it was inappropriate for a Harvard Professor's [wife] to be a Radcliffe student (because the function of a Harvard Professor's wife is to be a Harvard Professor's wife)." Mrs. Parry, however, advised Newhouse, p. 59, that, before going to Los Angeles she'd told Milman that she "wanted to go to Radcliffe and get my degree and prepare for something. And I said that I had helped him to have an education and now I wanted to have the same thing. And he agreed without any hesitation at all and it was a foregone conclusion." Of course, she added, "I don't think that he thought that I could ever do the work at Radcliffe."

246 "You don't actually miss him": Interview, Andrew Feld.

246 "trembling with anguish": Marian to brother Adam, 15 January, no year, but about 1968, Adam 012.

247 "I don't think that's entirely implausible": Interview, Stephen Parry.

247 "persuaded the officers": Sterling Dow's notes, Dow 5.

248 prospective visit: Telephone interviews, Christine Henry, Milman Youngjohn.

248 "This is too dreadful for words": This and other condolences mostly from December 1935, Harvard. Milman's colleague Mason Hammond wrote Mrs. Parry: "Classical scholarship in general has lost the one younger man who had hold of a really significant idea. Any one of the others of us would have been less missed than Milman."

248 "sympathy and deep sense of loss": Minutes, 10 December 1935, Department of Classics, 1927–42, Harvard.

248 single *Boston Globe* article: "Parry Brilliant Scholar, Say Harvard Associates," *Boston Globe,* 4 December 1935.

248 "The ceremony held here": John Finley to IP, 17 February 1936, Youngjohn.

249 books and records: *Kirkland House Alumni News,* 1935–36. "Mrs. Milman Parry presented the House with the late Professor Parry's collection of about 60 records, predominately compositions by Mozart."

249 French classes: These details from Mrs. Parry's Cal transcript. She earned her BA on 22 May 1937.

27—THE HOUSE OF ACADEME

250 "almost a taboo topic": Margaret Beissinger to author, 17 January 2017.

250 "My family is very reserved": Interview, Nate Lord.

250 gave a paper: ABL, "Homer and Huso I: The Singer's Rests in Greek and Southslavic Heroic Song," *Transactions and Proceedings of the American Philological Association* 67 (1936): 106–113.

250 from an abstract: MP's abstract appears in *Making,* p. 420. Some of the unpublished notes appear in Ćor Huso, Ibid., pp. 454–455.

251 "It was only when the Southslavic poetry": Ibid., p. 455.

251 "we can begin to reconstruct": ABL, "Homer and Huso I: The Singer's Rests in Greek and Southslavic Heroic Song," *Transactions and Proceedings of the American Philological Association* 67 (1936): p. 113.

252 "This book is about Homer": *Singer,* p. xxxv.

252 "that a theory of composition": Ibid., p. xxxvi.

252 "Then suddenly": Ivo Andrić, *The Bridge on the Drina,* trans. by Lovett F. Edwards. Chicago: University of Chicago Press, 1977, p. 34.

253 "The singer has to contend": *Singer,* p. 14. The other extracts appear on pp. 20, 21, 15, and 102, respectively.

254 "Typical Scenes": *Making,* p. 404,

254 "The Theme": *Singer,* chapter 4.

255 "The world never looked the same": Ruth Finnegan to Mary Louise Lord, 29 September 1991. Accession 13489, Harvard.

255 "it was decided that I should work": *EpicSingers,* p. 5.

256 there would be scholars who: See, for example, Joseph Russo, "Oral Theory: Its Development in Homeric Studies and Applicability to Other Literatures," in Marianna E. Vogelzang and Herman L. J. Vanstiphout, *Mesopotamian Epic Literature: Oral or Aural.* Lewiston, NY: Edwin Mel-

len Press, 1992, p. 8: "Parry's oral theory is familiar to, and used as an intellectual tool by, a large majority of scholars who have not read most of Parry's writings, and who cannot read Homer in Greek and probably do not know him very well in translation into their own vernacular."

256 "What he accomplished": John Miles Foley, *The Theory of Oral Composition: History and Methodology.* Bloomington: Indiana University Press, 1988, p. 36.

256 "gyrated in the American fashion": G. S. Kirk, "Adam Parry and Anne Amory Parry," *Gnomon,* 1972, p. 427.

256 "seems to me a terribly good idea": AP to ABL, 17 August 1958, Zabel 21.

257 the project was under way: AP to ABL, 7 December 1959, Zabel 20.

257 "much slower work": AP to ABL, 15 January 1960, Zabel 22.

257 "which means I am working": AP to sister Marian, 16 January 1960, Adam 011.

257 "the gates of horn and ivory": Wilson *Odyssey,* Book 19, line 567.

257 "There was nothing in it about Albert": Newhouse, p. 66.

257 "Homer as Oral Poet": Albert B. Lord, *Harvard Studies in Classical Philology* 72 (1967): 1–46.

257 "Homer as Artist": Anne Amory Parry, *Classical Quarterly* 21, no. 1 (May 1971): 1–15.

258 "the fuzzy repetitions": AP to unknown recipient, 8 July 1967, Adam 026.

258 "a very nice man": AP to William Whallon, ca. 1960, Adam 055.

258 "There is, of course, no longer need": C. A. Trypanis, review of *Making* in *American Journal of Philology* 94, no. 3 (Autumn 1973): 302–304.

258 "It is almost incontestable": Erich Segal, review of *Making* in *New York Times,* 15 August 1971.

259 came to an intersection: "Accident Corporel de la Circulation Routière," Gendarmerie Nationale, Compagnie de Colmar, 4 June 1971, Adam.

259 *A Bibliography:* Edward R. Haymes, *A Bibliography of Studies Relating to Parry's and Lord's Oral Theory,* Cambridge, MA: Harvard University Printing Office, 1973.

260 "almost never rhyme": Bruce A. Rosenberg, *The Art of the American Folk Preacher.* New York: Oxford University Press, 1970, p. 5.

260 "Keep your hand in God's hand": Ibid., p. 49.

261 "ethnographic impulse": Russo, "Oral Theory," p. 8.

261 "Parry's prize": Dorothy Wender, "Homer, Avdo Međedović, and the Elephant's Child," *American Journal of Philology* 98, no. 4 (Winter 1977): 327–347. See also review of *Meho,* by Barbara Kerewsky-Halpern, in *Balkan Studies* 19 (January 1, 1978): 215–217: "The song itself, with its wealth of verbal art and acoustical patterning, should be listened to, as Avdo's

audiences did. Reading it reveals a thrilling story, told with skill. Hearing it is an aural delight." On the long wait for *Meho,* Joseph Russo tells of a colleague "grumbling that it was taking forever," and that "he suspected Lord was afraid to show comparative material that would reveal the mediocrity of the Serbo-Croatian work and weaken the parallel to Homer." Joseph Russo to the author, 30 January 2018.

261 *The File on H:* See Ismail Kadare, *The File on H,* translated from the French of Jusuf Vrioni by David Bellos. New York: Arcade, 1998; Dominique Cassajus, "Retour Sur le Dossier H," *Paroles nomades. Écrits d'ethnolinguistique africaine en hommage à Christiane Seydou,* sous la direction de Jean Derive et Ursula Baumgardt. Paris: Karthala, 2005, pp. 47–70; Barbara Graziosi, "Homer in Albania: Oral Epic and the Geography of Literature," in Barbara Graziosi and Emily Greenwood, *Homer in the Twentieth Century: Between World Literature and the Western Canon.* New York: Oxford University Press, 2007, pp. 120–142; Erica Weitzman, "Ismail Kadare's *The File on H.* and the Comedy of Epic," *Modern Language Review* III, no. 3 (July 2016): 818–839.

262 "an unreflexive orthodoxy": Steve Nimis, in his introduction to an issue devoted to oral poetry and neoanalysis, *Critical Exchange* 16, 1984.

262 "Let me say": Merritt Sale, "In Defense of Milman Parry: Renewing the Oral Theory," *Oral Tradition* 11, no. 1 (1996): 374–417.

262 "certain excess": de Lamberterie, p. 411.

263 "Parry's theory": D. C. Young, "Was Homer an Illiterate Improviser?," *Minnesota Review* 5 (1965): 65–75.

263 "that the work of Milman Perry": *EpicSingers,* p. 39.

263 "the finger of God": H. T. Wade-Gery, *The Poet of the Iliad.* Cambridge: Cambridge University Press, 1952, pp. 38–39.

264 by then a commonplace: James P. Holoka, "Homeric Originality: A Survey," *Classical World* 66, no. 5 (February 1973): 257–296.

264 our own limited vocabulary: Martin Bernal, reply to Hugh Lloyd-Jones review of *EpicSingers* in *New York Review of Books,* 14 May 1992. For the comparison to Coltrane and Charlie Parker, see Roy Lotz, "Lotz in Translation" blog post, 1 May 2016.

264 "For Parry, Homer's poetry": Johannes Haubhold, "Homer After Parry: Tradition, Reception, and the Timeless Text," in Barbara Graziosi and Emily Greenwood, eds., *Homer in the 20th Century.* New York: Oxford University Press, 2007, p. 37.

265 landmark 1962 book: Thomas S. Kuhn, *The Structure of Scientific Revolutions,* 2nd edition. Chicago: University of Chicago Press, 1970.

266 "I have never done anything 'useful' ": G. H. Hardy, *A Mathematician's Apology.* New York: Cambridge University Press, 1st edition, 1940, p. 151.

Index

Page numbers in *italics* refer to illustrations.

ILLUSTRATION CREDITS

Robert Kanigel is the author of eight previous books, most recently *Eyes on the Street: The Life of Jane Jacobs.* He has been the recipient of numerous awards, including a Guggenheim Fellowship and the Grady-Stack Award for science writing, and for his biography of Milman Parry, a public scholar grant from the National Endowment for the Humanities. His book *The Man Who Knew Infinity* was a finalist for the National Book Critics Circle Award and the Los Angeles Times Book Prize. For twelve years he was a professor of science writing at MIT. He and his wife live in Baltimore, Maryland.

A NOTE ON THE TYPE

This book was set in Adobe Garamond. Designed for the Adobe Corporation by Robert Slimbach, the fonts are based on types first cut by Claude Garamond (ca. 1480–1561). Garamond was a pupil of Geoffroy Tory and is believed to have followed the Venetian models, although he introduced a number of important differences, and it is to him that we owe the letter we now know as "old style." He gave to his letters a certain elegance and feeling of movement that won their creator an immediate reputation and the patronage of Francis I of France.

Composed by North Market Street Graphics,
Lancaster, Pennsylvania

Printed and bound by Berryville Graphics,
Berryville, Virginia